T0342254

GLOBAL MACRO TRADING

Since 1996, Bloomberg Press has published books for financial professionals on investing, economics, and policy affecting investors. Titles are written by leading practitioners and authorities, and have been translated into more than 20 languages.

The Bloomberg Financial Series provides both core reference knowledge and actionable information for financial professionals. The books are written by experts familiar with the work flows, challenges, and demands of investment professionals who trade the markets, manage money, and analyze investments in their capacity of growing and protecting wealth, hedging risk, and generating revenue.

For a list of available titles, please visit our website at www.wiley.com/go /bloombergpress.

GLOBAL MACRO TRADING

Profiting in a New World Economy

Greg Gliner

Published by John Wiley & Sons, Inc., Hoboken, New Jersey.
Published simultaneously in Canada.

Library of Congress Cataloging-in-Publication Data
Gliner, Greg.
    Global macro trading : profiting in a new world economy / Greg Gliner.
       pages   cm—(Bloomberg financial ; 567)
    Includes bibliographical references and index.
    ISBN 978-1-118-36242-6 (hardback)—ISBN 978-1-118-42038-6 (ePDF)—
  ISBN 978-1-118-41714-0 (ePub)   1. International trade.   2. Investments.   3. Macroeconomics.
    I. Title.
  HF1379.G556   2014
  332.64'2—dc23
                                                                            2014013497

Printed in the United States of America.
10 9 8 7 6 5 4 3 2 1

FSC
www.fsc.org
MIX
Paper from
responsible sources
FSC® C132124

To My Family

Contents

CHAPTER 10
Commodities   195

CHAPTER 11
The Role of Central Banks in Global Macro   269

CHAPTER 12
Economic Data Releases and Demographics   315

Preface

Global Macro has been one of the most intriguing and most often-covered trading strategies, and it has also been responsible for creating some of the most legendary hedge fund managers. Conversely, it is also one of the most difficult strategies and possibly the least understood. After working as a Portfolio Manager in London I joined Tudor Investment Corporation as an Analyst, and I recall often feeling frustrated that there was no primer or reliable reference guide I could go to in times of need. Luckily, I was surrounded by extremely talented and brilliant people who gave me so much of their time. As I progressed, I found that more and more friends who worked for other hedge fund strategies had a lot of questions about Global Macro. It dawned on me that there existed a need for an introduction to the strategy of Global Macro and an explanation of how it is applied. The combination of my early frustrations and then becoming aware of this need is what compelled me to write a book on Global Macro Trading that could serve as both an introduction and a handy reference tool.

Global Macro Trading is separated into Part I and Part II. Part I provides a broad overview of Global Macro while Part II offers a deeper look into the foundation for Global Macro Trading. Part I spans Chapters 1 to 6 and Part II spans Chapters 7 to12. Additionally, you'll find Bloomberg Cheat Sheets at the end of certain chapters to help navigate ways to use Bloomberg for that specific chapter and topic.

Part I

Chapter 1 examines the landscape of Global Macro as an asset class. It provides an overview of the strategy and returns and discusses why managers allocate to the strategy. Chapter 2 provides a detailed explanation of the trading process, as well as how to size trades and evaluate performance. It includes information on different types of bias, stress testing, risk utilization, and other risk management tools. Then, in Chapter 3, we tackle the construction of basic backtests and queries and analogs and provide the reader with framework to make trading evaluations. Chapter 4 starts to look at the four product groups, which serve as the building blocks for Global Macro. Part II will cover these in greater detail. Chapter 5 provides detail on technical analysis, including different types of charts, trends, moving averages and various oscillators such as Elliott waves, Fibonacci numbers, parabolics, seasonals, cycles, and crowd psychology. Chapter 6 explores the basic construction of systematic models and trading, as well as some commonly used strategies.

Part II

Chapters 7 through 10 explore the individual product groups: foreign exchange, equities, fixed income, and commodities. Chapter 7 looks at foreign exchange, and Chapter 8 examines equities. These chapters aim to provide the reader with some background, as well as some ways to value the respective asset classes on a macro level. Chapter 9 delves into the different aspects of fixed income. Chapter 10 examines commodities and separates them into energy, precious metals, agriculture, and industrial metals. It also serves as a reference tool about the main producers and consumers, as well as crop calendars. Chapter 11 explores central banking and takes an in-depth look at the Fed, ECB, and some of the recent programs following the financial crisis, as well as the importance of the main central banks in Global Macro Trading. Finally, Chapter 12 looks at important data releases followed by every macro trader, which is also meant for use as a reference tool.

The thorough information provided in *Global Macro Trading* enables readers to navigate Global Macro markets with confidence. After reading this book, you will understand the basic concepts behind the asset class and ways to trade it. You will also have a reference guide that will serve as a valuable tool in navigating the various regimes and market conditions. This information will empower the reader with a confident and competent understanding of Global Macro.

Acknowledgments

I would like to thank Dave Abner, who I met when I started as an analyst at BNP Paribas. He ran their ETF business during my time at BNP, and we kept in touch through the years. Dave has served as both a personal and professional role model for me. He is the author of *The ETF Handbook* and *Visual Guide to ETFs* and is the best-selling author for ETF books. When I ran the idea of writing a book on Global Macro Trading by him, he was more supportive than I ever could have imagined. He helped by connecting me to Wiley and boosted my confidence throughout the entire process, especially at points when my morale was low or I was plagued by self-doubt. He was my mentor throughout the entire process, and I am truly grateful to him and greatly admire his craft. He is the best in the ETF market and one of the greatest people I have the privilege of knowing.

I would like to thank Amit Hampel, who brought me on to join his team at Tudor Investment Corporation. Amit was the greatest mentor and boss I could have asked for. A large part of this book can be credited to the foundation I built while working for Amit. He was always one of the first in the office, and his unrelenting persistence and aim for perfection still resonate with me today. To this day, every time I have an investment idea, I ask myself how Amit would respond to it. I am honored to have worked for him and to call him a friend, an older brother, and a mentor.

I have been fortunate to work beside some of the most brilliant and morally sound associates I could have found in any profession. I would like to thank everyone I worked beside in my professional career. I want to thank former and current colleagues for making me a better person and for being my friends. I want to thank Mark Mitten, Todor Georgiev, Brian Martin, Donn Davis, Frank Leitner, Pat O'Brien, Beau Cummins, and Amit Hampel for being my mentors over the years.

Given the broad coverage of this book, I am grateful that I was able to call on some close friends and former colleagues who were instrumental in getting me to the finish line. I am very lucky to have had feedback from these incredibly knowledgeable industry participants: Dave Abner, Namik Immelback,

Josh Smith, Frank Leitner, Kobi Platt, Charley Powers, Ray Fischer, Jay Hammarstedt, and Brett Steenbarger.

The expertise of the dedicated team at Wiley has been invaluable to me throughout the entire process. I want to thank Pamela Van Giessen, who helped me find this opportunity. Additionally, Evan Burton, Emilie Herman, Judy Howarth, Tula Batanchiev, and Steve Kyritz, who helped me take this book from conception to fruition, and I would like to thank Wiley as a whole for making this book a reality. Also, I would like to thank Mary Barbour, who I worked with as my editor for countless hours. I am grateful for all her care and attention; she is an extraordinary professional and I am grateful for her contribution.

Last, I want to thank my family for always being there for me. What they have achieved in the face of their many struggles served as my drive when I wanted to give up. I am so lucky to have parents who sacrificed so much to give me the life they never had. I love them and truly admire the example they set for me—I am so grateful to have inherited such high moral standards and to have had their support and encouragement throughout my entire life.

PART ONE

An Overview of Global Macro

CHAPTER 1

Surveying the Global Macro Landscape

Global macro, short for global macroeconomics, is the strategy of using economic theory, educated guesses about the macroeconomic environment, and geopolitical events to make large-scale investments around the world. It's one of the most important strategies for any global investor, no matter if they are retail or institutional, because global events have a substantial influence on the performance of any type of investment.

Global macro is often considered the most flexible and opportunistic hedge fund strategy, due to the scope of traded products and the number of markets it covers. Its aim is to preserve capital, using stringent risk management to limit drawdowns. Profits are made through trades in equities, currency, fixed income, and commodities. These trades can occur anywhere in the world, hence the term "global macro."

This chapter introduces the basic types of global macro strategies, historical returns of the strategy, and the various reasons why institutions choose to allocate to global macro.

Types of Global Macro Strategies

Like any hedge fund strategy, global macro can be categorized into substrategies. The four basic approaches of global macro are discretionary, systematic, high frequency, and commodity trading advisors (CTAs).

Discretionary and systematic macro strategies both have the potential to be extremely profitable and are powerful methods of analyzing markets and determining investments. These are the two most often used global macro strategies but, because the four are often used together, it's important to understand how all of them work.

Discretionary

Discretionary macro trading, as the name implies, relies on a trader's experience, intelligence, and knowledge to take subjective and often risky bets on various global markets in order to capture alpha and the best possible risk-adjusted return. With knowledge gleaned from studying global data, releases, economic data, and central bank action, among countless other factors, an investor can frame a top-down approach. This allows for a unique analysis of the risks and opportunities offered by industries, sectors, countries, and the macroeconomic situation at large.

Discretionary strategy requires serious organization and processing skills, since it involves such a large amount of data. The ability to analyze data across many different markets aids the trader in assessing whether or not a particular market is fully incorporating all factors into global asset prices.

The discretionary macro strategy is nimble and can also produce alpha in significant risk off markets. One example of a trader using historical patterns to capture alpha this way is Paul Tudor Jones's prediction of the Black Monday crash on October 19, 1987. Jones observed that the market behavior during that period could potentially experience a catastrophic crash. He expressed this view by going short and made an enormous return on Black Monday.

Global macro managers have the luxury of being able to trade a vast amount of markets and also to go against the trend, shorting the stock market while other hedge fund strategies and mutual funds remain long. Thus, discretionary traders have the potential to make a tremendous profit in a selloff, while equity managers tend to lose significant amounts of capital.

Discretionary macro traders may also determine trades based on direction and relative value. Directional trades are made in hopes of an asset moving in a particular direction. For example, if a manager is bullish he or she could go long copper and hope to capture returns on the move up.

Relative value trades aim to pair or group assets together to capture the relative value differential between those assets, and profit from a divergence or change in the price difference. Looking at the European crisis, if a discretionary macro trader believes that German yields will be less affected than Italian yields, the trader can short Italian five years and go long German Bobls. If matters worsen in Europe and Italy acquires more credit risk, it could see yields rise in relative terms.

Systematic

The second main type of global macro strategy is systematic macro. Systematic managers employ a top-down model that takes various economic indicators into account. By using large sets of quantitative data, systematic macro strategies seek to earn alpha by capturing these dislocations. Systematic macro funds typically employ many PhDs to "systemize" all these quantitative factors in order to produce a model of trading positions that removes the variable of human emotion. Systematic macro prides itself on its stringent process, strong back-tests, and the ability to operate solely on quantitative analysis, hence ensuring maximum returns (assuming that past risk-adjusted returns are predictive). Over long periods of time—several years or more—systematic funds can produce more consistent returns than discretionary strategies; however, in periods of high volatility, they tend to underperform discretionary macro, as they did in 2008. Holding periods for systematic macro can range from days to months, or longer.

Systematic macro hedge funds have significantly changed the landscape in Macro with the amount of capital they have attracted. AQR Capital Management, founded by Cliff Asness, and Bridgewater, founded by Ray Dalio, manage over $80 billion and $100 billion, respectively, and have revolutionized systematic trading. The ability to trade multiple liquid asset classes in systematic macro means that asset managers can oversee large amounts of assets at once. Since equities, fixed income, commodities, and foreign exchange are the most liquid markets, it allows these funds to grow assets to previously unseen levels. Additionally, since strategies are constantly back-tested and improved, large asset allocators such as pensions, sovereign wealth funds, and endowments that have large amounts of capital to allocate, find comfort in using a computer-driven process with predictable drawdowns. Many of these institutions have minimum allocations of greater than several hundred million dollars, so, in a way, size also attracts more capital.

It is worth noting that, while systematic macro is scalable and can take large allocations, it is wise to allocate to both discretionary and systematic macro in a fairly even manner. This will allow an asset allocator to gain the advantages of both strategies and hedge the disadvantages. Discretionary macro is negatively correlated during periods of stress and, since discretionary traders can get short in a nimble way, it can produce profit in economic situations where most people are losing money. Systematic macro, on the other hand, lets traders allocate safely and predictably with more assurance.

A good book on this topic is *Expected Returns* (John Wiley & Sons, 2011) by Antti Ilmanen of AQR Capital Management (formerly of Brevan Howard).

High Frequency Trading

A third type of global macro trading is high frequency trading. This is the process of using highly sophisticated computers and technology to trade very short-term (millisecond) dislocations that may exist in the market. High frequency trading in macro is not as large or scalable as discretionary and systematic macro. Holding periods can range from milliseconds up to a few hours depending on the strategy. In high frequency trading, processing speed is of the utmost importance to ensure that certain dislocations are captured.

Commodity Trading Advisors (CTAs)

According to the National Futures Association, a Commodity Trading Advisor (CTA) is an individual or organization that advises others as to the value or advisability of buying or selling futures contracts, options on futures, or retail off-exchange foreign exchange contracts. Since futures are traded on most global macro markets, CTAs are considered a global macro strategy. Many larger CTAs employ a model-driven approach that can be technical or fundamental. However, most CTAs utilize a highly automated trend-following strategy that is in some ways similar to systematic macro. The methodology on position sizing used by most CTAs, which we'll also be using in this book, originated with the Turtle Traders.

As with other trend-following strategies, CTAs perform very well over longer periods of time—as long as several years. They are, however, subject to large drawdowns (peak-to-trough) as a result. Man AHL and Winton Capital Management, both based in London, are widely regarded as the premier CTAs, each managing approximately $20 billion.

Return Profile and Allocations

Global macro as a strategy is very attractive because of its return profile. The Barclays Global Macro Index has achieved annualized returns of 10 percent from 2002 to 2012 compared to the S&P 500, which has been 2 percent over the same period. Additionally, the Barclays Global Macro Index has experienced lower volatility on an annualized basis compared to the S&P 500 over the same time period. As a result, global macro as a strategy has a higher Sharpe ratio, with the attractive investment characteristics of higher returns and lower volatility relative to other hedge fund strategies. Figure 1.1 demonstrates the outperformance of the Dow Jones Credit Suisse Global Macro Hedge Fund Index versus the S&P 500.

FIGURE 1.1   Global Macro versus S&P 500 from January 1995 to September 2013

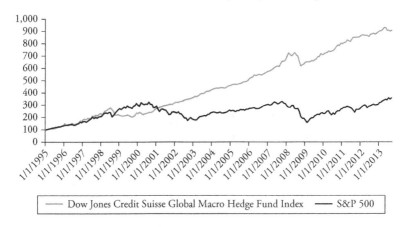

Source: Dow Jones, Credit Suisse, and Bloomberg.

Global macro has shown a low correlation to S&P 500 returns, particularly in periods of market stress. Since many macro traders short during bear markets, this allows global macro funds to make money even when the market drops precipitously (Figure 1.2). Having a low correlation to the S&P 500 and a negative correlation during market collapses is also a very attractive return profile, and one of the reasons money managers tend to like global macro. While global macro returns have come down from the 1980s, 1990s, and 2000s with fixed income yields at historical lows and an atmosphere of economic uncertainty, global macro has still seen profit in all markets, which is why it remains a popular hedge fund strategy.

As a result of the attractive uncorrelated return profile of global macro, investors have allocated to the strategy. Another attractive aspect of global macro is that it is one of the most, if not *the* most, liquid strategies in the hedge fund universe, considering that the assets traded are the most liquid to begin with. As a result of the very desirable return profiles and liquidity, global macro is the most popular hedge fund allocation by pension funds, as shown in Figure 1.3.

Hedge Funds and Global Macro

Some of the most famous hedge fund managers have emerged from global macro. In 1992, George Soros earned his fame on Black Wednesday, where

FIGURE 1.2 (a) Performance of Global Macro during the Top Five Losing Quarters in SPX since January 1995 and (b) Performance of Global Macro during the Top Five Best Quarters in SPX since January 1995

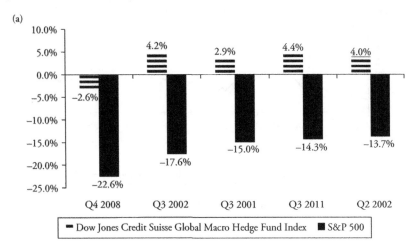

(a)

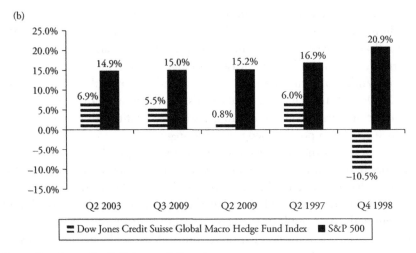

(b)

Source: Dow Jones, Credit Suisse, and Bloomberg.

he accurately predicted the devaluation of the British pound, making over $1 billion dollars in one day and earning himself the title of "The man who broke the Bank of England." As mentioned previously, Paul Tudor Jones also successfully shorted the stock market prior to the October 19, 1987, crash, characterizing the week preceding the crash as one of the most exciting weeks of his life.

FIGURE 1.3 Changes in Pension Funds' Allocations to Different Hedge Fund Strategies from 2009 to 2012

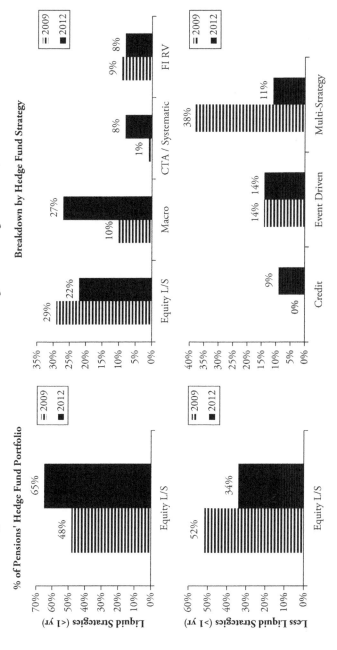

Source: Barclays Prime Services.

Louis Bacon, Stanley Druckenmiller, Bruce Kovner, Colm O'Shea, and Julian Robertson all earned their fame as discretionary macro traders able to profit in both bull and bear markets using the disciplined approach, stringent process, and analytic insight that are characteristic of global macro trading.

Summary

The goal of this chapter is to provide the reader with a brief introduction to the concept of global macro, the four basic strategies it encompasses, and why global macro is important to the macroeconomic situation at large.

CHAPTER 2

Trading Process, Sizing Trades, and Monitoring Performance

Regardless of what hedge fund strategy you are trading, there are implicit risks involved. The first rule in any kind of investing is to understand how much you stand to lose, rather than how much you stand to gain. Having a stringent trading process that fully accounts for risk is critical to a trader's long-term success. Like the old adage about pilots says: "There are old and bold fighter pilots, but rarely both." The inescapable fact is that any time a global macro trader puts a trade on, things can go wrong. Some of these risks can be stress-tested while others are unpredictable, but a global macro trader should be as educated as possible on potential outcomes of any given trade.

This chapter will examine some of the tools one can use in the trading process, as well as some implicit human biases that make us more prone to potentially catastrophic risks. No process is perfect and each trader must find the one he or she likes best. With that said, just as humans evolve over time, one's trading process should also evolve. This chapter will also outline some of the initial methods one can use to monitor and improve performance.

Understanding the different types of trading strategies and learning to monitor one's own performance serves many important functions. Whether one is trading discretionary macro, systematic macro, or high frequency, having a process in place is the key to success. The greatest traders of all time used a variety of different strategies, but what they all had in common was a stringent process and the ability to take losses and recover.

Maintaining a Stringent Process

The biggest advantage of systematic and high frequency strategies is that once the systems and algorithms are in place, the variables of human emotion and psychology are removed. Trading discretionary macro, on the other hand, requires having a stringent process to ensure that we avoid our human impulses as much as possible. As mentioned before, all of these strategies can lead to profit, but it's important for a trader to choose (and stick with) the strategy that feels most comfortable. For example, many people are skeptical of technical analysis; however, technicians can't live without it since it gives them the discipline to know when to get in and out of positions. There is no right or wrong strategy when it comes to trading; it's just important to figure out which one is the best for you and make sure your process is consistent.

A process should always evolve and improve. No one system or person is perfect and since the world of trading is constantly evolving, one's process must as well. Evaluating one's performance in a nonbiased and numeric fashion is an important part of driving process improvement. Oftentimes particular strategies may be making money while other strategies are not—so it's statistically probable that there is opportunity for process improvement.

For example, many fixed income traders who systematically trade the 2s/10s yield curve might want to adjust the way they trade flatteners and steepeners since, in many countries, there is a zero lower bound (ZLB) and the two-year likely won't react as much as it used to in years prior. This means that going further out in the yield curve will likely be a more effective move. If you aren't continuously evaluating and updating your process, you might miss out on simple moves like this that can help your profits.

One of the best ways to maintain a consistent process is to log all of your trades in a journal or spreadsheet along with your thesis, conviction level, and the outcome of the trade. This will be an invaluable reference for you when it comes to future trades and will help you develop objectivity by finding patterns across both profitable trades and losing trades.

Objectivity and Bias

Gut feeling in discretionary trading is a lovely gift, but the fact remains that having objective procedural indicators relies far more on process than instincts. This section looks at the following types of bias:

- Confirmation bias
- Availability bias
- Anchoring bias

Building indicators is not a scientific process. Ask 100 traders how they do it and you might get 100 different answers. But building a system, or combination, of important indicators can give some traders the discipline they require to stay true to their process. A big part of building a process is the understanding that we, as humans, are subject to biases that can impair our judgment; no one is immune. Making a checklist of questions and revisiting them often can help alleviate bias in one's decision making.

Confirmation Bias

Confirmation bias means favoring information that supports one's own argument, or favoring information that already has popular support. This tends to be the most common type of bias, as it is heavily aligned with human instinct.

Have you ever been to a social gathering where you were tempted to order fish, but when everyone else ordered a steak you followed suit? We all fall subject to confirmation bias in both trivial and significant ways.

1. If a trade moves against you, do you seek advice from others in the same position as you?

    Do you think it is likely that bears consult with other bears? If they have a conversation with a bull, how open would they be to changing their minds? Hedge fund traders tend to seek confirmation from peers who hold the same positions that they do in order to reaffirm their instincts. How useful do you think this is?

    One way to deal with this bias is to create a map of different trading scenarios and regimes. Some traders have an incredible ability to make money in bear markets but lose in bull markets, while others are great momentum traders but lose money when the market is choppy and mean reverts. If you can identify the trade you're likely to have on, you can get a different perspective by seeking the advice of a trader who has had success in situations where you have lost money.

2. How mutually independent is the information you use for developing an argument for your trade?

    It helps to log the reasons for your trade in your trade journal and then mark the points that are positive (+) and negative (−) for your argument. Examine these objectively and beware of how you may be skewing the facts to support your existing beliefs. The goal here is to try to outwit yourself by seeing the intentions behind your trade as objectively as possible, avoiding common pitfalls that can sometimes act in opposition to your process.

Availability Bias

Availability bias means overestimating the probability that something will occur, based on it being a vivid or memorable event rather than its relative likelihood. A great example is the fear of flying in an airplane. Many people have a fear of flying but have no problem driving a car. The fact is that the probability of dying in a plane crash is at least 2,000 times less likely than dying in a car crash, but because the fear of flying is one that is often discussed (i.e., it is "available"), people overestimate the chances that it will happen.

Imagine that your original thesis has been proven completely wrong, but the first data point you encounter after that fact is in support of your trade. How much weight should you give to this data as your new reason for keeping the trade?

This is a very important question and one without a clear answer. The best solution is to learn from past successes and mistakes by consulting your trade journal and analyzing your rationale for putting your trades on. This way you can get more familiar with the biases you tend to exhibit. Each time you feel a certain trade could be subject to this type of bias, you can revisit your journal where you outlined your original thesis for making a specific trade. You can track the outcome of prior trades and then objectively ask yourself whether it makes sense to stick with your original thesis or if you are overlooking some key information.

Anchoring Bias

Anchoring bias means prematurely establishing an estimated value for what the final value should be. The problem with anchoring bias is the inability to adjust that estimated value.

Are you married to a fair value price, level, or trade? Anchoring bias happens to all traders but it is probably most common among single stock investors. Single stock investors tend to do intensive fundamental analysis and arrive at a "fair value," which can be defined as book value and free cash flow yield, for instance. The problem is when they become too attached, or married, to their thesis, it makes it difficult for them to assess a trade objectively. Legendary trader Jesse Livermore is known for his statement that "losers average losers."

Tversky and Kahneman conducted a study to determine if two groups could guess the percentage of African countries that were part of the United Nations. Group One was asked if the population was more or less than 10 percent. Group Two was asked if it was more or less than 65 percent. The power of suggestion skewed the biases in different ways, resulting in the first group answering 25 percent and the second group answering 45 percent (Tversky and Kahneman 1974).

It is important to remember that no one is immune to these biases. If you have in your mind an idea of what price the asset should be trading at, be sure to question it lest you act with false confidence. The best thing one can do to fight anchoring bias is to seek out those who oppose your view and allow yourself to play devil's advocate. If, for instance, you think the euro should go to parity, find analysts who think the euro is undervalued and force yourself to understand why they would think so. Even if you continue to defend your position afterward, you will have a much stronger argument as a result.

Remedies

Fortunately, there are remedies for these biases. Keeping a stringent process will help you counteract any influence they might have on you. As discussed, keeping a journal that logs your trades, along with their rationales and outcomes, will be a great reference point to help you with trades going forward. Playing devil's advocate, performing extensive research on opposing views, and asking evenhanded questions can also help you avoid falling prey to these judgment biases.

Taking Losses

The ability to take losses is one of the most important attributes a trader can have. In *Reminiscences of a Stock Operator*, Jesse Livermore says, "A loss never bothers me after I take it. I forget it overnight. But being wrong—not taking the loss—that is what does damage to the pocketbook and to the soul."

Human psychology has us wired to take profits early and hang on to losing trades too long, which stems from Prospect Theory. But this strategy dooms us to lose money since it doesn't take into account the erratic behavior of market products. While this is a difficult instinct to overcome, we must acknowledge this fundamental human flaw and fight this urge as best we can. If a trade is losing, we need to cut it and take the loss—and if a trade is winning, let it run; traders actually need to do the exact opposite of what their instincts and psyche would have them do.

The first rule in investing is capital preservation; that is, limiting losses. Cutting losing trades and riding winning trades are the foundations of this rule. In *Market Wizards*, Paul Tudor Jones says, "I am always thinking about losing money as opposed to making money. The first thing I do is try to figure out what can go wrong." Every trader will have winning trades and losing trades. The ability to acknowledge when one is wrong and move on is of the utmost importance. Peter Lynch of Fidelity once said, "If you are right half the time you have a terrific score." Learning how to quickly cut a losing trade is more valuable (and realistic) than only making winning trades. Staying humble and being aware of the human tendency to err can save one a lot of money.

A stop-loss is a predetermined price to sell a long asset or buy back a short trade at a loss. The purpose of a stop-loss is to have a predetermined loss limit on any given trade. Putting in a stop-loss is, in a way, its own anchoring bias. However, there are procedural methods that try to ameliorate this bias. Sizing positions appropriately and accounting for historical volatility can help to mitigate anchoring bias and quantify a stop-loss. Technicians love using stop-losses because they signal when to get in and when to get out. A stop should be predetermined prior to the trade to avoid bias and, even though they face gap risk, using stops can limit downside risk. For bigger money managers and hedge funds, mental stops may be more appropriate so banks or dealers don't sit on your orders and act in a way that may not be beneficial to you.

Position Sizing

Analyzing what to buy and sell dominates most of what portfolio managers and traders think about when they trade. Position sizing is often overlooked by many market participants, but is arguably more important than knowing what position to buy or sell. Remember, the first rule of investing isn't to make money—it's to preserve capital and avoid loss. While this may seem like an issue of semantics, utilizing position sizing ensures that you are always aware of your downside risk, that is, the amount you stand to lose.

Position sizing aims to adjust each position for volatility. The importance of adjusting for volatility is that it equally normalizes all your positions such that if losses are incurred they are more predictable and statistically have the same probability of occurring, assuming that positions are weighted equally based on volatility. This allows traders to take positions in a broad range of markets and to have a measure by which to monitor risk.

This concept of position sizing was developed by the Turtle Traders, whose work has influenced many managers and CTAs. The Turtles calculated the volatility of a particular asset, which they referred to as "N," in which N is defined as the 20-day exponential moving average of the true range. The true range is defined as the maximum of the High on Day − Low on Day, High on Day − Previous Day's Close, or Previous Day's Close − Low. N ends up representing the 20-day average price move in the particular asset or volatility.

$$\text{True Range} = \text{Maximum (High − Low, High − Previous Day's Close,}$$
$$\text{Previous Day's Close − Low)}$$

$$N = \frac{19 \times \text{Previous Day's N} + \text{Today's True Range}}{20}$$

Unit Size

The Turtles have a specific methodology for calculating unit size but, for matters of simplicity, this book elects to take a slightly different approach to it. Let's assume that the portfolio has $100,000,000 under management. One hundred basis points (1 percent) of the portfolio is equal to $1,000,000 and 25 basis points equals $250,000. We will assume that each unit size is equal to 25 basis points. What this means is that on any particular trade of one unit, the portfolio is willing to absorb 25 basis points of losses before being stopped out. If someone had stronger conviction, he or she could risk 75 basis points, which is a unit size of 3, for example. This is done to limit the downside risk. Many successful discretionary macro traders use stop orders, since, unlike a systematic macro fund, humans are doing the trading and often need the discipline to take losses.

Volatility Adjusting Position Size

Once you have calculated N and Unit Size, deciding how to adjust your positions for volatility is a matter of personal preference. For Discretionary traders, when a position is moving against you, you get stopped out of the position and take the loss at a certain point. N is the volatility of a one standard deviation move, which means that on any given day you have a roughly 16 percent probability of being stopped out of any position due to the volatility of the asset (using just the left side of the distribution as losses). In other words, your prediction might be completely accurate, but sheer odds

FIGURE 2.1   Sample Normal Distribution

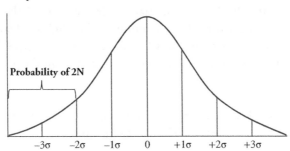

determine that you will still get stopped out almost one-sixth of the time on any given day.

How do you successfully monitor risk without being overly cautious to the point that you lose money on trades that should be making money? The best approach for this is to use 2Ns when calculating one's stop, which means you are using two standard deviations. By doing this, one has only around a 2 percent chance of being stopped out (using just the left side of the distribution as losses—see Figure 2.1). In other words, with 2Ns you get stopped out 2.3 out of 100 days, or one out of every 43.5 days as opposed being stopped out one out of every 6.25 days with 1N. This way, when each position is volatility adjusted, one knows exactly the risk per each unit. Remember, the first rule (second and third rule also!) of trading is to preserve capital and avoid loss.

Once you have calculated the 2N of a particular trade, you back into the dollar amount of capital you are willing to lose. In our example, one unit of 25 bps, or $250,000, is the amount of capital at risk. One should calculate how many contracts or how much notional to trade based on unit size.

Risk/Reward

By the time you factor in human error and transaction costs, one can only hope to be right about a trade around half of the time. For some of the best traders, this is more like 40 percent. Humbly acknowledging this, having a good risk/reward on each trade will make or break the long-term success of any money manager. Risk/reward is the concept of calculating basis points at risk along with estimating how much a trader believes he or she can make on the trade (reward). As a general baseline, one should always strive for a 1:3 risk-to-reward ratio, if not higher, and should also calculate risk by using the 2N volatility-adjusted position.

There are several disciplines that stem from this assertion. The first is based on the notion that, for every trade you put on, risking 25 basis points means you should expect to make at least 75 basis points. This should be assessed before each trade is put on and human emotions can get in the way. Once the trade is put on, the trader must stay true to his or her hypothesis and "suffer the pain of the gain." For example, let's assume the trade has initially made a positive return of 50 basis points and then comes into a 25 basis point profit. Can you stomach the moves? There is no question that this takes immense resolve and conviction, which is why one should set targets before the trade is executed to avoid the biases of irrational human decision making.

A key part of this process is for the trader to log his or her reasons for putting the trade on in the trade journal. It is always important to be able to move on a dime and if in fact an original thesis no longer holds true, then it may make sense to take the trade off. The key concept here is not to provide conditionality or excuses for taking a trade off early, but rather to demonstrate the power of what can go wrong in one's trading. For example, if a trader is executing trades without having a regard for risk/reward, he or she is essentially making losing bets over time, since after transaction costs, human error, and other risks, the trader stands a less than 50 percent chance of being right. Imagine if you knew when you were wrong, got out, and stayed in your winners. That is precisely the discipline we are trying to instill with risk/reward. Since you have a minimum 1:3 risk/reward, you can cut your losers early and ride your winners to make them more profitable. Assuming one is 60 percent wrong, losing 25 basis points on each trade, and correct 40 percent of the time, gaining 75 basis points, then one would have an expected return of +15 basis points (40% × 75 bps + 60% × –25 bps = 15 bps). Without this discipline, you fall into the trap that most traders do, which is selling winners too early and riding losers too long—the exact opposite of what you should do.

Correlation

Traders must know what assets they are trading on aggregate. If their entire portfolio has assets with a high correlation to one another, they need to be aware of that. If the market turns against them, they can be stopped out of all their positions more easily if their positions are highly correlated.

There are also offsetting positions where correlation is inverted. This means they can have bigger position sizes and it might be helpful to run the volatility (N) of the positions combined, as well to make sure that portfolio is sized appropriately. The more predefined rules and processes a trader has in making adjustments on position sizing on the portfolio level, the more successful the trade will be.

Gap Risk

Gap risk is one of the biggest risks when sizing positions. Gap risk is when the price changes in an asset without any trading in between. A great illustration is the act of carrying positions into the weekend. Let's assume the trader is short Euro Stoxx 50 (SX5E) and suddenly there is an agreement that the European Central Bank (ECB) will monetize Italy and Spain's debt. The SX5E would rally significantly as soon as it opened on Monday and the trader would not be able to cover their short until then, which might mean that this level is outside their stop. A recent example was in Cyprus on Saturday, March 16, 2013. The Eurogroup, ECB, and IMF agreed to provide aid to Cyprus to recapitalize its banks, and Cyprus agreed to charge depositors a one-time tax of 10 percent in exchange for the aid (an agreement that was later amended). Had someone been long Euro Stoxx over the weekend, on Monday they would have experienced an immediate drop of 2.3 percent on the open (see Figure 2.2).

FIGURE 2.2 Euro Stoxx 50 Chart March 15, 2013 – March 18, 2013

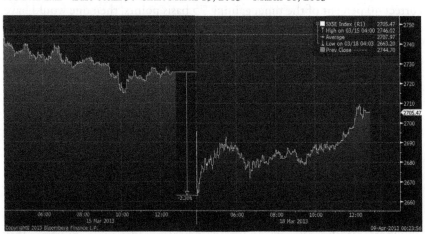

Source: Bloomberg.

Position Sizing Sheet

When trading discretionary markets, whether in fast markets or just observing trends, it helps to have a "cheat sheet" with all the products you trade, basis points at risk, and the amount of futures contracts for each variable amount of risk. By looking at the position sizing sheet and at ES1 (S&P E-Mini's), for example, and assuming the trader wanted to take two units of risk and go long, they would buy "X" E-Mini contracts. While a proper risk management system does provide this information, it is still useful to have this data readily available when trading in a fast market so as to avoid mistakes when many things are occurring simultaneously.

Thematic Trade

When people think of discretionary global macro trading, thematic trades often come to mind first. Bold statements such as "Europe is done," and "fiat money as we know it is over," point to thematic trades that, in this example, would likely lead to shorting the euro and being long gold, respectively. Discretionary traders tend to use a more defined framework. For example, a chart often used to argue the long gold trade is the increase in central bank balance sheets via the creation of electronic reserves and negative real rates. The idea being that as the central banks increase the money supply, the value of their currency relative to gold should decrease.

The point of thematic trades is that they can be very successful over longer periods of time. It is highly recommended that thematic trades be done in smaller size relative to shorter-term trades. This is because thematic trades often price in big moves. Another example of a thematic trade is shorting 10-year Japanese government bonds (JGBs). Clearly, the debt-to-GDP of Japan is not sustainable and its demographics are working against it. While these traders will likely be proven right, as they have recently, for years they all lost money because JGBs rallied and those who shorted were also short carry (see Figure 2.3). Even after Shinzō Abe got elected and announced a higher inflation target, 10-year JGBs still initially rallied. For this reason many people believe that JGBs should sell off drastically. As with any other trade, it is good to have an idea of one's downside and the maximum pain one is willing to absorb before cutting the position. Still, having said all this, those who have been long gold over the past 10 years have significantly outperformed. It is important to remember that with thematic trades, like any trade, it is easy to fall into many bias traps.

FIGURE 2.3   10-Year Japanese Government Bond Yields

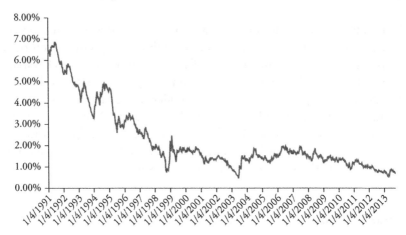

Source: Bloomberg.

Sharpe Ratio

The Sharpe ratio is defined as the expected return minus the risk-free rate divided by the standard deviation. Along with absolute returns, the Sharpe ratio is the most used measure of return.

$$\text{Sharpe ratio} = \frac{ER - R_f}{\sigma}$$

Where ER is the expected return, R_f is the risk-free rate, and σ is the standard deviation of the portfolio.

The Sharpe ratio aims to adjust all returns for volatility for both up and down days. All else being equal, given the same returns, investors prefer lower volatility; hence a higher Sharpe ratio is more desirable. When evaluating back-tested strategies, more often than not it is more effective to test Sharpe ratios of strategies rather than returns themselves. This is especially so in systematic macro when additional factors are added to a model. In this case, it makes the most sense to risk-adjust all returns, because, unlike discretionary macro traders, the returns on systematic macro are more predictable because of back-tests. (Keep in mind, however, that the biggest problem with the Sharpe ratio is that it does assume a normal distribution.)

Sortino Ratio

Since capital preservation is of the utmost importance, being able to measure downside in a portfolio is as important as knowing the return profile. The Sortino ratio, as defined by Bloomberg, is a return/risk measure developed to differentiate between good and bad volatility in the Sharpe ratio. It measures how efficient a fund is on a risk-adjusted basis instead of only on an absolute performance basis. The higher the ratio, the greater the return per unit of downside volatility. The ratio is given by the annualized average of the monthly returns of the previous year minus the yield of a risk-free investment, divided by the downside deviation during the same period.

The advantage of using the Sortino ratio is that it eliminates the volatility of up days, which allows one to better assess the downside performance of the portfolio. However, like the Sharpe ratio, the Sortino ratio assumes a normal distribution when not all returns are normally distributed. The Sortino ratio will also be more effective with returns over longer periods of time.

Drawdowns

A drawdown is defined as the measure from a peak in return performance (or high water mark) to its next trough. Drawdowns are very important on multiple fronts. For starters, when back-testing a successful strategy, it is helpful to know the maximum drawdown so that one can determine the maximum potential loss. CTAs, which have trend-following strategies over time, tend to make money but are subject to large drawdowns. Being able to project potential drawdowns based on past data is very useful. Additionally, for discretionary traders it may make sense to have a predefined drawdown limit. For instance, if discretionary traders have a 5 percent drawdown limit, as soon as they trigger it, they should close all positions and take a timeout as part of their process.

Value at Risk (VaR)

Value at Risk, or VaR, is the most widely used risk measure. The most common VaR measures are based on a 99% daily VaR and a 95% daily VaR confidence interval, but VaR can be measured over greater periods of time. The portfolio is then back-tested and sorted from worst to best days, creating a normal distribution of returns. Using a 99% daily VaR is very conservative, while using a 95% daily VaR is more aggressive. For example, using a 95% daily VaR, if a portfolio has a one-day 3% VaR, then it is expected that 1 out of 20 days the portfolio will lose 3 percent or more. In addition to the confidence interval, it is useful for the trader to predefine his or her limit at a certain percentage; for example, using a maximum 5 percent loss with a 95% daily VaR.

Risk Utilization

Using a 95 percent confidence interval, let's assume that the trader sets a maximum VaR limit of 5 percent for him or herself. If the trader is running at 2.5% VaR, he or she is utilizing 50 percent of the risk limit. If the trader is running 5.0% VaR, he or she is using 100 percent of the risk limit. That means that on the worst one out of 20 days, the trader can theoretically lose up to 5 percent. If, in our given parameters, 5 percent is the maximum amount of risk that we can take, does it make sense to always run at 5% VaR? Let's assume we are playing Texas no-limit poker and you are dealt two separate hands on two tables. Hand 1 is pocket aces (A-A) and Hand 2 is jack-queen unsuited (J-Q). Would you go all in with both hands?

$$\text{Risk Utilization } \% = \frac{\text{Portfolio VaR}}{\text{VaR Limit}}$$

The answer is no! For those who do not play poker, Pocket Aces are the best possible starting hand and have the highest probability of winning pre-flop. If you were dealt pocket aces, you would want to run 100 percent of your risk utilization, or 5% VaR, whereas when someone has less certainty about one's portfolio, less risk should be run. The most important factor to consider is that risk-taking is nonlinear (Figure 2.4), meaning that if you have 50 percent conviction, that doesn't mean you should run 50 percent of your risk utilization.

Assuming a $100,000,000 portfolio and strong performance, there are times when a trader can get rewarded with more VaR. Incremental VaR rewards traders who are making money by allowing them to take more risk. Let's assume that at the start of the year, if you are up 5 percent you pre-determine (remember, process is everything!) that you will allow your VaR limit to increase to 6 percent on a 95 percent confidence interval, and if you are up 10 percent you will allow your VaR limit to increase to 7 percent on a 95 percent confidence interval. This concept is widely drawn from the

FIGURE 2.4   Nonlinear Risk Utilization

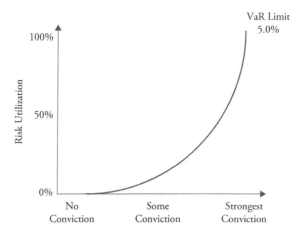

1962 book *Beat the Dealer*, by Edward Thorp, and also *Fortune's Formula*, by William Poundstone. This increase in risk can reward traders who have had a good year and enable them to make outsized returns. Since they are "playing with the house's money," so to speak, the incremental risk holds the original rule of capital preservation because it eats into profits, not our original capital. If the streak of strong performance diminishes, then the preset VaR limit of 5 percent reemerges if the portfolio is up less than 5 percent on the year.

By the same token, more important than incremental VaR is predefined risk limits on the downside. None of these numbers given are a rule but merely a suggestion. For instance, if a trader is down 2.5 percent on their portfolio, their VaR limit decreases from 5 percent in our example to 4 percent, and if they are down 5 percent on the year, then their VaR limit decreases to 3.0 percent.

Many traders liken these predefined rules to having their wings clipped, but it is important to incentivize intelligent risk taking both on the upside and downside. Furthermore, if traders are down on the year, cutting their risk not only punishes them but also takes away the moral hazard of the trader taking capricious risk and acting like a gambler ("punting"). Lastly, at the start of each new year, one should start the portfolio at 0 percent return even if the prior year was very strong. The intention is to create steady returns, while preserving capital and acknowledging that every year is a new start. This will help keep positions smaller than they would have been otherwise, as well as keep the trader honest and avoid blow-up risk.

Stress-Testing

Stress-testing aims to go beyond VaR to find out what the potential worst-case scenarios are. There are two useful methods for approaching stress-testing. The first is quite basic and involves running a historical back-test on one's P&L for the previous 500 trading days. There are roughly 252 trading days in a year, so 500 trading days amounts to around two years. Using this method, one would sort the P&L from best days to worst days and look at the average of the five worst days (so the worst one percent of all days) as well as the worst-day performance. This number will be greater than the VaR calculation. Knowing what the maximum loss outside of VaR could be helps traders know what they stand to lose in three standard deviation moves or "tail" events.

In long periods of low volatility, traders should be even more cautious. Let's assume that the past 500 trading days have been relatively tame. Looking at the average of the worst five days, and even the worst day, may not give traders the proper idea of how much they could lose. A solution for this is to look at the P&L of the portfolio during extreme events like the October 1987 crash, the 2011 Japanese earthquake, and the U.S. downgrade. By seeing the most extreme days of P&L volatility, the trader can unearth potential mines that may not appear on a VaR calculation or stress test in periods of low volatility. (See Table 2.1.)

TABLE 2.1   Sample Stress Test Days/Periods

Date	Event
October 6, 1973	Start of the Yom Kippur War (1973 Oil Crisis)
October 19, 1987	Black Monday
August 2, 1990	Start of Persian Gulf War
December 22, 1994	Peso crisis—abandoned target band
July 2, 1997	Asian crisis—depreciation of Thai baht
August 17, 1998	Russian default and devaluation of ruble
September 23, 1998	LTCM
December 23, 2001	Argentina defaults on $132 billion
March 19, 2003	Invasion of Iraq
September 29, 2006	Amaranth blowup
March 17, 2008	JPMorgan Chase offers $2 for Bear Stearns

Date	Event
September 15, 2008	Lehman bankruptcy
May 6, 2010	Flash Crash
March 11, 2011	Japan earthquake
March 18, 2011	G7 coordinated effort to sell Japanese yen
August 5, 2011	S&P downgrades U.S. credit rating

Monitoring Performance

Have you ever watched the baseball playoffs? The TV stations usually show a 3 × 3 matrix when a hitter comes to bat, which shows where the hitter's strengths and weaknesses are. The idea behind the grid is to be able to let the audience know which areas of the plate the pitcher should avoid, and which areas the pitcher should look to position the ball against the hitter (Figure 2.5). Ideally, the pitcher will already know these areas from studying the batter beforehand. Just as a hitter has a profile that can be studied, traders have weak and strong spots too.

Rather than guessing whether you are strong or weak in a type of trading, it makes sense to have a detailed blotter of all trades or relative value trades. Important attributes include fields like strategy, product groups, duration, and conviction level. The idea behind building this blotter is that it will give you several ways to retroactively evaluate your performance.

The four product groups are defined as foreign exchange, fixed income, equities, and commodities. The strategies could be defined as relative value, directional, or tactical, or have a theme, like "Hedge" or "Tail Trade." Duration is defined by the intended holding period of the trade, which could be 0–2 months, 2–6 months, and 6 months or more, which we will refer to as short-term, medium-term, and long-term, respectively. It is crucial that a trader be as objective as possible on each trading day and score each trade appropriately.

Conviction level is a very interesting field that not only helps you monitor performance, but also helps to potentially identify a bias in your trading. Let's assume a 0–10 scale, where 0 is no conviction and 10 is the highest conviction. If, for instance, a pattern emerges where you are making money on most of your lower-conviction trades (5–6 score) and losing money on your high-conviction trades (8–10), this could be indicative of a confirmation

FIGURE 2.5   Baseball Hot Spots in the Strike Zone

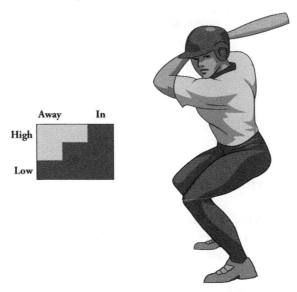

bias. Conversely, if you are consistently losing money on your low-conviction trades, perhaps you should stick strictly to high-conviction ideas.

The objective is to get the trader thinking about his or her trading style and how to best monitor performance. If one trades a lot of volume then it's helpful to have more fields. Again, the idea is that you always want to know what your revenue generators are, where you are losing money, and how you can improve. Table 2.2 is an example of how to break down P&L.

A few patterns emerge from the analysis of the returns in Table 2.2. It is clear that the bulk of the returns are attributable to trading foreign exchange and commodities, in short and medium terms. Imagine if one knew this ahead of time and could avoid areas of weakness; the P&L would be much stronger. It is worth noting that traders who have a fixed income background shouldn't avoid fixed income. They should decrease position sizes drastically to have little to no effect on the P&L and wait for performance and Sharpe to improve. Looking at the Sharpe ratios by strategy is also very telling. Even though the trader performed very well in foreign exchange, the Sharpe ratios in the commodity trades are the most attractive. It would make sense for the trader to add more risk to commodities and decrease risk elsewhere. If performance and Sharpe are maintained, then this is a winning strategy. But as soon as performance and the Sharpe begin to suffer, the trader can quickly

TABLE 2.2   Sample of Returns by Asset Class, Duration, and Sharpe Ratio

2013 Returns

	Short-Term	Medium-Term	Long-Term	Total
FX	2.1%	0.9%	0.3%	*3.3%*
FI	0.5%	−0.5%	−0.6%	*−0.6%*
Commodities	0.8%	3.2%	1.1%	*5.1%*
Equities	−0.3%	1.2%	−1.0%	*−0.1%*
X Sectional	0.3%	1.0%	−0.1%	*1.2%*
TOTAL	*3.4%*	*5.8%*	*−0.3%*	

2013 Sharpe Ratios

	Short-Term	Medium-Term	Long-Term
FX	1.62	1.80	1.00
FI	1.00		
Commodities	1.78	2.29	1.83
Equities		0.92	
X Sectional	0.60	0.91	

maneuver into products and duration where they are performing better, in order to maximize returns.

Again, the idea here is to have a firm process in place. As the great Sun Tzu said in *The Art of War*, "Each battle is won before it is fought." Trading markets is a never-ending battle. Learning one's strengths and weaknesses is the difference between making money and losing money.

Trend Analysis

Adding trend analysis to one's P&L record is another powerful monitoring tool. When both a short-term and long-term moving average are positive, the trader is said to be long the trend. Conversely, if the trader is short when both moving averages are positive, they are counter-trend. It is worth noting that when observing one's direction of trend, the starting point is the position of the trader. For example, if a trader is long but both moving averages are negative, the trader is still counter-trend.

The other two possibilities are trend reversal, and new trend. Trend reversal is when the short-term moving average is starting to turn negative. If one is a trend trader, knowing when the trend reverses is of absolute importance. If one is long the trend and the trend reverses, then, by definition, the trader is likely to lose money. The sooner the trader identifies the change in trend, the sooner he or she can exit. New trend is when the short-term moving average turns positive in the counter-trend. This can be the start of a new trend or a false breakout, so the trader should proceed with caution if going long the same direction as the shorter-term moving average (see Table 2.3).

Using moving averages, one can determine their trading style and P&L attribution. For example, if one considers themselves a trend trader, then he or she should try to be long the trend for as many days as possible. By being short the countertrend one is counted as being long the trend, reversing the signs of Table 2.3.

Table 2.4 shows an example of a whole year's trading P&L broken down by trend attribution. If one considers oneself a trend trader, he or she has done a good job of being in a trend 64 percent of the trading days for that year. Notice, though, that in Trend Reversal, they were down –2.4 percent for the year, even though that only accounted for 15 percent of the total trading days. If this particular trend trader wanted to improve, one thing he or she could do is

TABLE 2.3 Trend Types

	Short-Term	Long-Term
Trend	+	+
Trend Reversal	–	+
New Trend	+	–
Countertrend	–	–

TABLE 2.4 Sample of Annual Trend Breakdown

	No. of Days	% of Days	Return
Trend	162	64%	9.8%
Trend Reversal	39	15%	–2.2%
New Trend	29	12%	2.4%
Countertrend	22	9%	–1.1%
Total	*252*		*8.9%*

watch the shorter moving average more closely. If it begins to become negative, perhaps getting out of a position or decreasing position sizing would be appropriate. Using this methodology can improve trading performance. If traders consider themselves trend traders, there isn't any reason why they can't be long a trend 75 to 80 percent of the time. Clearly there is money to be made by staying long on trends. If they cut their positions before entering Trend Reversal, their strong performance would be even stronger and they could protect more gains. Remember, "the trend is your friend."

Bloomberg Shortcuts

PORT \<GO\>	Portfolio and Risk Analytics
MARS \<GO\>	Multi-Asset Risk System
BVAL \<GO\>	Bloomberg Valuation
MARS \<GO\>	Information on Bloomberg Valuation
HFA \<GO\>	Historical Fund Analysis
BT \<GO\>	Advanced Back-Testing and Optimization

Summary

Developing methods of risk management and the ability to evaluate your performance and improve your process are the bedrock of long-term success as a global macro trader. An established process gives you structure and helps you to avoid bias, but keep in mind that your process is not static and should evolve over time. The core concepts covered in this chapter are essential to growth in the discipline of global macro trading.

CHAPTER 3

Back-Tests, Queries, and Analogs

The old adage that "history repeats itself" is used by historians as the initial hook, or catchphrase, in explaining the value in studying history. Markets and human behavior are no different and having methods of analyzing past economic behaviors enables us to make more educated predictions about the future, which helps us become better traders and investors.

Anything you can do to further inform your trading and investing decisions, from a basic understanding of the ways markets have behaved in the past to performing complex back-testing of strategies, can help to prevent the same errors that have been made in the past. Doing so can help you avoid enormous losses of the kind traders have experienced in the past. Additionally, understanding the past in an economic sense can help traders identify potential trades and exit points. The ability to interpret the economic behavior of the past, using back-tests and analogs, and apply that knowledge to current scenarios gives a trader a powerful edge.

This chapter will show the reader how to run simple back-tests and queries. Understanding how these simple strategies work is critical for a global macro trader in order to be aware of risks that some of their trades might face. It will also help with generating short- to medium-term trade ideas. This chapter then examines historical correlations and analogs, which can be very helpful in determining longer-trend moves and predicting the future path of an asset.

Simple Back-Tests and Queries

The term "query" is the most-used term for observing a particular event and analyzing how particular assets behaved during past occurrences of the same event. For example, imagine that the Federal Open Market Committee (FOMC) meeting is tomorrow and the market expects the Fed to hike by 25 bps. What will happen to your portfolio? After the hike, what will happen to asset prices over the next week, month, or quarter? We can never have concrete answers to questions like these, but we do possess the hindsight that history affords us. We have the ability to look back in history during certain periods of time to see how markets behaved. Even though past performance is never a predictor of future performance, having an awareness of the effects of past events will ensure a trader has a much better sense of what is going on than someone who lacks this awareness. Even though the events cannot be predicted, your research will give you insights that others will not have. This is the power of creating queries.

Deciding which event to query is essentially identifying the problem you are facing. As the saying goes, "Identifying the problem is half the battle." Once the event is identified, solving for the output is relatively rudimentary. Central bank dates are always a great starting point. For instance, it would be useful to know whether the ECB is meeting tomorrow, because the announcement of the meeting will affect what happens to the euro, gold, SX5E (Euro Stoxx 50), and SX7E (Euro Stoxx Bank Index), bunds, and peripheral spreads. You'll want to narrow down the number of dates you're analyzing by finding other similarities in the economic climate at the time. Let's assume that the ECB rate is 0.75 percent and the market is expecting no change in the interest rate (0.75 percent). The more logical historical meetings to back-test are days when the ECB made no change to the rate. This way, when the ECB meets and no change is made (expected outcome), you have an idea of how assets performed under similar circumstances in the past, and might, conceivably, perform again.

An Example of Building a Query

Short-term trades can take many forms, which is why day traders have countless techniques for capitalizing on patterns and market momentum. We will explore two ways of using queries to aid short-term trading in global macro.

The first way is to trade on the day of news events. One example would be the Bank of England (BOE) minutes for June 2012 showed that the BOE had changed direction and voted 5 to 4 in favor of no quantitative easing (QE). (This is covered in further detail in Chapter 11.) However, since the economy continued to deteriorate in the UK and, as the country was already in recession, some traders knew that it was very likely that in the July meeting the

BOE was going to opt for more QE—which is what the public was predicting. Sure enough, at 7 A.M. on July 5, 2012, when the press release came out, the BOE opted for £50 billion in additional QE, which was bearish for the British pound. By expecting this beforehand, one could have shorted the GBP right before the meeting (Table 3.1).

To determine whether there may be a short-term trade or not, one would want to run a query that back-tests the past dates of quantitative easing by the Bank of England (Table 3.1).

Table 3.2 takes the historical dates from Table 3.1 and then looks at the asset returns of the FTSE 100 (UKX Index), U.S. Dollar Index (DXY Index), British Pound (GBP Curncy), gold in British pounds (XAUGBP Curncy), gold in U.S. dollars (XAU Curncy), WTI Crude (CL1 Comdty), FTSE Banking Sector (F3BANK Index), 2-year gilts (GUKG2 Index), 5-year gilts (GUKG5 Index), and 10-year gilts (GUKG10 Index). The objective is to see what the best or worst performers are in order to evaluate whether or not to make a short-term trade, or if one's portfolio could be potentially exposed in a way not previously thought. Queries are an extremely powerful tool for predicting asset behaviors in this way.

The first box is the average return right after the BOE QE announcement. For example, we would expect the FTSE 100 (UKX Index) to rally 30 bps, on average, the day of a BOE QE announcement, and 170 bps +4 days out. The second and third boxes are up and down days. Since there were six observations, the corresponding data for up and down days will sum to 100 percent. Sticking with the FTSE 100, on the day of the announcement we can see that the FTSE went up 83 percent of the time. The FTSE 100 (UKX Index) traded up five times and down one time the day of BOE QE, and four

TABLE 3.1 Bank of England—Quantitative Easing

Date	Amount	Total
March 5, 2009	£75 billion	£75 billion
May 7, 2009	£50 billion	£125 billion
August 6, 2009	£50 billion	£175 billion
November 5, 2009	£25 billion	£200 billion
October 6, 2011	£75 billion	£275 billion
February 9, 2012	£50 billion	£325 billion

Source: Bank of England.

TABLE 3.2 BoE Quantitative Easing—Query Output of Expected Returns

	Average Return						
	+1 Day	+2 Days	+3 Days	+4 Days	+5 Days	+2 Weeks	+1 Month
	7/5/2012	7/6/2012	7/9/2012	7/10/2012	7/11/2012	7/19/2012	8/6/2012
UKX Index	0.3%	0.6%	1.2%	1.7%	1.6%	2.2%	4.0%
DXY Curncy	0.2%	0.1%	-0.1%	-0.1%	-0.4%	-1.7%	-1.2%
GBP Curncy	-0.3%	-0.2%	-0.5%	-0.6%	-0.6%	0.9%	1.2%
XAUGBP Curncy	0.8%	0.6%	1.0%	0.7%	1.2%	1.2%	1.3%
XAU Curncy	0.4%	0.4%	0.4%	0.1%	0.6%	2.1%	2.5%
CL1 Comdty	0.1%	0.5%	2.0%	1.4%	0.4%	5.1%	7.4%
F3BANK Index	0.5%	0.8%	1.2%	2.0%	1.3%	4.0%	6.3%
GUKG2 Index	0.00	0.00	-0.02	-0.03	-0.06	-0.01	0.05
GUKG5 Index	-0.04	-0.07	-0.07	-0.07	-0.10	-0.14	-0.07
GUKG10 Index	-0.03	-0.06	-0.05	-0.06	-0.09	-0.15	-0.07

	Up						
	+1 Day	+2 Days	+3 Days	+4 Days	+5 Days	+2 Weeks	+1 Month
	7/5/2012	7/6/2012	7/9/2012	7/10/2012	7/11/2012	7/19/2012	8/6/2012
UKX Index	83%	67%	83%	100%	83%	83%	100%
DXY Curncy	67%	50%	50%	50%	33%	33%	50%
GBP Curncy	17%	50%	33%	50%	50%	67%	50%
XAUGBP Curncy	67%	33%	67%	100%	100%	67%	50%
XAU Curncy	33%	50%	67%	50%	67%	67%	67%
CL1 Comdty	50%	50%	67%	67%	50%	83%	67%
F3BANK Index	50%	67%	83%	50%	67%	83%	50%
GUKG2 Index	50%	67%	33%	50%	33%	33%	67%
GUKG5 Index	50%	67%	17%	50%	17%	33%	33%
GUKG10 Index	67%	50%	50%	33%	17%	33%	17%

Down

	+1 Day	+2 Days	+3 Days	+4 Days	+5 Days	+2 Weeks	+1 Month
	7/5/2012	7/6/2012	7/9/2012	7/10/2012	7/11/2012	7/19/2012	8/6/2012
UKX Index	17%	33%	17%	0%	17%	17%	0%
DXY Curncy	33%	50%	50%	50%	67%	67%	50%
GBP Curncy	83%	50%	67%	50%	50%	33%	50%
XAUGBP Curncy	33%	67%	33%	0%	0%	33%	50%
XAU Curncy	67%	50%	33%	50%	33%	33%	33%
CL1 Comdty	50%	50%	33%	33%	50%	17%	33%
F3BANK Index	50%	33%	17%	50%	33%	17%	50%
GUKG2 Index	50%	33%	67%	50%	67%	67%	33%
GUKG5 Index	50%	33%	83%	50%	83%	67%	67%
GUKG10 Index	33%	50%	50%	67%	83%	67%	83%

Standard Deviation

	+1 Day	+2 Days	+3 Days	+4 Days	+5 Days	+2 Weeks	+1 Month
	7/5/2012	7/6/2012	7/9/2012	7/10/2012	7/11/2012	7/19/2012	8/6/2012
UKX Index	2.2%	2.4%	2.8%	2.0%	2.8%	2.4%	3.9%
DXY Curncy	0.4%	1.1%	1.5%	1.6%	1.6%	2.8%	2.5%
GBP Curncy	0.5%	1.0%	1.9%	2.0%	1.8%	2.6%	3.8%
XAUGBP Curncy	1.4%	1.9%	1.9%	0.9%	0.9%	2.8%	6.0%
XAU Curncy	1.2%	1.6%	1.5%	1.4%	1.6%	3.4%	5.0%
CL1 Comdty	2.5%	3.1%	3.4%	4.1%	5.0%	6.3%	11.5%
F3BANK Index	5.0%	5.7%	6.9%	4.3%	7.1%	6.6%	15.9%
GUKG2 Index	0.03	0.05	0.09	0.09	0.14	0.25	0.27
GUKG5 Index	0.09	0.18	0.14	0.16	0.16	0.15	0.28
GUKG10 Index	0.14	0.27	0.25	0.26	0.27	0.25	0.17

Source: Bloomberg and Bank of England.
Note: Gilts are quoted in terms of basis points of change, not percentage.

days out trades up six times and down zero times (or up 100 percent of the time). This means that UK stocks have historically rallied 83 percent and 100 percent of the time, respectively.

The last box shows standard deviation. The small sample size sacrifices some of the accuracy in the prediction, but it can still be useful to examine even a small number of observations. For example, the FTSE 100 had a standard deviation of 220 bps. Within one standard deviation we would expect the returns to be –190 bps to 250 bps (30 bps ± 220 bps). XAUGBP (gold in British pounds), on the other hand, had an 80 bps average the day of BOE QE with a 140 bps standard deviation. This provided a one-standard-deviation expected return of –60 bps to 220 bps, which is a more attractive return profile (30 bps ± 220 bps). With larger samples, this can be used to calculate Sharpe ratios for each trade. Had you traded XAUGBP or the FTSE 100, however, you would have lost money. Figure 3.1 shows how the British pound fell as the query results predicted.

Keep in mind that while queries are very useful, like all strategies, they can't be perfectly accurate and you can still lose money. The objective here is not just to show how to build a query but also to show that not all queries promise a profitable outcome.

FIGURE 3.1   British Pound Intraday Performance on July 5, 2012

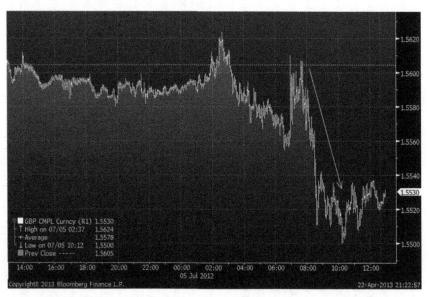

Source: Bloomberg.

Queries are a very helpful tool that can help all traders, investors, and strategies during particular events with large volatility. For those interested in a great resource on queries, Robert Hanna from QuantifiableEdges.com does some fantastic work on this topic.

False Positives

False Positives occur in all back-tests and trading signals, otherwise queries and analogs would be foolproof. The key with false positives is understanding that they can, and often do, happen. Once you recognize a situation in which a false positive is occurring, especially on a short-term query trade, it is critical to cut your losses as soon as possible. Certainly a loss can reverse, but if you are playing a central bank or data release, and the position moves against you, you need to identify where you were wrong, cut the trade, and move on. In our example from the Bank of England announcement, had traders been long the FTSE instead of being short the British pound, they would have lost money (Figure 3.2). False positives are living proof that queries, while useful, do not always work. Queries are very useful for assessing overall risk to

FIGURE 3.2 FTSE Intraday Performance on July 5, 2012

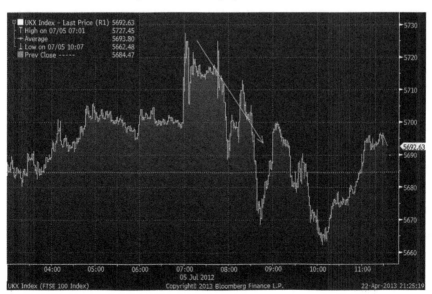

Source: Bloomberg.

a portfolio, but if you use queries for short-term trades then you should cut your losses as soon as you realize you are wrong. After all, remembering that a trade is short-term should keep a trader honest and avoid bias.

Historical Correlations and Analogs

Analogs, like queries, should not be used to predict the future in any absolute way, but they can provide a helpful roadmap that guides a trader toward more likely outcomes in different scenarios. The objective is to utilize what you do know rather than haphazardly guess about what you don't know.

Price action in the Dow Jones Industrial Average (DJIA) is something that can be confusing and perplexing for everyone. Let's take a closer look at how using analogs can help us examine this data.

Let's look closely at the 100-day period of July 22, 2011, to December 12, 2011 (Figure 3.3). The chart shows just how choppy the market was, with volatile moves both upward and downward. Many traders and market participants were confused by this volatility. Did it indicate another Great

FIGURE 3.3   Dow Jones Industrial Average Price Chart from July 2011 to December 2011

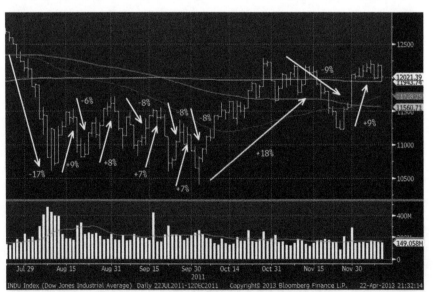

Source: Bloomberg.

Depression on the horizon, or would stocks finally rally to new highs after this consolidated period?

To run a proper analog, or historical correlation, of an asset, one must freeze the price performance and then compare it to periods of high correlation in the past.

Let's look at the U.S. Dollar Index (DXY) as our asset of choice when observing analogs and, for purposes of simplicity, run data from 2005. The ideal scenario is one that has the least number of variables—that is, a high correlation with a similar economic environment. For instance, if a historical asset's correlation is around 80 percent and both periods were recoveries, that will likely deliver a more meaningful output than comparing periods where the asset prices moved in different ways and existed in different economic climates.

The next variable one must determine is the amount of days the period will span, which we'll refer to as our "analog period." For this example we will assume 180 days, from March 16, 2011, to November 21, 2011 (Figure 3.4) when observing the U.S. Dollar Index.

In August 2011, the stock market fell precipitously and, as a result, risk-on assets fared poorly. The dollar started to rally, however, and the volatility of the market was very choppy and hard to read. This was also true in the foreign exchange market and for the dollar.

According to Figure 3.5, the period ending October 20, 2008, had the highest correlation with the analog period, which was 79 percent. The beginning part of the analog time range for that 180-day period was February 12, 2008, right before the time of the Bear Stearns collapse. The period also includes the Lehman Brothers bankruptcy, which occurred in September 2008. Granted, our analog period does not possess the same stress, although there was certainly a considerable amount of confusion and talk of a double-dip recession.

After the analog period in 2008, the dollar continued to rally to the right of the vertical line in Figure 3.6. What we find is that, in 2011, the original period in which we began running historical correlations also ended up rallying. If the additional days were included in the original analog period of 180

FIGURE 3.4 Analog Period Time Series

FIGURE 3.5   U.S. Dollar Index Historical Correlations to 180-Day Analog Period

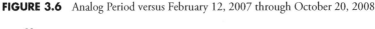

Source: Bloomberg.

FIGURE 3.6   Analog Period versus February 12, 2007 through October 20, 2008

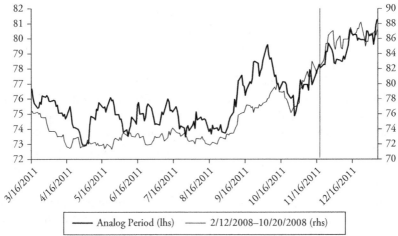

Source: Bloomberg.

and were extended as in the chart, the correlation ran higher than 85 percent. This demonstrates that even though past performance is not an infallible predictor of the future, it can provide valuable insight into future performance. Those who have researched the correlations shown in Figure 3.6 could have profited in this period of uncertainty by making sure they were long on the U.S. Dollar Index.

Summary

This chapter is intended to give the reader a framework for constructing simple back-tests and queries on important events. Since past events can have a big impact on one's profit and loss, it helps to back-test prior occurrences in order to observe how particular assets have reacted. Additionally, grasping how historical analogs work can help with understanding confusing price action and also improve chances of profitability by observing historical patterns in price moves.

CHAPTER 4

The Building Blocks of Global Macro Trading

The Importance of Equities, Fixed Income, Foreign Exchange, and Commodities in Global Macro

Most capital markets can be subcategorized into one of the four product groups: currencies (foreign exchange), equities, fixed income, and commodities. This chapter aims to give a basic introduction to the four groups and describe their role in global macro. Having an insight into these groups and their relationships to one another is critical to developing an understanding of global macro.

The Four Product Groups

Let's start by discussing the markets in broad categories. Table 4.1 aims to highlight the biggest and most important markets in each of the four categories. This list is by no means exhaustive, but will serve to demonstrate the nature of each market.

Currencies

The first product group we cover is currencies. For the purposes of this chapter, let's look at them from the perspective of major currency pairs and commodity currencies.

TABLE 4.1 The Four Product Groups

Currencies	Equities	Fixed Income	Commodities
USD, EUR, JPY, GBP, AUD, CAD, CHF, BRL, MXN, RUB	S&P 500	United States	Oil
	Nasdaq	Germany	Gold
	Euro Stoxx 50	Italy	Copper
	Nikkei	Japan	Corn
	Shanghai Composite	United Kingdom	
	Bovespa		

FIGURE 4.1 Foreign Exchange Market Turnover by Currency Pairs

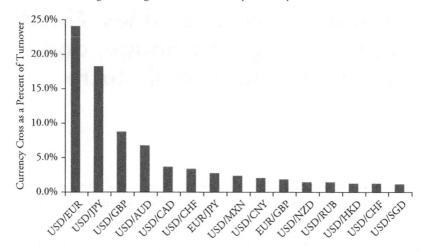

Source: 2013 Triennial Central Bank Survey: Bank for International Settlements. As of April 2013.

Generally, the best way to view major global currencies is against the U.S. dollar. One can observe the price changes of currencies on a daily basis in combinations of pairs. Major global currency pairs—EUR/USD, GBP/USD, and USD/JPY—and the U.S. dollar's strength alone are the starting point for currencies, as they are the most traded by volume (see Figure 4.1).

The aforementioned combinations of pairs are significant because they are the most heavily traded. These currencies can be used to gauge both risk-on and the fixed income market. For example, when GBP/USD rallies, this typically denotes a risk-on day, so we would expect the S&P 500 to rally as well. Commodity-based currencies consist of some of the following pairs of countries:

- AUD/USD
- NZD/USD

- USD/CAD
- USD/BRL
- USD/ZAR
- USD/RUB
- USD/CLP

These countries are a mix of emerging and developed markets, but all are commodity exporters. On a day when commodity prices are falling across the board, we would expect most of these currency pairs to weaken versus the U.S. dollar. For example, Canada is the largest supplier of crude oil to the United States and this accounts for a large percentage of their exports. Since 1996, the correlation of the Canadian dollar to WTI Crude Oil is almost 80 percent. Figure 4.2 illustrates the interrelatedness of cross assets.

Currencies alone have a number of important characteristics that are explored in more depth later in the book. The idea in this chapter is to demonstrate that currencies are more interrelated with other product groups than many traders realize.

Equities

The second group is equities, which are discussed in depth in Chapter 8. The S&P 500, Nasdaq, Euro Stoxx 50, and Nikkei are the best barometers for

FIGURE 4.2   Canadian Dollar versus WTI Crude Oil

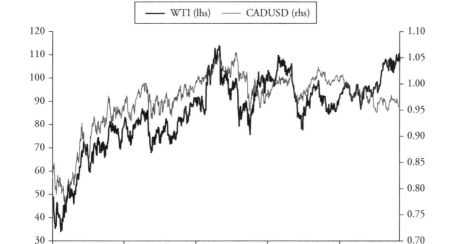

Source: Bloomberg.

global equity prices in the developed world. They are also the largest in terms of GDP of the underlying countries or regions they represent (except China): the United States, Europe, and Japan. The Dow Jones Industrial Average (INDU Index) is also an important index, though it is not as broad as the S&P 500. The S&P 500 in the United States is considered to be the most important equity index. The Nasdaq is watched by traders in order to get a sense of business in the technology and growth sectors. The Euro Stoxx 50 Index is the standard for watching European equity markets and is a collection of the largest 50 blue chip companies in the Eurozone.

In addition to watching the developed world, keeping an eye on the Bovespa, KOSPI, Hang Seng China Enterprise Index (HSCEI), and Shanghai Composite will offer the best insight into how the emerging market equities are behaving. These indices have a large beta to the S&P 500 and typically react in a magnitude of the S&P 500. The Bovespa and the Shanghai Composite are largely composed of commodity and bank companies, which makes them more volatile. Equity indices as a whole are the standard of risk markets and are at the core of risk-on/risk-off.

Fixed Income

The fixed income market is in many ways the most important of the four product groups. One reason it is so critical is that, in equities, fixed income and money markets act as a discount rate for investments, where the rate affects the value of virtually every asset in the long run (future value) and, in currencies, affects factors like carry. The United States, Japan, Germany, and the United Kingdom are the best starting points for looking at sovereign fixed income.

The challenge of fixed income today is that it is no longer the free market it once was. In the United States, the United Kingdom, Japan, and Europe, the central banks have become the largest players in buying schemes. For instance, one famous macro trade many people like to propose is selling 10-year Japanese government bonds (JGBs). With a debt-to-GDP of over 200 percent and an aging demographic population that will eventually have to sell their holdings, it is only a matter of time till yields rise. But how can a country with so much debt borrow at around 1 percent for 10 years? The far better question is not *if* you should short 10-Year JGBs, but *when* you should short them.

In fact, as it turns out, Japan's debt-to-GDP has risen since 2006 and yields on 10-year JGB's have fallen (see Figure 4.3)—the opposite of what one would predict. A similar example is in U.S. fixed income markets. The

FIGURE 4.3 Japan Debt to GDP Ratio and 10-Year Japanese Government Bonds

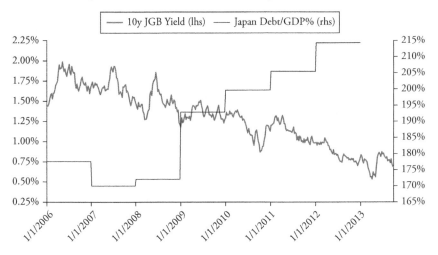

Source: Bloomberg.

old mantra is "don't fight the Fed," yet by shorting U.S. fixed income during quantitative easing, you are doing just that—fighting the Fed. So, while fixed income markets are the main drivers of global capitalism, trading "fixed" markets against central banks is difficult. Sadly, the action by central banks has become more the rule in global markets than the exception, which is contributing to the decline of free-market capitalism as we know it.

Commodities

The final product group is commodities, which includes energy, precious metals, industrial metals, agriculture, and livestock. For the best snapshot of the global commodity atmosphere, we can start by looking at oil, gold, copper, and corn. There are a number of subcategories within the commodities group, but we cover those in Chapter 10.

- Gold has, in a way, become the anti-fiat currency trade (i.e., it acts as a currency). Its several-decade bull market is evidence that people are losing faith in fiat money. Real negative yields in recent years have also been a big factor.
- Crude oil is the benchmark of energy markets and can offer a sense of global growth and global political stability.

- Copper is the best industrial metal to watch and one of the strongest risk-on assets in global markets. Many economists and market participants claim that "copper has a PhD in Economics," due to the fact that it is often a leading indicator.
- Corn is the agricultural product with the deepest liquidity. It acts as a complement to, and substitute for, other products like wheat, soybeans, and even gasoline, since roughly 30 percent of corn demand is ethanol-based in the United States.

Assessing the Relationships between Assets

What makes global macro trading so fascinating is how closely connected all assets really are. Let's look at some examples to get a better sense of the inter-relationships in global macro markets.

Figure 4.4 shows copper prices versus CLP/USD (Chilean pesos). Typically Chilean pesos are quoted in USD/CLP, but for purposes of this chart we are using the inverse to show the relationship to copper. It turns out that Chile is the largest exporter of copper in the world. Hence, their balance of trade and capital flows are largely influenced by the price of copper.

FIGURE 4.4   Copper versus the Chilean Peso

Source: Bloomberg.

Knowing this, it makes perfect sense that copper and Chilean pesos are correlated almost at 90 percent. Essentially, one can look at the price of copper or Chilean pesos to determine what the other is doing. This is a powerful depiction of the correlation between markets and also illustrates the benefits global traders stand to gain from watching all markets.

When GDP growth is stronger than expected in a country like the United States, we would expect corporate profits to do well (S&P 500 rallies). This might mean the companies need to expand, causing a need for new buildings, which in turn might cause demand for copper and iron ore to increase, and so on. This is a perfect demonstration of how tightly connected all the markets really are.

Risk On/Risk Off

Risk on refers to assets in the four product groups that benefit from strong growth or the perception of more growth than the markets have priced. Risk off is typically defined as a perception of less growth than the markets have priced. Think of the two as an on and off switch. Risk on means that risk assets, such as equity indices, oil, copper, and commodity currencies, are rallying in the same period. When such assets sell off in the same period, it's referred to as risk-off. What we find in global macro markets, is that risk-on events not only occur in equities but are intertwined within all global markets. For example, if someone told you that the S&P 500 was trading 2 percent higher on the day, without looking at any other prices, you could reasonably guess that copper prices, the Australian dollar, and oil prices would all be trading higher.

There are several reasons for this, one of which is correlation, which we cover in the next section. The other reason is the economic interrelationship between each product.

If the United States is growing at a great rate (S&P 500 up on the day), then China will benefit because this is when U.S. consumers spend more. This in turn means that Chinese equities will perform better, resulting in the Chinese building more; that is, their demand for copper will increase. From this information, we could infer that copper prices will increase as well as the Australian dollar. Because Australia exports a lot of its commodities to countries like China, the Australian dollar moves in line with these risk assets. This is the basic concept of risk-on.

Conversely, if the S&P 500 trades lower, or risk-off, we would expect oil prices, the Aussie dollar, and copper prices to trade lower. Clearly, on a day-to-day basis, this relationship is not 100 percent accurate, but this formula tends to hold true. For instance, if the S&P 500 is trading 2 percent up on the day, but the Reserve Bank of Australia (RBA) unexpectedly cuts interest rates by 25 basis points, then the Australian dollar could potentially trade lower. What this demonstrates is that risk-on/risk-off is a general relationship that typically holds true, but is by no means set in stone.

The concept of risk-on/risk-off is very important because if one believes that assets will rally, one wants to be in the position to long the asset that will move the greatest percentage. For example, if the S&P 500 for a particular month is up 2 percent but copper, oil, and risk-on currencies are all up greater than 5 percent for the month, traders will feel like they did not have enough risk-on, or possibly missed the trade window.

Lastly, on a day-to-day trading basis, risk-on/risk-off is a crucial gauge because it gives you a sense of the mood for the day and also allows you to keep an eye on the intraday movements. If stocks are up 1 percent in the early morning trading and closed down 1 percent by the end of the day, clearly sentiment has changed intraday. This can typically be seen through all risk assets. The strength of these assets moving together is a relationship referred to as correlation.

Correlation

Correlation is critical to understanding global macro trading and other trading strategies. For purposes of this book we examine the correlation of global macro assets in order to better understand the interrelationships of markets. A perfect correlation is 100 percent. What this means is that as the price of asset A moves 1.5 percent, we would expect the price of asset B to also move exactly 1.5 percent, and these assets would move in line through a time series. Of course, in the real world we never see perfect correlation. Anything greater than 75 percent is defined as "strong correlation," though correlation lower than that still shows strong relationships. In the context of risk-on/risk-off, we can see why correlation matters—it is the very thing that holds all of these interrelationships together.

If a trader has a position where he or she is long the S&P 500 and long copper, when correlations run high, they can be almost twice as long the S&P 500 as they may want to believe. Why is this? If the S&P 500 rises, we would anticipate that the price of copper would typically also rise. Conversely, if the price of the S&P 500 falls, we would expect the price of copper to fall, hence the trader has effectively twice the amount of risk-on as they probably thought. This is critical because it is always important to know exactly what risk one is facing when trading an entire portfolio. It is very important to note

FIGURE 4.5   Four Individual Assets from the Four Market Categories during the 2008 Financial Crisis

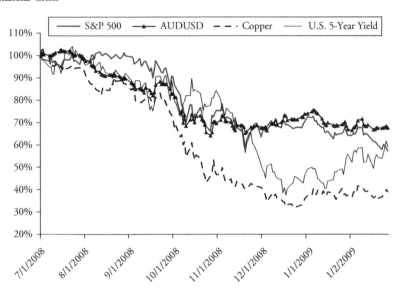

Source: Bloomberg.

that the correlation of rising markets tends to be weaker than falling markets. Figure 4.5 shows a chart of the four product groups during the September 2008 Lehman bankruptcy. The chart demonstrates that when markets are under duress, correlations typically run very high. When markets rally, as we have seen in recent years, assets tend to be less correlated, as we can see in Figure 4.1. The general relationship is that, in times of stress, correlation amongst different assets tends to be higher than in periods of calm or rising equity prices.

Summary

The goal of this chapter is to introduce the four main product groups: currencies, equities, fixed income, and commodities, and to explain the ways they are relevant to each other. These product groups are the foundation of global macro trading, and understanding how they work as well as the effects of risk-on/risk-off and correlations will help serve as a foundation for successful trading. Later chapters discuss these product categories in further detail.

CHAPTER 5

Technical Analysis

Technical analysis is a very effective means of examining past price moves and volume to help predict future moves in a particular market. Its roots can be traced back to the seventeenth century in the Netherlands with *Confusion of Confusions* by Joseph de la Vega, and even before that to Japan with the rice trader who developed what we now know as candlestick charts.

Even for the nonbelievers who follow only fundamentals, having a basic understanding of technical analysis can prove useful in many macro markets. Technical analysis gives many traders the discipline to know when to enter a trade and how to look for appropriate risk/reward ratios on their trades. Since much of technical analysis uses charts to measure potential price moves, it is a very effective tool for providing macro traders with the discipline of putting on trades that they believe can give them the appropriate risk/reward balance.

This chapter introduces the reader to the strengths and weaknesses of technical analysis. It also discusses the different types of charts, trends, and moving averages, and various oscillators such as Elliott Waves, Fibonacci numbers, parabolics, seasonals, cycles, and crowd psychology.

Strengths and Weaknesses of Technical Analysis

One of the greatest strengths of technical analysis is that it gives a trader the discipline to get in and out of a trade. Traders are subject to many biases and technical analysis can serve as a useful anchor to help them cut losses. Momentum and trend-following over the long run can be a profitable trading strategy, especially in commodities. While momentum has been viewed as its own category for evaluating assets, it is ultimately a technical indicator.

People and market participants are irrational. The point of technical analysis is to use methodologies to identify market extremes and biases. Technical analysis also helps traders identify patterns in history by examining certain price movements from past regimes. This can then help them predict future market behavior and establish their risk/reward on each trade. Utilizing technical analysis in one's process can be a great way to avoid bias and set objective profit-taking levels and stop-losses that meet one's risk/reward targets. There is no right or wrong way as long as the trader makes money with their system. In *Market Wizards* by Jack Schwager (John Wiley & Sons, 2006), Marty Schwartz says, "I used fundamentals for nine years and then got rich as a technician."

Not everyone buys in to the value of technical analysis. The greatest argument *against* it is the efficient market hypothesis, which asserts that past prices cannot predict the future. Furthermore, Eugene Fama, from the University of Chicago, has found significant evidence that the efficient market hypothesis is valid. An extension of that is the random walk theory, which asserts that prices of assets move randomly regardless of what the intrinsic value is.

Another argument that is used against technical analysis is that it is valid merely because so many people believe in it and becomes a self-fulfilling prophecy. For instance, if an asset breaks a bullish trend line, many would assert that it is not necessarily a short. Technicians would assert that, valid or not, the fact that people buy in to technical analysis just means it's another reason to use it, while opponents argue that a self-fulfilling prophecy is not a basis for investment decisions. Some would argue that the fact that it is such a hotly contested topic makes it one worth discussing.

Types of Charts

Traders use several different types of charts in their analyses and each one has advantages and disadvantages. It's important to recognize that charts have different periodicity. For example, if you're looking at a shorter time horizon, such as one year, it might make more sense to use a daily chart, while if you're looking at a multidecade chart, it would make more sense to look at weekly or monthly price changes, depending on your needs. For a day trader, an intraday, hourly, or minute chart is most useful.

The basic types of charts are:

- Line chart
- Bar chart

FIGURE 5.1 Line Chart of the S&P 500

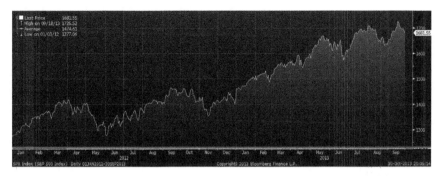

Source: Bloomberg.

- Candlestick chart
- Point and figure chart
- Logarithmic scale chart

Line Chart

A line chart is the most basic chart. A daily chart uses a line to connect an asset's closing price points (Figure 5.1). Line charts are very clean and easy to read, but the problem is they do not show how prices change for each period. For example, if we were looking at a daily line chart we would be unable to ascertain the intraday price action.

A line chart can be created on Bloomberg simply by selecting an asset and then entering GP <GO>.

Bar Chart

Bar charts are the most commonly used charts among technicians for two reasons. They are easy to read and construct and they also provide the trader with more detail than a simple line chart (see Figure 5.2). The vertical bar going up and down represents the high and low price of the asset for the day. The horizontal line to the left of the vertical line represents the opening price of the asset and the horizontal line to the right represents the closing price of the asset.

They are called bar charts because the vertical line that represents the high and low of the day is a vertical bar. Figure 5.3 shows a full bar chart of the S&P 500. Daily bar charts are the most common, followed by weekly charts. One of the advantages of looking at a bar chart instead of a line chart is that

FIGURE 5.2   Sample of a Single Bar on a Bar Chart

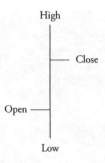

FIGURE 5.3   Bar Chart of the S&P 500

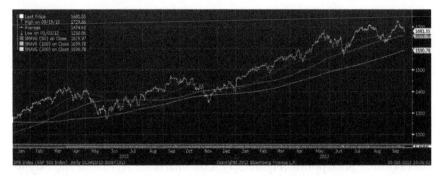

Source: Bloomberg LP.

price gaps can be identified. Many technicians follow the adage that "gaps get filled." This means that if the price gap is higher, you would predict that the price would fall and eventually fill the gap.

Bar charts are created on Bloomberg by entering GPO <GO> after most assets.

Candlestick Charts

Candlestick charts are similar to bar charts and record the same prices: the high, low, opening, and closing prices. Figure 5.4 shows the basic construct of a candlestick chart.

Figure 5.4 shows two candlesticks, one where the price closes up on the day and one where the price closes down on the day. The main difference between candlestick and bar charts is the candlestick's body, which gives more visual information and has more patterns for technicians to use. If the real body is white, that means that the price, open to close, was higher. Conversely,

FIGURE 5.4   Sample Candlesticks

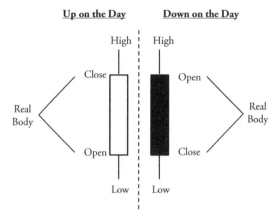

FIGURE 5.5   Candlestick Chart of the S&P 500

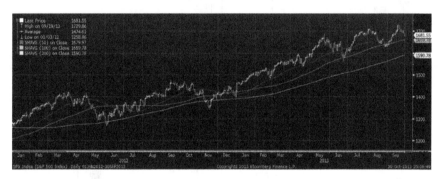

Source: Bloomberg.

if the real body is black, that means that the closing price was lower for that period. Figure 5.5 shows a candlestick chart representing the S&P 500 for the same period as in the bar chart in Figure 5.3.

Candlesticks also offer additional patterns that are unique to this type of chart. Certain patterns are indicative of bullish or bearish signals. Many traders use these signals in trading. It is difficult to quantify the magnitude of these moves, however, which leaves much of the interpretation to human judgment. Figure 5.6 shows a sample of some basic and more complex structures. A gray body means that it will hold true regardless of whether the body is white or black.

A candlestick chart can be created on Bloomberg with GPC <GO> on most assets.

FIGURE 5.6 Major Japanese Candlestick Signals

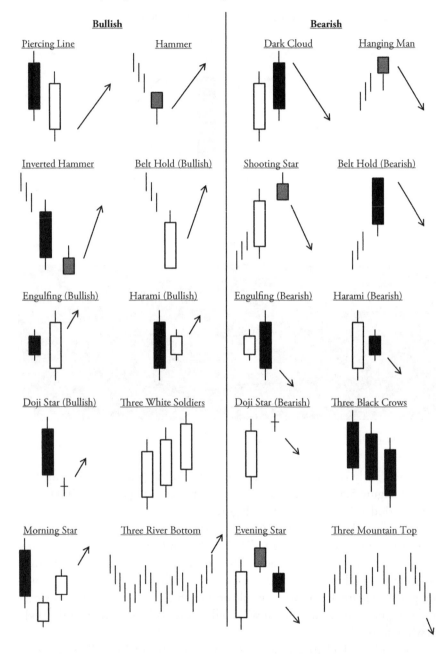

Point and Figure

Point and figure charts are unique in that all other charts plot time on the x-axis, whereas point and figure charts plot only the price changes. If you were to look at the x-axis, you would not be able to tell how much time has elapsed. Point and figures are constructed using X's and O's, where the X's mean the asset price has moved higher and O's signify the price going down. The y-axis is the price. Point and figure charts are described by their box size and reversal size. For example, 10 × 3 is a very common chart. This means that the incremental box size is 10 points. If one is plotting X's, another X is drawn for every 10-point price increase. Figure 5.7 demonstrates the mechanics of the box size. The reversal size means that 3 (from 10 × 3) times the box size is the minimum move required to switch to O's, which is down 30 points. In Figure 5.7, when the price goes from 1050 to 1040 and to 1030, that isn't enough for an O. Once the asset falls 30 points to 1020, then O's are marked for 1040, 1030, and 1020 (Arrow 1). This may not be intuitive at first, but the rationale here is to avoid noise. If there was an X or O for every 10-point change up or down, the chart would be cluttered and not as useful. After a 30-point fall, every subsequent 10-point drop gets an O (Arrow 2). In order to move along the x-axis to the next X, the price change again would need to be at least 30 points to the upside.

Figure 5.8 is a more developed point and figure chart. It demonstrates that on the x-axis, we have no idea how much time has elapsed. It could be one month or even a year. Over time, point and figure charts give technicians patterns on what the market may do and the magnitude of each move. Perhaps the best book on point and figures is *The Definitive Guide to Point and Figure* by Jeremy Du Plessis.

Point and figure charts can be seen on Bloomberg with PFP <GO>.

FIGURE 5.7 Point and Figure Chart—First Steps

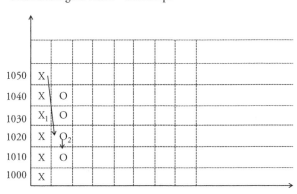

FIGURE 5.8 Point and Figure Chart

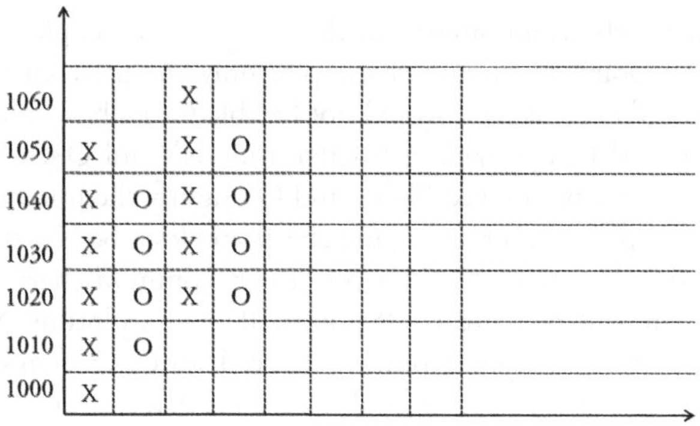

1060			X							
1050	X		X	O						
1040	X	O	X	O						
1030	X	O	X	O						
1020	X	O	X	O						
1010	X	O								
1000	X									

FIGURE 5.9 Arithmetic Scale and Logarithmic Scale

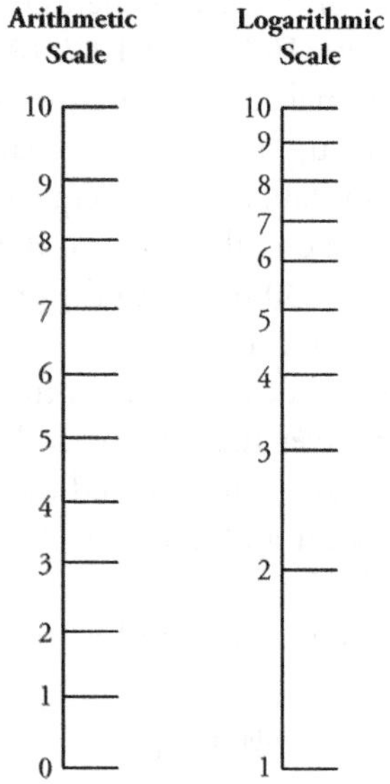

Arithmetic Scale	Logarithmic Scale
10	10
	9
9	8
8	7
	6
7	5
6	4
5	
	3
4	
3	2
2	
1	
0	1

Logarithmic Scale Charts

All the charts described thus far use arithmetic scale, meaning that the y-axis has an equidistant measure among points. In instances where assets have moved substantially over longer periods of time, or the asset has become a parabolic, it helps to use a logarithmic scale to get a different perspective of the asset price move (see Figure 5.9).

One great illustration of the use of a logarithmic scale can be found by looking back to the Dow Jones Industrial Average from the 1920s, when it

FIGURE 5.10   Dow Jones Industrial Average: (a) Regular Chart and (b) Lognormal Chart

(a)
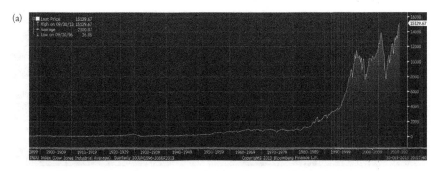

(b)
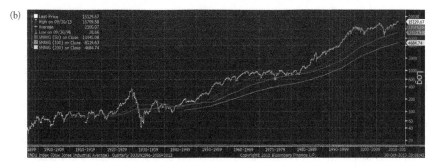

Source: Bloomberg.

traded below 100. Today, the DJIA trades above 15,000. If you were using a regular arithmetic scale you wouldn't be able to see significant price changes that occurred, since 100 compared to more than 10,000 today is such a small percentage (see Figure 5.10 for a comparison). Another great example for a shorter-term chart is the price of gold. In the new millennium, the price of gold is a parabolic chart. Because we are looking at a period that is longer than a few years, it makes sense to look at a logarithmic chart of gold to see price moves prior to the big move we have experienced over the past decade.

This chart can be made on Bloomberg with GPL <GO>.

Volume and Open Interest

After price change, volume and open interest are the next most important factors to monitor. Volume applies to all markets, whereas open interest only applies to the futures market. Volume is the total amount of a particular asset

FIGURE 5.11   Bar Chart and Volume of the S&P 500

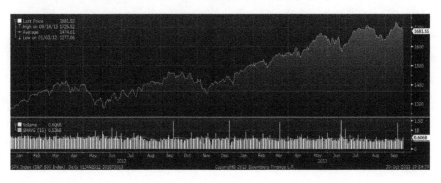

Source: Bloomberg.

that is traded (see Figure 5.11). The magnitude of volume can provide insight on price moves and potential sentiment. On volume charts, the volume is below the price chart.

Open interest is the total number of long or shorts that are currently outstanding in a futures contract. It is important to distinguish the fact that a futures contract must have one buyer and one seller to create one contract. When the open interest is calculated, the buyer and seller create a contract and are not double counted. Changes in open interest can confirm the strength of a move in a particular asset. This report comes from the Commodity Futures Trading Commission (CFTC) website and is also found on Bloomberg.

CFTC Positioning

Understanding positioning is an important technical indicator. You can look at plot positioning historically to see if speculators ("specs") are too long, or too short. According to Bloomberg, the Commitments of Traders reports provide data from the CFTC, as well as from UK ICE and NYSE LIFFE (London International Financial Futures and Options Exchange) exchanges. The CFTC report provides a breakdown of each Tuesday's open interest for markets in which 20 or more traders hold positions equal to or above the reporting levels established by the CFTC.

This can be seen on Bloomberg with CFTC <GO> and is shown in Figure 5.12.

Bloomberg further states that one can determine whether futures contracts are primarily being bought (long) or sold (short) and then correlate

FIGURE 5.12 Commitments of Traders Report

C A Comdty | 1) Search | Commitments of Traders Report

All Data | CBOT Corn | Report Date: 10/15/13

1) US CFTC | 2) UK ICE | 3) NYSE Liffe

	Futures Commit	Chg	F & O Commit	Chg	Futures Traders	Chg	F & O Traders	Chg
Non-Commercial								
Long	344347	7767	304209	5188	155	2	184	9
Short	473407	12726	413343	8665	210	-3	238	-3
Spreading	145628	-2392	567295	3635	170	4	258	0
Net Position	-129060	-4959	-109134	-3477				
Bullish (%)	-27.3		26.4					
Commercial								
Long	599076	11623	755469	14958	261	-3	305	-2
Short	382311	8095	519875	12921	257	-5	297	-3
Net Position	216765	3528	235594	2037				
Bullish (%)	56.7		45.3					
Total								
Long	1089051	16998	1626974	23782	522	-1	637	2
Short	1001346	18429	1500513	25221	549	-6	654	-3
Net Position	87705	-1431	126461	-1439				
Bullish (%)	8.8		8.4					
Total OI and # Traders	1237489	22022	1811735	28010	711	-10	784	0
Non-Reportable								
Long	148438	5024	184761	4228				
Short	236143	3593	311222	2789				
Net Position	-87705	1431	-126461	1439				
Bullish (%)	-37.1		-40.6					
Total Net Long	-216765	-3528	-235595	-2038				

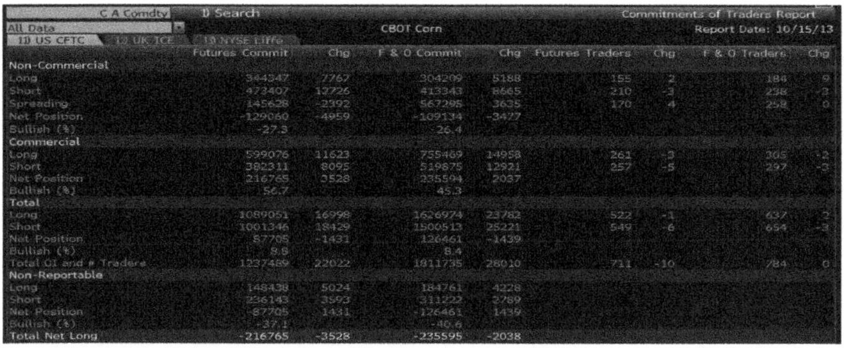

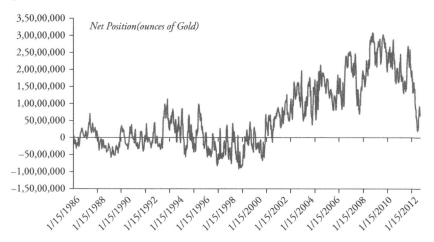

Source: Bloomberg, CBOT, CFTC, and NYSE.

FIGURE 5.13 Gold CFTC Net Positioning of Noncommercial and Nonreportable Speculators

Note: Includes Net Long/Shorts for Noncommercial and Nonreportable Speculators.
Source: Bloomberg, CBOT, CFTC, and NYSE.

the reasons behind the trends (e.g., weather could be detrimentally affecting a specific crop, thus causing more traders to take a long or short position depending on conditions). Commitment of Traders enables one to display additional analytics, such as spread data, regression, and seasonality. As was the case in the fall in gold prices in 2013, the CFTC positioning saw a drastic decline in net long positions among noncommercial and nonreportable speculators to 10-year lows on long positions.

FIGURE 5.14 Nikkei Historical Price Chart with Trends

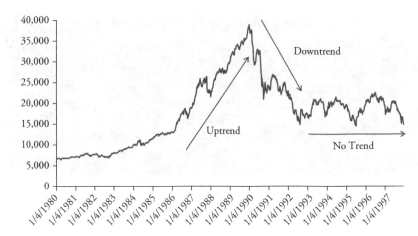

Source: Bloomberg.

Trend

Trends are one of the most important tools in technical analysis. Simply defined, trends are the direction in which an asset is moving. The old saying amongst technicians is "the trend is your friend." There are uptrends, downtrends, and sideways, or horizontal, trends (see Figure 5.14). Typically, an uptrend is defined as a move with higher highs and lower lows. A sideways market is usually range-bound. When looking at trends, it also helps to identify one's time horizon, whether it is hourly, daily, weekly, or monthly.

Support and resistance levels also play a key role in trends. Support level is a line that connects lows and tends to support the price level. This means that as a result of behavioral finance, the price does not usually fall below the line. The longer a support line exists, the greater the significance when it is broken. This will typically result in an asset price falling. Conversely, a resistance level is typically followed by selling pressure. When support or resistance levels are broken, they reverse roles. For instance, if a support line is broken it can become the new resistance level.

Moving Averages

A moving average is an average of past trading days. A 50-day simple moving average is simply an arithmetic mean of the past 50 days. Moving averages are used to give a more quantitative sense of a trend and also to indicate entry and exit points. For a trend trader, using moving averages is an essential part of a trading strategy.

Moving averages can be used in a couple of ways. They are typically used in at least two time periods, one shorter and one longer. Most people use two or three moving averages simultaneously. The advantage of the shorter-term moving average is that since it contains fewer data points, the first derivative, or change in the shorter moving average, happens faster. This makes it easier to observe a change in trend more quickly. The advantage of using a longer-term moving average is that it provides a sense of the general trend rather than shorter-term changes. One of the most common moving average combinations is the 50- and 200-day moving average.

Crossover points are one method that many technicians use for trading with moving averages. If we are in an upward trend, seeing the shorter-term moving average cross over the longer-term moving average typically means the market is bullish. The opposite holds true when the shorter-term moving average crosses below the longer-term moving average.

Another method that technicians use when they trade moving averages is to identify the direction of the shorter- and longer-term moving averages. If both moving averages are positive, then one is long a trend. Since trend traders, by definition, want to be long when both the shorter- and longer-term moving averages are positive, many technicians use exponentially weighted moving averages (EWMA), which weight current days more heavily than past days. The idea is to catch the trend more quickly by weighing recent prices more heavily than older prices.

Bollinger Bands

John Bollinger developed Bollinger Bands in the 1980s. He created two trading bands, one above and one below the actual price of the asset. The two bands, or envelopes, are calculated by using two standard deviations of the last 20-day moving average. Using two standard deviations aims to target a 95 percent confidence interval that the data will fall between that range. When the price hits the upper Bollinger Band, it is interpreted as overbought and when the price hits the lower band, it is interpreted as oversold (see Figure 5.15).

Bollinger Bands can be created on Bloomberg by entering BOLL <GO>.

Reversal Patterns

In technical analysis, trend reversal patterns aim to identify when trends are likely to end and reverse. In order for a reversal pattern to emerge, there needs

FIGURE 5.15 Bollinger Band Chart of the S&P 500

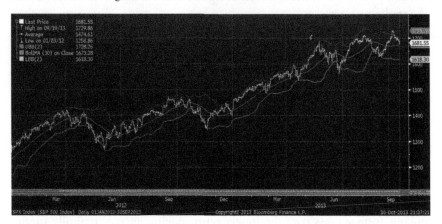

Source: Bloomberg.

to be an original trend. Typically, the longer the trend and move, the bigger the reversal pattern has the potential to be. Many technicians rely heavily on volume and open interest as tools in trying to determine reversal patterns.

Head and Shoulders

Head and shoulders are probably the most well-known and important reversal patterns. There is a head and shoulder reversal top and a head and shoulder reversal bottom, with the difference being which direction the original trend was going and which direction the asset will reverse.

There are four parts to a head and shoulders pattern. On a head and shoulders top, the neckline acts as a support line and the price rises and falls in a way that resembles a drawing of a head and shoulders. It first outlines a left shoulder, then rises, and falls again to make a right shoulder.

One of the keys to the head and shoulders pattern is the volume. The high of the left shoulder has the highest volume. The head makes a new high, but does so on less volume. Upon the formation of the right shoulder, volume is typically even less than the head. After the right shoulder, the price should fall to the neckline. Once the price reaches the neckline, in a classic head and shoulders pattern, the price breaks the neckline by about 3 percent, according to Edwards and Magee, then rallying back to the neckline and then falling by the distance of the head and neckline (see Figure 5.16). According to Robert Edwards and John Magee, as described in their book *Technical Analysis of Stock*

FIGURE 5.16 Sample Head and Shoulders Pattern

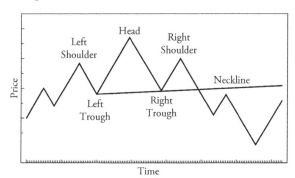

Source: Carol Osler, "Identifying Noise Traders: The Head-and-Shoulders Pattern in U.S. Equities" (Federal Reserve Bank of New York, February 1998).

Trends, a proper head and shoulders pattern should take about 18 months to form, though many technicians will trade hourly and daily head and shoulder patterns. An additional advantage to trading these patterns is that the risk/ reward is very favorable. Since the magnitude of the move is large, even if the pattern doesn't hold true all the time, risk/reward is skewed in your favor.

Trend Lines

Trend lines are an important tool for examining trends. In an uptrend, a trend line connects the lows and in a downtrend, consecutively lower highs form a trend line. Trend lines are very important to trends because they can signal a reversal. When trading a trend line break, it is helpful have a predefined set of rules to avoid losses due to a false breakout. This means that even though the trend line has been broken, the asset price may revert back to the trend. There are occasions where a trend line is broken; an example is given later in the chapter. For example, according to *Technical Analysis of Stock Trends* by Edwards and Magee, once the neckline has been broken on a head and shoulders pattern, one would expect a 3 percent selloff in a bearish head and shoulder followed by a 3 percent rally before breaking down lower. Sizing positions appropriately is also helpful in stomaching the initial noise around the trend line break, prior to the reversal move.

Triple Tops and Bottoms

Triple tops and bottoms are similar to head and shoulders patterns except that the prices in a triple top have one resistance line and prices in a triple bottom

FIGURE 5.17   Sample Triple Bottom Pattern

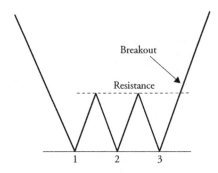

Source: Author.

have one support line. These patterns are rare and are the equivalent of a three-river bottom or three-mountain top in a candlestick chart. The distance of the breakout move is usually equal to the distance between the support line (in the case of a triple bottom) and the peak of the range (see Figure 5.17).

Continuation Patterns

When a trend is formed, sometimes it takes a pause and sometimes it goes into a reversal pattern. Continuation patterns aim to identify when a trend is moving sideways and the direction of the next breakout, which coincides with the original trend. Usually continuation patterns take much less time to form than reversal patterns.

Triangles

Triangles are probably the easiest continuation patterns to observe. In a symmetrical triangle, the price action that forms in the triangle is often called a coil. Symmetrical triangles are formed when both lines are at, or close to, the same angle. In ascending triangles, the lower line will be rising while the top line is horizontal. The opposite is true of a descending triangle where the top line is declining and the bottom line is horizontal (see Figure 5.18). Triangles are also important to Elliott Wave Theory, which is discussed later in this chapter.

Traders should be wary of broadening formations. These are triangles that are inverted—the opposite of the symmetrical triangle—where the triangle is expanding and not closing. Broadening tops are reversal patterns and are

FIGURE 5.18 Types of Triangles

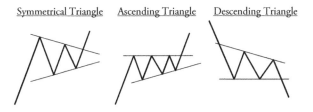

FIGURE 5.19 Chart of Nasdaq in Broadening Top Formation

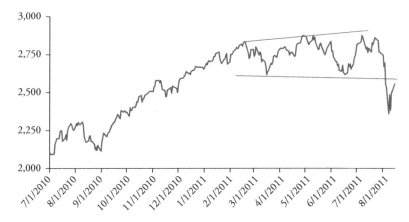

Source: Bloomberg.

often followed by violent moves in the opposite direction. In August 2011, the Nasdaq showed a broadening top, signaling a large market drop in equity and risk assets (Figure 5.19).

Oscillators

Oscillators are most useful in nontrending markets where the price is range-bound and many trend-following strategies may not work. Oscillators are most valuable when they reach extremes, which many technicians refer to as overbought or oversold conditions. While oscillators are most useful in nontrending markets, they can help technicians time the end of a trend. On their own, oscillators are not as powerful as other technical tools like a price chart or trend analysis, and must be used in conjunction with other indicators in order to be useful. Oscillators are generally plotted on the bottom of a price chart where the midpoint is referred to as a zero line, even if the scale is

0 to 100 (where 50 is the zero line). When oscillators reach an extreme in the upper range of the indicator, the asset is overbought and if the value reaches the lower range of the indicator, it is oversold. Oscillators are useful in gauging oversold and overbought periods, and can also be used when the oscillator crosses the midpoint or zero line. When oscillators cross the midpoint from above, they generate a buy signal and when they cross from below the midpoint line, they generate sell signals. There are many types of oscillators, but the ones we will explore are MACD, RSI, and stochastics.

MACD

MACD, or moving average convergence-divergence oscillator, was developed by Gerald Appel in the 1970s. The MACD observes two exponentially weighted moving averages and compares the two lines to observe changes. The two lines are the difference between the exponentially weighted moving average of a 12-day and 26-day period (known as the 12/26 day) and the 9-day exponentially weighted moving average. The faster line is the 12/26 and the slower line is the 9, sometimes referred to as the signal line. When the fast line (12/26) crosses above the slower line (9) this is a bullish signal and when the fast line crosses below the slow/signal line this is a bearish signal (see Figure 5.20).

MACD charts can be created on Bloomberg by entering MACD <GO>.

RSI

The relative strength index, or RSI, is an oscillator developed by J. Welles Wilder and published in his book, *New Concepts in Technical Trading Systems.*

FIGURE 5.20   S&P 500 Bar Chart with MACD

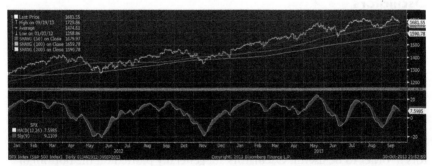

Source: Bloomberg.

RSI measures the strength or weakness of asset price closes. For daily charts, a 14-day is used as the time horizon, and for weekly charts, a 14-week chart is used. The shorter the time period, the more sensitive the RSI becomes. RSI ranges from 0 to 100. When the RSI reaches above 70, it is said to be overbought, and when it reaches below 30, it is oversold (see Figure 5.21).

RSI charts can be created on Bloomberg by entering RSI <GO>.

$$RSI = 100 - \frac{100}{1 + {}^*RSI}$$

$${}^*RSI = \frac{\text{Average of } x \text{ days up closes}}{\text{Average of } x \text{ days down closes}}$$

Stochastics (%K/%D)

Stochastic oscillators were developed by George Lane. They are most useful in sideways markets and not helpful in trending markets. The idea is that as prices rise, closing prices tend to reach an upper bound of a price range and the opposite holds true for prices going down. Stochastic oscillators produce two lines, %K and %D.

$$\%K = \frac{C - L_{14}}{H_{14} - L_{14}}$$

* C = Current Closing Price
* H_{14} = Highest High in last 14 periods
* L_{14} = Lowest Low in last 14 periods

FIGURE 5.21   S&P 500 Bar Chart with RSI

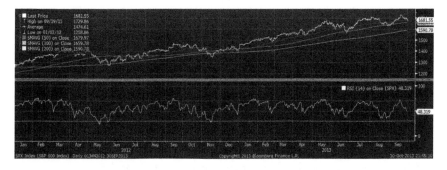

Source: Bloomberg LP.

FIGURE 5.22 S&P 500 Bar Chart with Stochastics

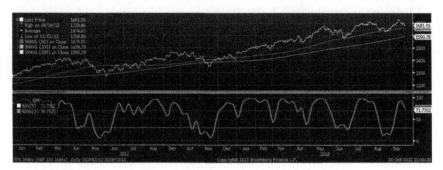

Source: Bloomberg.

The %K formula provides us with a 0–100% range on, where the closing price is relative to the total high/low price range. This is a dangerous assumption in trending markets and precisely why stochastics should be used primarily in nontrending markets. A number over 70 percent would indicate that the asset is overbought while lower than 30 percent indicates the asset is oversold. The second line is the %D, which is a three-period moving average of the %K line. The %K is the fast line and the %D is the slow line. Most technicians use the %D line for trading signals.

Stochastic charts can be created on Bloomberg by entering TAS <GO> and the check the "%K/%D" box (Figure 5.22).

Elliott Wave Theory

The Elliott Wave Theory was developed in the 1930s by Ralph Elliott and is used as a key technical tool by many technicians today. The Elliott Wave Theory is largely behavior-based. It has a strict five-wave pattern, 1 – 2 – 3 – 4 – 5. The motive or impulse wave is composed of 1, 3, and 5 on and Elliott count and corrective waves are 2 and 4. Following a five-wave pattern, Elliott Wave Theory then assumes that there is a corrective A – B – C pattern (see Figure 5.23). Elliott Wave also uses ratio analysis to determine the magnitude of retracements. *Elliott Wave Principle*, by A. J. Frost and Robert Prechter, is the recognized authority for the Elliott Wave Theory.

There are several rules that may not be broken in Elliott Wave Theory:

- Wave 3 can never be the shortest among Waves 1, 3, and 5.
- Wave 2 can never go below Wave 1.
- Wave 4 can never go below Wave 1.

FIGURE 5.23   Elliott Wave Basic Pattern

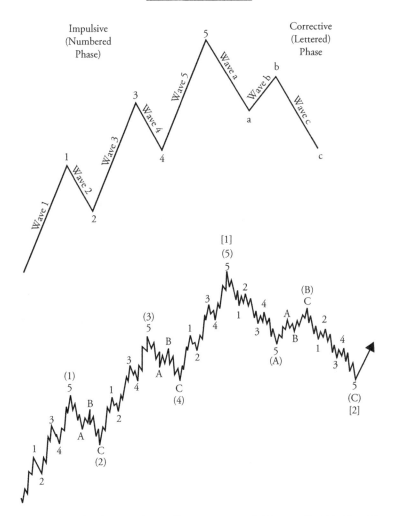

Source: A. J. Frost and Robert Prechter, *Elliott Wave Principle* (Gainesville, GA: New Classic Library), 23–25.

- Wave 3 must go beyond Wave 1.
- Wave 5 must go beyond Wave 3 (unless failed fifth).

   In Elliott Wave Theory, a failed fifth (or "truncation" according to Prechter), is when the fifth wave fails to go beyond the third wave. Failed fifths are reversal patterns, and in a bullish Elliott Wave they become bearish, while in a downtrend they become bullish.

Corrective Waves

Corrective waves occur in the second and fourth position in Elliott Waves. The fourth wave is generally the most complex and involves zigzags, flats, and triangles. Corrective waves are never five waves (1 – 2 – 3 – 4 – 5) and occur prior to the continuation of the motive wave in position 3 or 5.

Zigzags

Zigzags are a three-wave corrective pattern that usually comes in a 5 – 3 – 5 pattern where Wave B is shorter than Wave A. In the most complex patterns, double zigzags and triple zigzags occur, but they all occur in an A – B – C pattern. In a bull market, the zigzags overall direction is lower, and in a bear market the zigzag moves higher. Figure 5.24 displays these different variations.

Flats

Flats differ from zigzags in that they occur in a 3 – 3 – 5 pattern. In a zigzag, Wave A is a five-wave structure, unlike a flat, which is a three-wave structure. Since Wave A in a flat is a three-wave pattern, it doesn't run as deep as a zigzag and typically resembles more of a consolidation pattern than a corrective pattern. However, it largely depends on the magnitude of Wave B and whether it exceeds Wave A and the magnitude of the five-wave structure of C in the flat (Figure 5.25).

Triangles

More than any other corrective pattern in Elliott Wave Theory, triangles tend to almost always occur in the fourth position, prior to the fifth wave. Triangles are considered consolidating. They are corrective patterns that move sideways with lower volatility. Simple triangles form an A – B – C – D – E pattern in a 3 – 3 – 3 – 3 – 3 wave structure. There are four types of triangles identified by Elliott Wave Theory, which are ascending, descending, symmetrical, and expanding. Figure 5.26 displays the different variations of triangles.

FIGURE 5.24   Zigzags in Elliott Wave

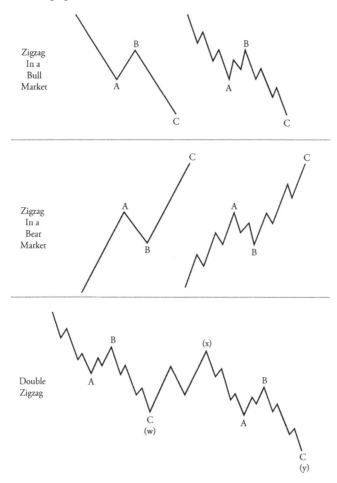

Source: Frost and Prechter, *Elliott Wave Principle*, 43–47.

Truncation

Truncation is the term used in Elliott Wave Theory to refer to a failed fifth wave, meaning that the fifth wave does not extend beyond the third wave. A truncated fifth wave is a reversal pattern with the move in the other direction generally being very aggressive. Prechter provides two examples of truncated fifths. The first is in 1962 during the Cuban missile crisis where, in a bearish market move, the market failed to make a new low

FIGURE 5.25 Flats in Elliott Wave

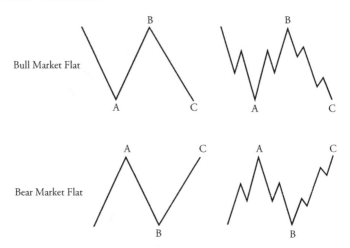

Source: Frost and Prechter, *Elliott Wave Principle,* 45–46.

fifth wave, which resulted in the market rallying. The second example occurred at the end of 1976 when, during a bull market, the fifth wave failed to make highs above the third wave, which later resulted in a selloff (Figure 5.27).

Fibonacci

Elliott Wave Theory also introduced Fibonacci ratios to the study of technical analysis. The idea behind using Fibonacci retracements is to forecast the magnitude of the move in the next wave. Since some of the impulse waves extend more than the other waves, Fibonacci ratios aim to measure the magnitude of these moves. Many times in an Elliott Wave, Fibonacci retracements are evident in alarming numbers.

The standard Fibonacci number sequence is as follows: 0, 1, 1, 2, 3, 5, 8, 13, 21, 34, 55, 89, 144, 233, and so on. It is calculated by taking the prior two numbers and adding them together. The sequence can go on infinitely. When looking at Fibonacci ratios in technical analysis, 0%, 23.6%, 38.2%, 61.8%, 76.4%, and 100% are the most common numbers observed. For instance, $(\sqrt{5} - 1)/2 = 0.6180$ is one of the calculations in Fibonacci ratios. The reflexive power of 61.8% or .618 is quite intriguing upon further examination. Dividing 1 by .618 equals 1.618, which is the only positive decimal

FIGURE 5.26 Corrective Wave (Horizontal) Triangles

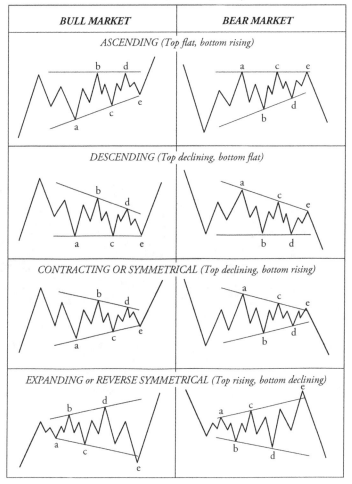

Corrective Wave (Horizontal) Triangles

Source: Frost and Prechter, *Elliott Wave Principle*, 50.

that, when divided into 1, equals itself plus 1. All of these numbers are used to forecast market moves. Corrective moves tend to retrace 61.8%, 38.2%, or 23.6% of the prior move. In continuation patterns, Fibonacci retracements are generally targeted at 61.8%, 138.2%, and 161.8% of the prior impulsive move (wave higher). Figure 5.28 shows a chart of the S&P 500 selling off 61.8% before rallying.

FIGURE 5.27   Bull Market Truncation (Failure)

Source: Frost and Prechter, *Elliott Wave Principle*, 35.

FIGURE 5.28   S&P 500 Chart with Fibonacci Retracements

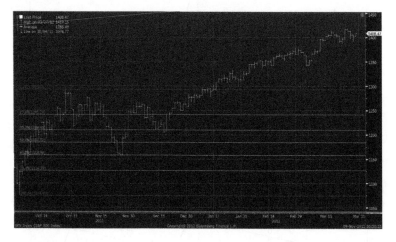

Source: Bloomberg.

Parabolics

Parabolic moves have a herd-like or bubble-like mentality. Calling the peak
is nearly impossible and is typically involves a venture that loses money.
As John Maynard Keynes said, "Markets can remain irrational longer than
you can remain solvent." This is one that many contrarians can relate to.
Parabolics have euphoric rises, often times leaving people to believe that
they are never-ending. But almost all parabolics collapse just as quickly
as they rise. There are countless examples: the Nikkei in 1989, Nasdaq in
2000, and silver in 1980 (see Figure 5.29), just to name a few. It involves
more than just looking back in time and picking out parabolic rises, but
even knowing nothing other than past price performance, one can see that

FIGURE 5.29 Historical Price Chart of Silver, 1977–1980

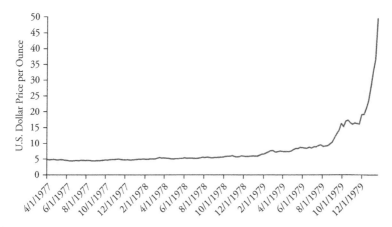

Source: Bloomberg.

FIGURE 5.30 Historical Price Chart of Gold, 1920–2012

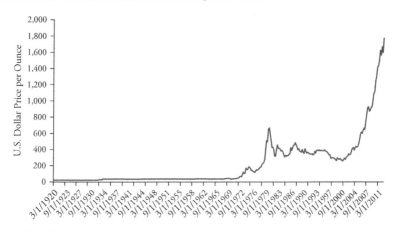

Source: Bloomberg.

prices during past parabolics do mean revert. The question isn't if they will, but when they will.

Most recently, one can argue that gold has had a parabolic rise (see Figure 5.30). Factors like negative real rates and the expansion of fiat currency certainly solidify the argument for higher gold prices. But have we gone too far? The question about gold is a complicated one. Many bullish technicians believe we are in a fourth wave and have more room to go, while others believe gold has become too big of a bubble. If we are, in fact, in a fourth wave as many Elliotticians suggest, then gold has a lot of room to go higher. But if global markets get out of the rut from the financial crisis and real yields continue to rise, it is likely gold will continue to sell off.

Seasonals

Many markets experience seasonal effects. A simple illustration is the way retailers have higher sales in the month of December than they do in January because of Christmas sales. Seasonal variables affect each asset class and product differently. In a trading sense, seasonals refers to a general move that an asset has over a given period of time, usually a one-month performance. For instance, in agriculture, different crops have different seasonal price action based on various indicators. Knowing the seasonal history is critical when trading many assets because it can increase your odds of being right or wrong on a trade. Planting seasons, industrial demand, holidays, election years, and countless other factors can be determinants of seasonality. During a U.S. presidential race, stocks typically perform well. The year before elections stocks also perform strongly, while the first and second year after an election tend to be weaker.

Figure 5.31 shows the price performance of corn from 1970 to 2010 on a monthly basis. Where the return is positive, it is counted as "up" and if the return is negative then it is counted as "down." Additionally, the returns

FIGURE 5.31   Corn Seasonal Data, 1970–2010

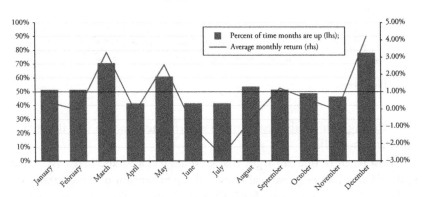

Source: Bloomberg.

are averages for each month over the time horizon. We can quickly observe that certain patterns emerge. March and December are the best months to be long corn, however June and July are the worst months to be long since 59 percent of the time corn trades lower. So, even though one might have a bullish view on corn, they may want to think twice about going long in the month of June (unless, of course, a drought is coming, as it did in the summer of 2012).

Cycles

Cycles are periodic price changes that occur in common, repeated patterns. The objective of looking at cycles is to try to pinpoint when markets will move in a particular direction in order to project regime shifts. In other words, in capitalism the economy never improves in a straight line up. Instead, we face expansions and recessions. Cycle analysis aims to measure many different factors that could result in a pattern. Different patterns in cycle analysis have unique time durations. When observing cycles, phase, amplitude, and period are the most important characteristics. The phase is a measure of where we are in the actual cycle as it unfolds. Amplitude measures the height of the cycle, high to low. The period measures the distance between the troughs. What follows is a discussion of different types of cycles.

Kondratiev Wave

Russian economist Nikolai Kondratiev discovered long-term cycles in the 1920s, identifying them as roughly 50-year cycles. He asserted that all economic cycles experience expansion, slowdown, and recession, driven by strong growth investment, which then leads to credit booms and eventual credit busts. One example is the wave that occurred during the Industrial Revolution of the 1780s. It peaked around the War of 1812 and then saw a huge economic decline followed by a depression. In the late 1890s, the U.S. economy started to boom (with the exception of the Panic of 1909) and benefited from World War I and the Roaring Twenties, which led to the Great Depression. While the Kondratiev wave is difficult to measure precisely, it is certainly important to note that throughout the history of man there have booms and busts in the economy. Kondratiev waves attempt to measure this and acknowledge that this is a repeated force over longer periods of time.

Kuznets Cycle

Simon Kuznets won the Nobel Prize for his work on the Kuznets curve in the 1970s. He also came up with ideas on how cycles relate to investment. He identified that economic waves of roughly 10 to 20 years occur in relation to changes in investment. By monitoring the inflow and outflow of capital, infrastructure, and building, one can better gauge economic cycles. What makes the Kuznets cycle uniquely clever is that investment is typically the most volatile component of GDP and a great barometer for future growth.

Juglar Cycle

The Juglar cycle focuses on fixed investment as opposed to infrastructure investment, like the Kuznets cycle. It was developed by French economist Clement Juglar in the 1860s. It is measured from 7 to 11 years and aims to measure changes in fixed capital as a cause of cycle and regime changes. Juglar is often credited as being a pioneer in cycle analysis and he found that "the only cause of depression is prosperity."

Kitchin Inventory Cycle

The Kitchin cycle, named for British statistician Joseph Kitchin, is the shortest cycle that we discuss, ranging from three to four years. The idea behind the Kitchin cycle is that economic cycles emerge based on extremes of fixed capital and building of inventory. On the onset of a recovery, companies typically do not have enough inventory, so they tend to hire more and create more inventory. However, as an economy overheats, companies typically are not nimble enough to decrease production at the onset of a decrease in demand, which in turn causes a buildup in demand. Once this buildup of inventory continues, there is continually less demand, which causes a contraction. The Kitchin cycle teaches us that observing inventory buildup of goods, services, and commodities can be a predictor of excessive economic cycles.

Crowd Psychology and Contrarian Views

Understanding crowd psychology and knowing when it reaches its peak can help a macro trader make huge profits. It is one of the hardest things to predict and quantify, since much of it is dependent on human psychology and behavior. There are some indicators that analysts use in order to determine if there is a herd mentality. The best book for studying historical examples is *Extraordinary Popular Delusions and the Madness of Crowds*, by Charles Mackay.

Initial Public Offerings (IPOs)

IPOs tend to be good sentiment indicators for market peaks. After all, who is best suited to be able to sense when a market is at or near a top? The expert in that field is. A great recent illustration can be found in the commodities market. The bull market in commodities has been very robust over the past decade or two. The euphoria over quantitative easing, growing populations, China, and emerging market growth have helped propel commodities to new zeniths. In May 2011, Glencore, the commodities conglomerate, went public. No one knew when the peak in commodities would occur, but it is logical to see how a firm that specialized in commodities may have had a better sense of the market top than most. Sure enough, this move precipitated near the all-time highs in the CRB Index (Figure 5.32a). The same was true with the Goldman Sachs IPO in 1999 prior to the tech bubble collapse (Figure 5.32b) and Blackstone's IPO in June 2007, just before U.S. Investment Grade Corporate Bond Yields to 10-Year U.S. Treasuries blew out (Figure 5.32c).

FIGURE 5.32 Charts of Respective Markets when the Market Leader Had Their IPO

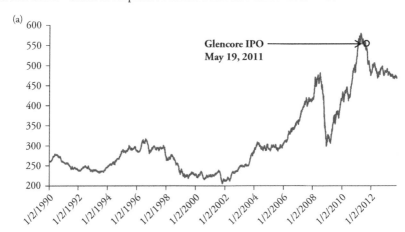

CRB Index and the Glencore IPO

Source: Bloomberg and Company websites. (*continued*)

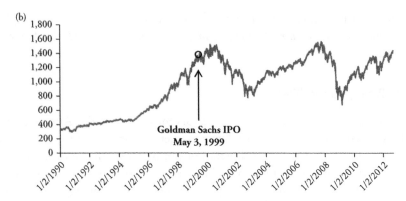

S&P 500 and the Goldman Sachs IPO

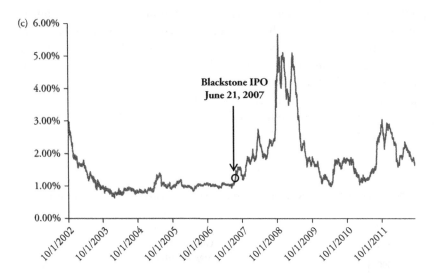

U.S. Investment Grade Corporate Bond Yield/U.S. 10-Year Yield Spread and the Blackstone IPO

FIGURE 5.32   (Continued)

Magazine Covers

Another great source for illustrations of market extremes can be found on the covers of magazines, such as *Time*. Magazine covers have an uncanny ability to time market peaks and troughs. One great illustration of this was on September 14, 1987. *Time* magazine had a bullish cover on the stock market. One month later, on October 19, 1987, the S&P 500 fell 20 percent on the day now known as Black Monday. Several weeks later, the Time

FIGURE 5.33 Chart of the S&P 500 during the October 1987 Crash

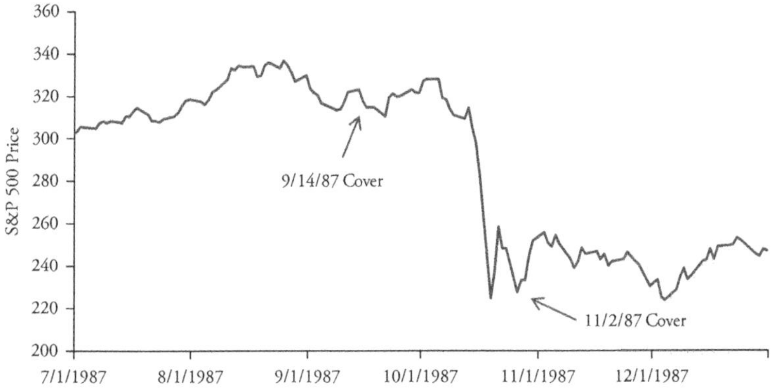

Source: Bloomberg.

Magazine released on November 2, 1987, had a cover titled "The Crash: After a Wild Week on Wall Street, the world is different." Subsequently the S&P 500 reached its lows and rallied significantly. Figure 5.33 attempts to display the release of such magazine covers against a chart of the S&P 500.

During the late 1990s, the S&P 500, Nasdaq, and technology sector experienced a boom that saw P/E ratios soar to never-before-seen zeniths and many companies saw unprecedented valuations with no earnings. All equity markets soared and technology companies became some of the biggest companies in the world, something we still see today. The velocity of the rise in the stock market was of a euphoric and bubble-like proportion. Timing the burst of any bubble is impossible. Using magazine covers is not an accurate method; however, it is useful as a sentiment indicator. In September 1999, *Time* magazine had a cover with the headline "GetRich.com" about the riches of the new tech boom. It took another six months for the Nasdaq to reach its highs in March 2000, with a P/E ratio reaching above 200 at one point.

Chartered Market Technician (CMT)

The CMT program is certified by the Market Technicians Association (MTA) and designates the individual holder of the CMT certification as having expertise in technical analysis. Like the CFA, the CMT has three levels of examination to get certified and the exams are offered twice a year by the MTA.

Bloomberg Shortcuts

Charts—Historical

GP <GO>	Graph historical prices
GPO <GO>	Historical price chart
GPC <GO>	Candle chart
GPL <GO>	Logarithmic chart
PFP <GO>	Graph a point and figure chart

Charts—Intraday

GIP <GO>	Tick chart
GIPS <GO>	Scrunch chart
GIPT <GO>	Scrolling tick chart with B/A and volume
GIPW <GO>	Sliding window chart
IGPC <GO>	Intraday candle chart
IGPO <GO>	Intraday bar chart
ISGP <GO>	Graph 30 days of intraday spreads or ratios
MGIP <GO>	Graph intraday ticks for multiple securities

Technical Indicators—Historical

IRSI <GO>	Intraday relative strength index
MACD <GO>	Moving average convergence/divergence
TAS <GO>	Stochastics for a selected security
DMI <GO>	Graph directional movement
ROC <GO>	Highest and lowest rates of price change
CMCI <GO>	Commodity Channel Index
WLPR <GO>	Williams %R graph
BOLL <GO>	Graph Bollinger Bands
GOC <GO>	Graph Ichimoku Cloud chart
GPF <GO>	Graph prices and Fibonacci lines
PTPS <GO>	Stop-and-reversal (SAR) trading points
MAE <GO>	Moving average envelopes
GM <GO>	Graph prices and money flow
CHKO <GO>	Display the Chaikin oscillator
GPCA <GO>	Graph historical corporate actions
CNDL <GO>	Candle patterns
KAOS <GO>	Hurst exponent
MCCL <GO>	McClellan oscillator

| OBV <GO> | On-balance volume for a selected security |
| PIVG <GO> | Pivot points graph |

Technical Indicators—Intraday

IMAC <GO>	Moving average convergence/divergence
ITAS <GO>	Intraday stochastics systems chart
IDMI <GO>	Intraday directional movement calculator
IROC <GO>	Intraday rate of change
ICCI <GO>	Commodity Channel Index
IWLP <GO>	Intraday Williams %R graph
IBOL <GO>	Graph intraday Bollinger Bands
IGOC <GO>	Intraday prices graph
IGPF <GO>	Graph prices and Fibonacci lines
IPTS <GO>	Intraday parabolic systems chart
IMAE <GO>	Moving average envelopes
GIM <GO>	Graph intraday money flow

Summary

This chapter introduces the reader to technical analysis and how it is useful in global macro. It examines the types of charts, trends, and moving averages that traders can use to aid their trading strategies. There are a number of tools that are also helpful in analysis, including oscillators, Elliott Wave Theory, Fibonacci numbers, parabolics, seasonals, cycles, and crowd psychology. Technical analysis is incredibly useful in global macro.

CHAPTER 6

Systematic Trading

The purpose of this chapter is to provide the reader with a general understanding of systematic trading models. Systematic macro can be used to observe some of the same things as discretionary macro. Where systematic trading and discretionary macro strongly differ, however, is that systematic trading is a method of using rule-based models to find trade opportunities, while discretionary macro leaves room for human emotion and therefore can often lead to less risk control. In a systematic model, predefined factors will result in buying or selling a certain asset.

This chapter will provide the basics of a systematic model by showing which assets, strategies, and risk factors are useful for initial construction. As the chapter progresses, it will introduce risk premia, risk parity, and high frequency strategies and how they are used in global macro.

A Brief Definition of Systematic Trading

Systematic trading is a way of using predefined rules and models in order to create a desired portfolio. This type of trading is typically generated using computer-based models, with strategies that are strenuously back-tested to optimize performance, maximize Sharpe ratios, and minimize drawdowns. One of the main advantages of systematic trading is that predefining the rules, measure, and risk takes the element of human emotion out of the equation. As Cliff Asness of AQR Capital Management astutely points out in the book, *How I Became a Quant* (Schachter and Lindsay 2010), there are several advantages and disadvantages to systematic/quant trading.

Advantages

- Quants are data miners.
- Quants have huge advantages over quals in terms of product design and risk control, such as market neutrality and separating alpha from beta.

Disadvantages

- LTCM's blowup shows the limits of quantitative investing.
- Quants are "driving with the rear-view mirror" (the data mining critique).

Systematic macro strategies are the fastest growing subsegment in macro. Few can argue with the strategy given the size and the speed at which many of these funds have been able to raise capital. *Expected Returns* by Antti Ilmanen is a tremendous resource for background on systematic macro.

Framework for Constructing a Systematic Model

There are several components that must be categorized in systematic trading. First and foremost, one must define which asset groups one intends to target. Once you have determined this, you can identify the strategy styles you plan to use. Strategy style refers to the main strategy a trader is examining. These include value, carry, trend, and fundamentals and they have their own unique factors that when combined give you the whole strategy output. Once these have been defined, you must examine underlying risk factors, such as trading costs and tail risks. You start by defining the first asset, applying the strategies to it and then overlaying it with risk factors. This categorization establishes a systematic output (see Figure 6.1).

Assets or Product Groups

In systematic trading, assets are divided into different categories. These can be a part of global macro, single stocks, risk parity, and various other strategies. In this book, the four assets are currencies, equities, fixed income, and commodities. There are two portfolio strategies that can be deployed in these

FIGURE 6.1 Construct and Framework of a Systematic Process

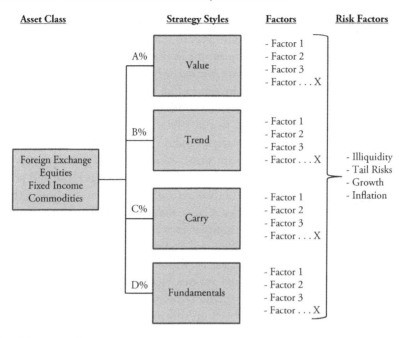

Note: Σ(A,B,C,D%) = 100%

assets: directional and relative value. Relative value is more desirable for capturing various factors over time and requires greater leverage and position sizes relative to outright directional trades. Systematic trading can include both relative and directional trading.

Strategies

Each asset has an overlay of factors (see Figure 6.1) that can help define the expected value of each strategy as being under- or overvalued. For purposes of this chapter we examine value, trend, carry, and fundamentals as our strategies. The sum of these four strategies on any given asset is 100 percent. One must identify the weights of each strategy to calculate their weights relative to one another. If one wanted to equally weight each strategy, then value, trend, carry, and fundamentals would each weigh in at 25 percent. However, running a back-test may show that this is not optimal. It is also important to observe maximum drawdowns when identifying the weights that will minimize drawdowns and maximize Sharpe ratios.

Value

Value is broadly defined by *Webster's Dictionary* as relative worth, or monetary or material worth. Equities are a safe asset to start with when examining value. Value investing has long been a hot topic in the investing arena starting with Benjamin Graham's *The Intelligent Investor*, which helped Warren Buffett to become arguably the best value investor of all time. Firms like Dimensional Fund Advisors, who manage over $200 billion in assets, employ the principles of Fama and French, who in the 1990s produced important research in the field that has influenced many of today's asset managers in the world.

As mentioned earlier, there are some value metrics that help assess the relative value of an equity index: price/book, price/earnings ratio, and price/free cash flow yield. Calculating all these separately and then combining them together can provide a trader with a relative measure for value. There are other factors that one can observe in equities as well. For instance, in the paper "Buffett's Alpha" (Frazzini, Kabiller, and Pedersen 2012), the authors try to break down the factors that have led to Warren Buffett's success throughout his spectacular career. They tested various factors such as small minus big companies, buying high book-to-market stocks/shorting low book-to-market stocks, buying stocks that have been up/shorting stocks that have been relatively down, and so on. Their findings were fascinating. The t-stats from the factors provided no substantial alpha. Rather, what they found is that low beta stocks and quality stocks were the two single factors that led to Buffett's success. The beta factor as defined by the paper, is betting against beta, which is buying low-risk assets and shorting riskier assets with a higher beta. As Buffett said in the Berkshire Hathaway 1989 Annual Report, "It's far better to buy a wonderful company at a fair price than a fair company at a wonderful price." These factors are not all easily converted to Equity Indices from single stocks, but it is these kinds of tests that shed new light on different factors.

When looking at currencies (foreign exchange) as an asset class, there are various useful factors that contribute to value. Over longer periods of time, purchasing power parity has proven to be a useful value measure. Another factor that is useful in foreign exchange value is terms of trade, which, on a comparative basis, is useful and a strong measure of value among currencies.

Trend

In a relative value systematic model, it is important to identify the constraints of trend. On a single asset, the phrase "the trend is your friend" has long been used by many traders and is the crux of many strategies similar to that which

CTAs implement. A study by Erb and Harvey shows that from December 1982 to May 2004, buying the four best-performing commodities over the last year and shorting the four worst performing commodities gave a 0.55 Sharpe ratio. They were able to get an increased Sharpe ratio by diversifying their trend-following strategy. In the article "Value and Momentum Everywhere" (Asness, Moskowitz, and Pedersen 2009), the authors demonstrate that basic trend-following strategies are profitable across various asset classes. Their work also showed that trend fared worst for fixed income and has been losing efficacy in foreign exchange since the 1990s.

In a relative value model, assets such as currencies, equities, fixed income, and commodities tend to mean revert on a comparative basis over time. In the short run, momentum, especially in commodities, has a strong positive return profile. Over time, momentum does run out of steam, so the ideal scenario is to catch the short-term momentum move, and then take a mean-reverting approach. It is important to remember that as a trend plays out over time, you are taking a negative bet against a positive trend not on a single asset but on the differential of an asset as compared to its peers (i.e., relative value). For comparative purposes, consider an economic cycle where an economy recovers, grows, and peaks only to eventually enter a recession. You want to be long the short-term positive trend in the recovery and growth phase, and, ideally, short at the peak. This is what the trend strategy aims to capture. Assets when measured against one another can only extend so much before they mean revert to their comparable group of assets. A useful approach is to use short-term trend indicators and longer-term indicators. The ideal is to be long the short-term trend indicator and short the longer-term trend indicator. In this scenario you are effectively trying to time the reversal of the trend. When both the short-term and longer-term trends are moving in the same direction, it certainly makes sense to be long that trend. However, the ideal scenario is when the shorter-term trend is moving in the opposite direction of the longer-term trend. One of the main reasons for this is that, as the momentum of the trend continues, the value component in your model will not show attractiveness—hence trend and carry tend to be negatively correlated. When the short-term trend indicator moves opposite to the longer-term trend, both value and trend become attractive, since we weight the short-term trend favorably. This is where position sizing should increase.

Trend and value are negatively correlated, and both valuable to systematic trading. When they are both indicating a long or short position, it is a very attractive time to increase position sizing in an attempt to capture a move. If you are wrong, the short-term trend will once again be in the same sign as the longer-term trend and will be negatively correlated, so the model will self-adjust and decrease position sizing. The success of the model depends on catching the move right as it happens.

Carry

Whether you are a discretionary macro trader or one who uses a systematic model, being long carry is generally a profitable strategy. Most good discretionary traders are right about 50 percent of the time at best, so imagine if someone has an asset that is negative carry. On day one, not only do you need to be right on direction but you need to make extra returns on a trade just to pay for the short carry you have on. The ideal situation is to be long an asset that has positive carry and, to the extent that it is possible, always be long carry.

In a systematic model, carry is an essential strategy. Currency carry is a classic starting point. Being long high-yielding currencies and shorting lower-yielding currencies is a profitable strategy in the long run. Being long a currency carry strategy is in many ways like being short volatility and long risk assets since the correlation to risk assets is high. Conversely, when markets sell off, currency carry strategies do not fare well and are subject to large drawdowns.

Sample of Large FX Carry Drawdowns:

- October 1987 (equity market crash: FX carry strategy returned –11%)
- October 1998 (aftermath of the Russian default/LTCM crash: FX carry returned –12%)
- October 2008 (virtually all markets crashed: FX carry returned –11%)

  Source: UBS FX Carry Index, Deutsche Bank FX Carry Basket, JP Morgan Global FX Carry Index, and Bloomberg.

Some effective ways of measuring currency carry are three-month LIBOR differentials, as well as three-month LIBOR/OIS spreads. Another way of looking at LIBOR is setting it equal to OIS + (LIBOR – OIS). The OIS component is effectively "risk free" while (LIBOR – OIS) is the credit component. There are numerous methodologies for systemizing currency carry; combining several can improve efficacy.

When analyzing other assets like commodities, it is also possible to compute carry. For example, the shape of the futures curve in any commodity is a proxy for carry. If the futures curve is in contango, then one is short carry when long, and if the curve is in backwardation, then one is long carry. All else being equal, these factors will enhance returns over time if observed properly.

Additionally, one can also monitor seasonality. Commodities are specifically prone to seasonality, due to weather conditions, planting cycles, and various other factors. As a result, the shape of the futures curve will price many of these factors, so overlaying contango and backwardation with historical seasonal performance can also increase the effectiveness of commodity carry predictions.

As far as equities go, Ilmanen points out that net buyback-adjusted dividend yield (the sum of dividend yields and buybacks, less issuance) has the highest correlation with next quarter equity market returns and is a more appropriate ex ante equity carry measure than dividend yield on its own.

Fundamentals

Fundamental indicators are laid out in many of the product chapters in this book because they are a useful starting point. However, there are countless methodologies and we advise that traders back-test their own strategies. Fundamentals are a critical strategy component and have an impact on a particular asset. For instance, in foreign exchange in emerging markets, monitoring the equity index versus the currency is helpful. As demonstrated with the Bovespa and the Brazilian real, there is a clear correlation. One can explain this with capital inflows. If there is bullish sentiment for the Bovespa and Brazilian equities, the Bovespa will rise, joined with the fact that investors will be more long the real as a result. This factor is particularly clear in emerging markets (EMs). The credit component of an EM is also critical and worth monitoring via credit default swaps (CDSs). If the credit risk component worsens, it's likely the currency is less desirable.

In addition to these, modeling in GDP growth, industrial production, inflation, and unemployment are also examples of fundamental indicators. For many macro traders, the list of fundamental factors is endless, so again, it is useful to personally construct a list of meaningful factors and back-test a group of strategies.

Factors

Each strategy is composed of factors (see Figure 6.1). The various factors under each strategy give the systematic model strength or weakness levels for each strategy. For instance, if one was observing equities and looking specifically at the value component, some basic factors would include P/E ratio, price/book, and price/free cash flow. Each factor gets a weight and when the weights are summed together they represent the value strategy. Assuming that value was the only strategy, and it yielded a result that indicated that value was very attractive, then the model would go long based on this strategy alone.

Risk Factors

Risk factors are other factors that can alter one's expected return outside the strategy styles previously outlined (see Figure 6.1). Having an eye out for various risk factors can optimize returns and eliminate unintentional risk. One of the risk factors Ilmanen highlights is inflation risk. Running a systematic model on a fixed income portfolio will yield a portfolio that is net long or short fixed income by country and as a whole portfolio. Inflation is a big risk in fixed income, in that increasing inflation hurts fixed income, and decreasing inflation is more bullish fixed income. In additional to fixed income, equities, energy-related commodities, and foreign exchange are also affected by inflation.

Liquidity is also a risk factor that must be modeled. Irrespective of what a particular model may suggest as an appropriate position, it is a good idea to model the bid/offer spread. On more liquid assets this is less of a risk but, in some emerging markets, the bid/offer spread can eat away at returns, especially for more high-frequency strategies. Additionally, illiquidity risk can get more complex when modeling downside risk. When markets fall sharply, as they did during the financial crisis, bid/offers widen and volume decreases, which represents additional risk because a back-test may not catch this. The Bank of England and Citigroup both publish useful liquidity indices. The hard part about modeling illiquidity is that it is impossible to predict crashes—and during periods of crisis, one is more hurt by illiquidity.

Other useful predictors for illiquidity risk are the yields on high-quality to medium-quality corporates. As worries arise, capital flows from medium-quality corporates to higher-quality corporates, which can be a leading indicator.

Selecting Risk Factors

The basic construct of a systematic model involves breaking each strategy style apart and selecting the factors for value, trend, carry, and fundamentals that give the highest Sharpe ratio possible and lowest drawdown ex ante (see Figure 6.1). Prior to summing the four strategy styles together, one must take factors such as illiquidity, tail risks, growth, and inflation into account. For example, a model may suggest that a large EM position is appropriate. However, it could be that there is little liquidity in the market currently so as a result that particular EM currency is trading very wide. Even though the model suggests trading a particular amount, it makes sense to optimize the output by taking these kinds of risk factors into account. Once the risk factors have been combined in each strategy, then one combines all the strategies together.

Back-Testing Factors

When factors are observed within each strategy, it is critical to back-test each new factor individually to identify its efficacy. If there is an attractive return profile, then one must back-test each factor amongst other factors already in the model. The idea is to find the optimal weights for each in order to maximize the expected return of the systematic model. It's possible that a factor one believes to be useful may yield a lower Sharpe than the current model, which makes it difficult to justify adding it.

Risk Premia

Risk premia are the premia traders are compensated for when they take risks beyond market beta risk. The idea behind risk premia is that the investor captures a risk premium in exchange for the risk of possible loss. Some well-known examples of risk premia are equity risk premium and selling equity volatility over the long run (Table 6.1). Risk premia in macro apply to the major asset classes—currencies, equities, fixed income, commodities—and other strategies such as volatility and credit risk. Many discretionary macro strategies, such as FX carry and selling volatility, have risk premia embedded in them. Risk premia also offer an elegant simplicity and ease in systematizing. Other advantages of risk premia strategies include liquid and scalable strategies, easily identifiable risks, and additional excess return to a portfolio with a positive expected Sharpe. The downside to risk premia strategies is that they are subject to large drawdowns. Especially since these strategies have become more popular and crowded, there is likely greater tail risk present that back-tests may not capture. Lastly, components of systematized models have risk premia embedded in them.

TABLE 6.1   Examples of Factors and Risk premia

	Carry	Value
Foreign Exchange	FX Carry	Relative PPP Absolute PPP
Equities	Dividend Yield	Book/Price Sales/Price FCF/Price
Fixed Income	Carry and Rolldown	Real Rates RV Current Account% GDP Debt/GDP %
Commodities	Futures Curve Carry (Contango/Backwardation)	Mean reversion* Scarcity Shocks

Source: Author.
*Cliff Asness, Tobias Moskowitz, and Lasse Pedersen, "Value and Momentum Everywhere,"
Journal of Finance 68, no. 3 (2013): 929–985.

FIGURE 6.2   Efficient Frontier

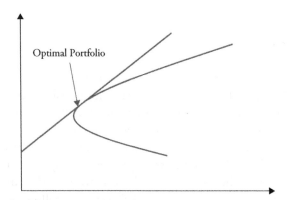

Risk Parity

The concept of risk parity (RP) strategies dates back to the 1950s when Harry
Markowitz won the Nobel Prize with the introduction of the efficient frontier
(see Figure 6.2). The basic concept is that portfolio diversification can lower
risk and increase Sharpe ratio. The benefit of an RP strategy is that over time
it has shown better returns to an asset class than standard allocations.

Risk parity has lately been one of the hottest allocations for pensions,
endowments, and asset allocators, due to its attractive return profile and

FIGURE 6.3 Historical Total Return of Indexed Risk Parity—60% S&P 500/40% Barclays U.S. Aggregate Bond Index

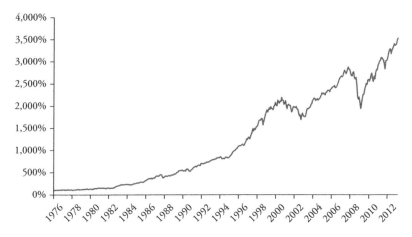

Note: Assumes compounding.
Source: Bloomberg.

risk management and its low fees (they do not always charge 2 percent and 20 percent). Bridgewater and AQR Capital Management were pioneers in many modern-day RP strategies. However, their RP strategies have diversified into other assets besides equities and fixed income, such as inflation and risk premia. The benchmark for RP is 60% S&P 500 and 40% Barclays U.S. Aggregate Bond Index (see Figure 6.3).

Risk

Risk is at the core of RP, since the opening premise is that portfolio diversification lowers risk. In the classic RP strategy, equities get an allocation of approximately 60 percent. This translates to roughly 90 percent of the risk of the portfolio. Even though, in the classic RP strategy, roughly 40 percent of the remainder is in fixed income, almost 90 percent of the risk in such a portfolio is in equities. So, while the traditional RP portfolio is diversified, from a risk perspective the portfolio is heavily weighted toward equities. Table 6.2 outlines correlations of equity, commodity, and Treasury returns to demonstrate its diversification of risk.

The traditional 60% S&P 500 and 40% Barclays U.S. Aggregate Bond Index portfolio has two problems. The first is an overallocation to risk in equities and the second is that the portfolio is static in its allocation. From

TABLE 6.2 Correlation of Asset Returns 1958 to 2011

	Equity Returns	Commodity Returns	Treasury Returns
Equity Returns	1.00		
Commodity Returns	0.13	1.00	
Treasury Returns	0.16	−0.11	1.00

Source: Lee Partridge and Roberto Croce, "Risk Parity for the Long Run" (white paper, Salient Partners, 2012).

a systematic approach, one knows the exact allocation at all times, but this can be a less optimal portfolio since there is no volatility rebalancing. One method to maximizing expected returns on a RP portfolio is balancing the portfolio according to risk. This approach aims to rebalance the portfolio sizes based on a fixed risk allocation. By targeting a fixed volatility, this RP portfolio remains systematic and also becomes more dynamic, optimizing returns and potentially decreasing drawdowns in turbulent times.

Positions

The optimal RP portfolio is one that consists of uncorrelated, low equity risk assets with diversification to do well in most environments. As a result, a portfolio of traditional equities and fixed income is the classic benchmark portfolio for RP. However, while equities and fixed income are necessary allocations in an RP portfolio, that does not mean that the portfolio cannot be optimized further. For example, outside of equities and fixed income, many funds have selected other categories of products to optimize returns. One of these allocations includes inflation protection, which can also take the form of commodities, mortgage-backed securities (MBS), or real estate investment trusts (REITs). Since inflation can erode returns over the long run, having a balanced portfolio of inflation protection has shown efficacy. Some of these products include TIPS and commodities (more specifically, energy-related commodities). Other categories that have been explored and added to portfolio mixes include risk premia, which include strategies like foreign exchange carry and selling volatility premium. Back-tests have proven that expanding beyond equities and fixed income, in combination with a dynamic position shift and maintaining a fixed volatility, can maximize Sharpe ratios and minimize drawdowns.

Summary

Systematic trading is a method of using rule-based models to find profitable trade opportunities. It has fewer variables and offers more risk control than discretionary trading. In order to establish a systematic trading strategy, one must identify an asset, determine which strategies to use within that asset, and then account for the underlying factors in order to guarantee the highest Sharpe ratio and drawdown.

PART TWO

Global Macro Trading Foundation

CHAPTER 7

Foreign Exchange in Global Macro

This chapter aims to provide several valuation methods and factors that allow traders to analyze the currency market and, in turn, model this efficiency in other markets. Every country around the globe uses currency to express the price of goods and services. In global markets, currencies can only have value relative to other currencies. Of the four product groups we examine in this book, currencies, or foreign exchange, are the most liquid and heavily traded; $4 trillion is the average daily turnover. Foreign exchange markets are open 24 hours a day starting at 8:15 PM GMT Sunday, and closing at 10 PM GMT on Friday, making it a very accessible product to trade. Currencies are also critical because they are the primary medium of exchange and affect trade, investment, and inflation. Foreign exchange is often considered the most efficient market in the world.

The Role of the U.S. Dollar

The U.S. dollar accounts for 85 percent of all foreign exchange (FX) transactions (see Figure 7.1). The foreign exchange market is disproportionately U.S. Dollar-centric as a result of its reserve currency status.

Central Bank Holdings of U.S. Dollars

Central banks maintain baskets of currencies as a part of their reserves. The U.S. dollar is also the major reserve currency of global central banks, accounting for more than 60 percent of their reserves (see Figure 7.2), though it has

FIGURE 7.1   Foreign Exchange Market Turnover by Currency as a Percent of Volume

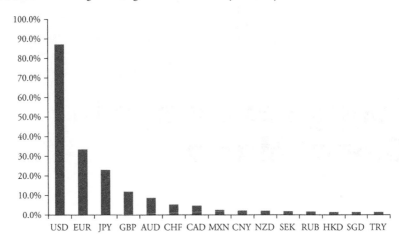

Note: The sum is equal to 200 percent, since currencies are traded in pairs.
Source: 2013 Triennial Central Bank Survey, Bank for International Settlements. As of April 2013.

FIGURE 7.2   Central Bank Holdings of Currencies

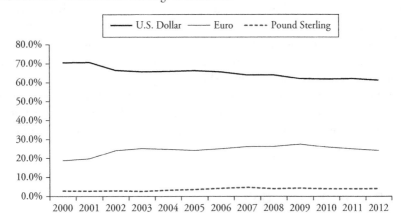

Source: IMF, Currency Composition of Official Foreign Exchange Reserves.

been on a gradual decline over the last decade. Reserve currencies are currencies that central banks and institutions hold in large quantities.

Dollar Index

The U.S. Dollar Index is the relative value of a basket of foreign currencies
against the dollar. While the euro does account for more than half of the
Index, it provides a relative measure for the strength of the U.S. dollar on any

day or period. The basket has only been changed once, in 1999, upon the creation of the euro. It trades as a futures contract (DX) and as an exchange-traded fund (UUP).

EUR Euro 57.6%
JPY Japanese Yen 13.6%
GBP British Pound 11.9%
CAD Canadian Dollar 9.1%
SEK Swedish Krona 4.2%
CHF Swiss Franc 3.6%

Source: Bloomberg.

Trading Currencies

The Bank for International Settlements divides currencies into four liquid markets and each of the markets moves in sync with one another. Figure 7.3 shows the four FX trades and their share of liquidity. Most foreign exchange today is traded through the derivatives market.

Currency Forwards

Currency forward contracts are over-the-counter (OTC) contracts used to buy or sell a particular currency at some date in the future. These are more commonly used by real hedgers as opposed to speculators who need to hedge

FIGURE 7.3 Currency Turnover by Market

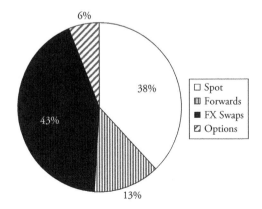

Source: 2013 Triennial Central Bank Survey, Bank for International Settlements.

their currency exposures. A prime example would be a multinational company that may have local currency obligations during a certain period of time and does not want the risk of currency exposure. Since the project may not be done at T_0 (today), it makes sense for many companies to enter into a currency forward agreement to hedge whatever future obligation or capital expenditure they may have. The cost of a project is determined during the budgeting process. Corporations assume today's rate and are not in the business of taking foreign exchange risk.

Non-Deliverable Forwards (NDFs)

A non-deliverable forward (NDF) is a forward contract used on foreign exchange in countries where the local government either bans or heavily restricts FX trading. NDFs are most common in emerging markets in South America and Asia, and it is estimated that 60 to 80 percent of volume is speculative (Lipscomb 2005). A great example of the way NDFs are used is trading Chinese renminbi (CCN+12M <Curncy>) (see Figure 7.4). They are traded on a particular currency and the notional trade is defined at trade inception. However, the contract typically cash settles, meaning that the profit or loss is settled in cash.

FIGURE 7.4 Chinese Renminbi versus Chinese Renminbi 12-Month Nondeliverable Forward

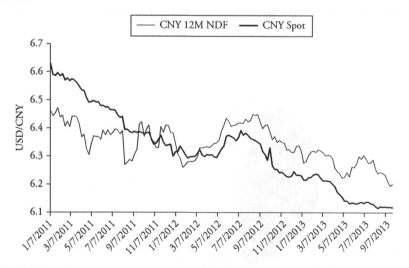

Source: Bloomberg.

Spot Market

The most tangible example of a spot market is currency exchange. Other spot transactions include receipts that are converted into other currencies from exports and large transactions between banks. Spot markets in foreign exchange are typically small.

Futures Market

One can trade futures in the currency market just like the other three product groups. Many currency futures trade on the CME, including DX (Dollar Index), EC (euro), BP (British pound), JY (Japanese yen), SF (Swiss franc), and PE (Mexican peso). The most liquid and traded futures contracts all expire quarterly in March (H), June (M), September (U), and December (Z).

Options

Like futures, options are traded in all of the four product groups, but they make up the smallest amount of transactions. Currency options provide the owner with the option, but not obligation, to buy (call) or sell (put) a particular currency at a certain price over a certain period of time.

Currency Regimes

When trading currencies, one must be aware of each currency's regime. This refers to the level of intervention the central bank has in regard to currency. This has a huge impact on a currency's value and the potential path it could take in the future.

The level of a central bank's intervention in a currency helps determine to what extent the value of the currency is subject to the bank's control. Clearly understanding this principle is of the utmost importance because no model will be of help if, for example, a currency is pegged. We will observe three types of currency regimes: fixed currencies, frequent intervention, and floating. One must remember that virtually all currencies have experienced intervention at some point, so the term "floating with no intervention" implies that *generally* there are no currency interventions and that the central bank's main policy tool does not include intervening frequently in the foreign exchange market.

Fixed	Floating (Frequent Intervention)	Floating (No Intervention)
HKD	JPY	USD
DKK	BRL	EUR
LVL	CNY	GBP
AED	CHF&EUR/CHF	AUD
	TRL	NZD
	MXN	CAD
	INR	SEK
		NOK

Fixed Currency

Fixed rate regimes can be achieved in a few different ways but historically have been on a gold or silver standard. In more recent years, we have seen the Bretton Woods system, pegs, and special drawing rights (SDRs), which we discuss in this section.

Bretton Woods

Bretton Woods was initially proposed to help avoid another serious downturn like the Great Depression and to maintain a single reserve currency: the U.S. dollar. Global free trade relied on a stable global currency system. For instance, during the Weimar Republic in Germany (from 1919–1933), the collapse of Germany's currency resulted in hyperinflation, which ultimately led to the rise of Hitler and World War II. During the advent of the Great Depression in the 1930s, the free-floating currency system experienced tremendous fluctuations, which helped deteriorate global trade.

There was no international central bank and the gold standard didn't seem feasible in a global economy, with the challenges of storage and transportation costs on countless transactions. The beauty of the U.S. dollar at the time was that the United States was on the gold standard, so U.S. dollars were convertible into the gold held at Fort Knox. By making the U.S. dollar the global reserve currency, it effectively became a derivative of the gold standard. As a result of the meeting at Bretton Woods in July 1944, the U.S. dollar officially became the global reserve currency. Forty-four nations attended the Bretton Woods conference and Harry Dexter White of the U.S. Treasury and John Maynard Keynes of Britain drafted the key documents.

The Fall of the Gold Standard

In the 1970s, the cost of the Vietnam War pushed inflation higher and put the United States in a balance of payments deficit for the first time in the twentieth century. As the economic picture in the United States continued to worsen, the French president, Charles de Gaulle, demanded delivery of gold in exchange for his U.S. dollars. The continuous pressure on U.S. fiscal spending and ultimate fiat money creation led Richard Nixon to put an end to the gold standard on August 15, 1971. This was effectively the end of the Bretton Woods system, making the U.S. dollar a pure fiat currency (backed by the full faith of the U.S. government). However, the legacy of the reserve currency still persists today as a result of Bretton Woods.

Peg

A peg is when a country decides that it wants to hold the value of its currency constant against another currency or in some defined band—typically, but not always, with a big trading partner. Some recent examples of pegs include the Danish kroner against the euro, the Swiss franc against the euro, and the Hong Kong dollar against the U.S. dollar. The Hong Kong dollar peg is highlighted hereafter in its own section.

Special Drawing Rights (SDRs)

The International Monetary Fund (IMF) describes special drawing rights (SDRs) as follows:

> The SDR was created by the IMF in 1969 to support the Bretton Woods fixed exchange rate system. A country participating in this system needed official reserves—government or central bank holdings of gold and widely accepted foreign currencies—that could be used to purchase the domestic currency in foreign exchange markets as required to maintain its exchange rate. But the international supply of two key reserve assets—gold and the U.S. dollar—proved inadequate for supporting the expansion of world trade and financial development that was taking place. Therefore, the international community decided to create a new international reserve asset under the auspices of the IMF.
>
> The SDR is neither a currency, nor a claim on the IMF. Rather, it is a potential claim on the freely usable currencies of IMF members. Holders of SDRs can obtain these currencies in exchange for their SDRs in two ways: first, through the arrangement of voluntary exchanges between members; and second, by the IMF designating members with strong external

FIGURE 7.5   Basket of Currencies in SDRs

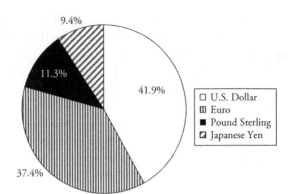

Source: IMF, as of October 2013.

positions to purchase SDRs from members with weak external positions. In addition to its role as a supplementary reserve asset, the SDR serves as the unit of account for the IMF and other international organizations.

The value of the SDR was initially defined as equivalent to 0.888671 grams of fine gold—which at the time was also equivalent to one U.S. dollar. After the collapse of the Bretton Woods system in 1973, however, the SDR was redefined as a basket of currencies, today consisting of the euro, Japanese yen, pound sterling, and U.S. dollar [see Figure 7.5].

General allocations of SDRs have to be based on a long-term global need to supplement existing reserve assets. Decisions on general allocations are made for successive basic periods of up to five years, although general SDR allocations have been made only three times.[1]

The Hong Kong Dollar

Fixed exchange rates occur when one country decides to link its exchange rate to another currency, usually defining a desired fixed exchange rate. For economies like Hong Kong's, it provides a stable exchange rate and credibility during a financial crisis (e.g., the Asian Crisis). However, it comes at the expense of higher inflation and an artificially weak currency, as in the case of the Hong Kong dollar.

The modern-day fixed exchange rate to the U.S. dollar goes as far back as nineteenth-century history. In 1863, the Hong Kong government declared

---

[1]IMF, "Special Drawing Rights (SDRs)," October 1, 2013, https://www.imf.org/external/np/exr/facts/sdr.HTM.

TABLE 7.1 Exchange Rate Regimes for the Hong Kong Dollar

Date	Exchange Rate Regime	Features
1863–November 4, 1935	Silver Standard	Silver dollars as legal tender
December 1935	Link to Pound Sterling	HK$16 = £1 (December 1935–November 1967)
	Link to pound sterling	HK$14.55 = £1 (November 1967–June 1972)
July 6, 1972	Link to the U.S. dollar with ± 2.25% intervention bands around a central rate	HK$5.65 = U.S.$1 (July 1972–February 1973)
	Link to the U.S. dollar	HK$5.65 = U.S.$1 (July 1972–February 1973)
November 25, 1974	Free-float	Exchange rates on selected days HK$4.965 = U.S.$1 (November 25, 1974) HK$4.6 = U.S.$1 (March 6, 1978) HK$9.6 = U.S.$1 (September 24, 1983)
October 17, 1983	Link to the U.S. dollar	HK$7.80 = U.S.$1 HK$7.75 = U.S.$1 (September 1998)

Source: Hong Kong Monetary Authority.

silver dollars as its legal tender. By 1935, the price of silver had risen dramatically during a global silver crisis and there was shrinkage in the money supply. This forced the Hong Kong government to adopt a local currency: the Hong Kong dollar. The initial peg of the Hong Kong dollar to the pound was HK$16 = 1£. The unfavorable exchange rate was a result of Hong Kong being a colony of the United Kingdom as well as the pound sterling being a major reserve currency (Table 7.1; Figure 7.6).

In November 1974, the U.S. dollar had weakened significantly and the Hong Kong government decided to free-float the currency. The free-floating currency resulted in very volatile and inconsistent levels of inflation and GDP growth. In certain years, both were 10 percent or more and in some years less than 1 percent. As a result, and in combination with negotiations over the United Kingdom's agreement to transfer power, confidence fell, which led to food shortages and ultimately resulted in depreciation of the Hong Kong dollar.

To stem the attack on the Hong Kong dollar, on October 17, 1983, it was pegged to the U.S. dollar at a rate of HK$7.8 = $1. The main objective

FIGURE 7.6   Hong Kong Dollar Exchange Rate, 1935–2005

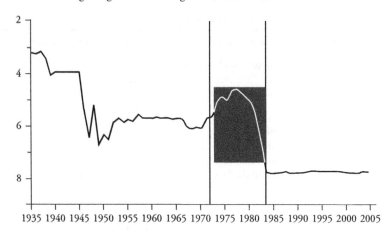

Source: "Hong Kong's Linked Exchange Rate System," Hong Kong Monetary Authority, available at www.hkma.gov.hk/media/eng/publication-and-research/background-briefs/ hkmalin/04.pdf.

was to provide the Hong Kong dollar stability and credibility as a currency. In May 2005, the Hong Kong government expanded the band of the peg from HK$7.75 to HK$7.85.

Advantages	Disadvantages
Stable currency	Artificially weak HK$
Monetary anchor	Lack of monetary policy control
Credibility during crisis	Inflation

Floating with Frequent Intervention

The Brazilian Real

Many currencies are free-floating but have frequent intervention for various reasons. The Brazilian Central Bank (BCB) frequently intervenes in its currency markets and unofficially uses its currency as a monetary policy tool. Due to the attractive carry and the strong performance of commodity prices, the Brazilian real has appreciated very strongly against the U.S. dollar in the past 10 years (Figure 7.7). As a result, retail sales and the middle

FIGURE 7.7   U.S. Dollar/Brazilian Real Price Chart

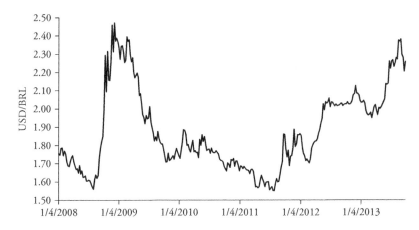

Source: Bloomberg.

class in Brazil have been flourishing. However, a negative externality of the strong real is that the export and manufacturing sector can suffer. To combat this, the BCB has in the past aggressively sold Brazilian real in the FX swap market when needed.

Inflation is another negative externality of depreciating the real. In May 2012, when equity markets and risk assets sold off, the combination of the BCB's FX intervention and sell-off in risk markets (which resulted in the dollar rallying against the real) caused a double whammy, in which the real depreciated to 2.10 at the end of May 2012. It ended up selling off from 1.70 at the end of February to 2.10, which was more than a 20 percent depreciation, a size that ultimately has inflationary implications. The BCB has explicitly targeted an inflation band of 2.5 to 6.5 percent, and has shown it will intervene in the FX market when it feels it is necessary (Table 7.2).

Additionally, since carry on the Brazilian real has been so attractive, the Brazilian government has enacted a tax known as IOF. The IOF is a tax on financial transactions that dissuades fast money from doing transactions in Brazil. It was steady at 6 percent, but was recently changed to 0 percent. The BCB must dance a thin line between avoiding too much inflation and making sure growth is not stunted. This example in Brazil is just one of many in which a country chooses to free-float its currency but is still affected by a variety of other factors.

TABLE 7.2 Table of Recent Interventions

Date	Description	USD/BRL Level
October 19, 2009	Increase in financial transactions tax (IOF) rate on inflows for equities (including ADRs) and fixed-income investments from 0% to 2%.	1.71
November 18, 2009	Reduction in financial transactions tax (IOF) rate on foreign investment in ADRs from 2% to 1.5%.	1.72
October 4, 2010	Increase of IOF on investments in fixed income, from 2% to 4%. Investments in equities remain subject to the IOF of 2% (imposed in October 2009).	1.69
October 18, 2010	New increase in IOF tax rate on inflows for the purchase of fixed-income securities, from 4% to 6%.	1.66
January 6, 2011	The central bank imposes reserve requirements on banks' short dollar positions.	1.69
January 10, 2011	The reserve requirement will be charged on 60% of the short positions in dollars that exceed the lower of $3 billion and the arithmetic average of the institution's tier-1 capital. It will be deposited with the central bank in local currency and will be remunerated. Bylaws allow sovereign funds to operate in the FX market.	1.69
March 29, 2011	The government establishes a 6% IOF levy on foreign financing with maturity below 1 year.	1.66
April 6, 2011	Extension of the 6% IOF tax on external loans for issuances with average maturity in up to two years BRL.	1.61
July 8, 2011	BCB reduces the exemption threshold to U.S.$1.0 bn (from U.S.$3.0 bn), in which banks don't need to pay the 60% reserve requirement on short U.S.$ positions in the FX spot market.	1.55
July 27, 2011	The government extends the IOF collection to FX derivatives. (IOF of 1% is charged on increases in the net long BRL exposures built through derivatives from the previous day that exceed $10 m, applied to the adjusted notional value; all investors are subject to this new IOF.)	1.54

Date	Description	Value
December 1, 2011	Exemption of IOF on foreign equities investment (from 2% to 0%); on venture capital (from 2% to 0%); on ADR cancellations (from 2% to 0%) and on nonresident applications in private bonds with maturity longer than 4 years (from 6% to 0%)	1.81
February 6, 2012	BCB to resume FX spot auction	1.72
March 1, 2012	Extension of the 6% IOF tax on external loans for issuances maturing in up to 3 years.	1.72
March 1, 2012	Exports prepayment (PA) limited to 360 days (unlimited before) and only importers will be allowed to fund it (before, banks were also able to fund it).	1.72
March 12, 2012	Extension of the 6% IOF tax on external loans for issuances maturing in up to 5 years.	1.79
March 15, 2012	IOF exemption on exporters' short positions in derivatives.	1.80
June 14, 2012	The government reduces the maturity of loans subject to the IOF levy from 5 years to 2 years.	2.07
June 28, 2012	Rules on advance payment transactions are extended to financial institutions and other companies.	2.09
December 4, 2012	The maximum term for the advance payment of export transactions is extended from 1 year to 5 years.	2.11
December 5, 2012	The government reduces the maturity of loans subject to the IOF levy from 2 years to 1 year.	2.10
January 30, 2013	The government reduces the tax on financial transactions (IOF) levied on foreign investments in shares of real estate investment funds from 6% to 0%.	1.99
June 4, 2013	The government reduces the tax on financial transactions (IOF) levied on foreign investments in fixed income from 6% to 0%.	2.15
June 12, 2013	The government withdraws the tax on financial transactions (IOF) levy of 1% on increases in short positions in financial derivatives whose settlement value has been affected by FX rate changes.	2.15

Source: JP Morgan (May 25, 2012), Credit Suisse (June 12, 2013), Bloomberg, and BCB.

Valuation Techniques for Foreign Exchange

Trading foreign exchange while predicting the future path of currencies is one of the hardest things to do in global macro trading. There are countless valuation techniques using fundamental and technical analyses that can be performed. Some traders utilize these in different weights and some don't use them at all. This section focuses on fundamental analysis and carry trades. It is recommended that traders run a mean regression to get a sense of efficacy.

Equity Index Price Performance

There are three ways to use equity performance to estimate currency moves. The first is basic equity price performance on a relative 12-month basis. This can be a very effective method of estimating foreign exchange moves, especially in emerging markets. The idea is that as the performance of equity markets continues to rise, it will attract foreign money flow; and capital flows in turn strengthen the currency. In Brazil, the Bovespa and Brazilian real are over 80 percent correlated (see Figure 7.8).

The second measure of equity market performance is earnings forecast revisions. Access to earnings forecasts is a powerful tool: comparison to changes in forward-looking forecasts can provide insight into currency appreciation. For example, if earnings forecasts were revised 10 percent higher, one would expect both equity markets and currency to perform well.

FIGURE 7.8   Brazilian Bovespa and Brazilian Real

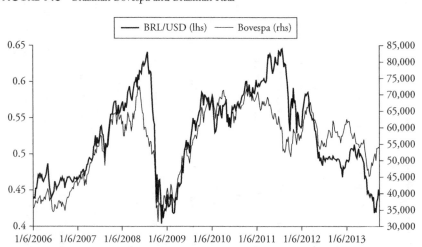

Source: Bloomberg.

The third effective way to help monitor equity performance as it translates to currency moves is flows into the equity markets. This information is not readily available for many markets; however, it is possible to retrieve such information for certain countries (foreign direct investment, local pension allocations, mutual fund flows, etc.).

Credit

For emerging market countries, it's useful to monitor five-year CDS relative to the currency. Figure 7.9 looks at the five-year CDS of Mexico and the Mexican peso, which have ~ 75 percent correlation. Generally, one would find that as the credit of an emerging economy deteriorates, its currency becomes less desirable.

Another powerful tool is to create a basket of EM currencies against a basket of EM five-year CDS. This is useful if one wants to trade baskets of currencies. Figure 7.10 demonstrates a simple pair of spread between Australia and Mexico. Using five-year CDS is effective in carry or basket strategies where currencies can be compared on a relative basis. CDS is covered in more depth later in the book.

Sentiment

One of the most useful indicators for sentiments is looking at call-put skew on three-month risk reversals. If someone is long GBP and needs to maintain a long

FIGURE 7.9   Mexican Peso versus Mexico Five-Year CDS

Source: Bloomberg.

FIGURE 7.10 Australian Dollar/Mexican Peso Cross versus Australia/Mexico Five-Year CDS Spread

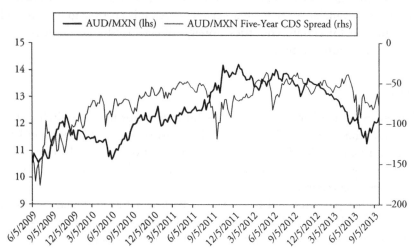

Source: Bloomberg.

bias, they could buy out-of-the-money puts when their view turns bearish and finance the hedge by selling out-of-the-money calls. If this happens frequently, the implied volatility on the puts will rise relative to that of calls (and this relationship will become increasingly negative). This relationship would be negative GBP and would run a high correlation to the currency (see Figure 7.11). It is worth noting that the three-month risk reversal should be back-tested on a currency-by-currency basis. With this indicator, some currencies do not correlate well in calm periods but have higher correlations in periods of distress. Measuring for overall equity market performance as an overlay can improve a factor's efficacy.

Trade

Competitiveness in global trade is a key fundamental driver of currency. Current account is a great measure of global trade and demand for a particular currency because it measures a country's trade and capital inflows/outflows.

Current Account = Changes in Net Foreign Assets[2]

---

[2]Net Foreign Assets is the Trade Balance + Investment Income + Service Transactions + Unilateral Transfers.

FIGURE 7.11   British Pound versus Three-Month British Pound Risk Reversals

Source: Bloomberg.

Table 7.3 shows the current account surplus/deficits for the G7 countries, including the Eurozone and China. If one were to compare the United States and United Kingdom on the forecasted change and relative forecast alone, the U.S. dollar should appreciate relative to the pound sterling. In 2012 alone, the United Kingdom ran a current account deficit 1.1 percent greater than the United States. However, over the next three years, the United Kingdom is expected to improve its current account deficit relative to the United States, which is arguably a more important metric for currency appreciation.

An interesting fact to point out is that since the Chinese renminbi is a controlled currency with frequent intervention (and artificially low), this helps China consistently run a current account surplus.

Trade-Weighted Index

Using a trade-weighted index (TWI) is an effective method for indexing a currency against its trading partners and then monitoring the performance of that basket. The weighting is done based on how much trade the base country does with its trading partners. So, for example, the Canadian TWI depends mostly on the U.S. dollar (over 80 percent) since most of Canada's exports go to the United States. The index base is set to 100 and is widely viewed as

TABLE 7.3 G7 Historical and Forecasted Current Account Surplus/Deficit

| Country | Current Account | | | | | | Three-Year |
	2011	2012	2013E	2014E	2015E		Forecasted Change
United States	-3.0%	-2.7%	-2.5%	-2.5%	-2.5%		0.2%
United Kingdom	-1.5%	-3.8%	-3.6%	-2.8%	-2.6%		1.2%
Japan	2.0%	1.0%	1.3%	1.9%	2.0%		1.0%
France	-1.8%	-2.2%	-2.0%	-1.8%	-1.5%		0.7%
Germany	6.2%	7.0%	6.6%	6.0%	6.0%		-1.0%
Italy	-3.1%	-0.5%	0.6%	1.0%	1.0%		1.5%
Canada	-3.0%	-3.7%	-3.0%	-2.6%	-2.3%		1.4%
Eurozone	0.1%	1.4%	2.1%	2.1%	2.3%		1.0%
China	2.7%	2.3%	2.4%	2.3%	2.4%		0.1%
						Max	1.5%
						Min	-1.0%

Note: Eurozone and China included in G7 for illustrative purposes.
Source: IMF and Bloomberg. As of September 2013.

a great measure for real effective exchange rate. Deutsche Bank has TWI on Bloomberg for many countries:

- TWI USSP <Index> = United States
- TWI EUSP <Index> = Europe
- TWI BPSP <Index> = United Kingdom
- TWI JPSP <Index> = Japan
- TWI ADSP <Index> = Australia

Economic Activity

Future economic performance of a country is one of the most powerful tools in predicting asset price moves because it lays the foundation for growth and inflation. Some key economic drivers that help one assess economic activity are GDP growth, inflation, unemployment rate, and consumption to name a few.

Another technique involves taking an average of forecasts from investment banks and using outside data providers who have a history of compiling data accurately to see what the market expects growth to be. Let's assume in the United States the 2013 GDP growth is forecasted to be 2.9 percent.[3] If all investment banks are in line with this forecast but two months later shift their forecasts to 3.2 percent GDP growth, markets are likely to adjust over time. This is very powerful information and, since the 2.9 percent projection was already "baked in the cake," identifying these changes early can generate significant alpha. This approach can be applied to a broad range of economic indicators and should get appropriate weights if one is building a forecasting model.

Export Partner Growth and Direct Exports

Many emerging markets like Brazil and Russia are export-driven. When risk assets sell off and commodity prices fall, it is logical that the local currency (BRL and RUB) decreases in value. Having a tool that can predict this on a macro level is critical to trading currencies.

One of the methods used to forecast how a currency will perform is to look at the growth and strength of a country's exporting partners. For Australia, the top five exporting countries account for 65 percent of total

---

[3] Midpoint of FOMC projection materials, April 2012.

TABLE 7.4 Australia International Merchandise Exports,
Top Five Countries from 2010 to 2011 (A$ in millions)

Country	Amount	Percent
China	$64,856	40.7%
Japan	46,967	29.5%
Korea	22,556	14.2%
India	15,761	9.9%
Taiwan	9,109	5.7%
	$159,249	

Source: Australian Bureau of Statistics.

exports (see Table 7.4). As one would expect, China is the leading exporting country and would command the biggest weight.

To understand the effect China, Japan, Korea, India, and Taiwan have on Australia, we must break each country down individually. As far as China, relative equity performance is one of the factors used to determine its strength. Using the Shanghai Composite (SHCOMP Index) and price performance, one should model its price change over a time horizon.

Another indicator of country performance is PMI manufacturing. This is a leading indicator that provides us with a glimpse into what the manufacturing sector might look like. For China, it is recommended to use the HSBC PMI manufacturing number since it is not surveyed by the government and this likely makes it a more valid number.

Further, it is useful to look at overall relative GDP growth as one factor and then combine it with changes to GDP forecasts to see if forecasts are disappointing or not. If GDP forecasts are being revised higher in China, it is more than likely that Australia will benefit as well, resulting in an appreciation in the Australian dollar.

Direct Exports

Direct exports are another useful indicator in currency valuation. For example, energy accounts for roughly 60 percent of Canada's total exports. Knowing this, it shouldn't come as any surprise that the change in the price of oil will have an effect on the Canadian economy and ultimately on the Canadian dollar (Figure 7.12).

FIGURE 7.12 Canadian Dollar versus WTI Crude

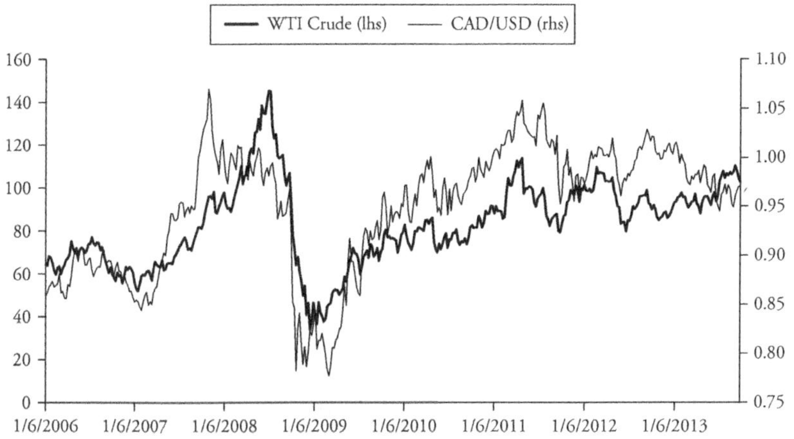

Source: Bank of Canada and Bloomberg.

Debt to GDP

Debt to GDP attempts to measure a country's debt relative to its GDP. As debt grows, many economists have argued that GDP growth will more than compensate for the additional debt added on. As the book *This Time is Different* by Ken Rogoff and Carmen Reinhart (Princeton University Press, 2009) demonstrated, trouble looms ahead for any country that is not keeping its debt to GDP ratio in check. Logic would hold that a high debt and low GDP means a country is in financial crisis, but this is not always true. Let's look at the case of Japan, for instance. On a debt to GDP basis, Japan seems doomed; however, the JGB market has rallied for years (lower yields). There are many factors that keep Japan afloat, such as a high savings rate that encourages locals to purchase sovereign debt and local banks to buy as well.

Debt to GDP is not always an accurate measure of a country's financial standing, as it can take years, if not decades (as in the case of Japan), before the credit deterioration leads to a fall in the currency and sovereign credit (see Figure 7.13).

Absolute and Relative Purchasing Power Parity

Absolute purchasing power parity (PPP) reflects the theory that, in the long run, exchange rates will adjust to their relative purchasing power of goods and

FIGURE 7.13   2012 Country Debt to GDP

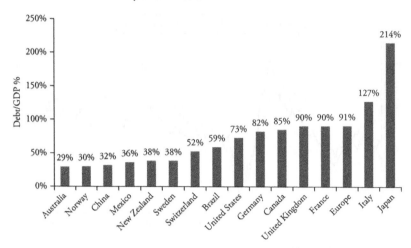

Source: Bloomberg and World Bank.

services. The theory is derived from the theory of one price, which effectively states that the price of a good will, over time, evens out to the same value anywhere in the world (as in the Big Mac Index). For example, if the price of a computer in the United States is $1,000 but the same computer costs $2,000 in Canada, over time people in Canada would begin to buy the same computers from the United States and prices in the United States and Canada would converge until the Canadian consumer was no longer more inclined to buy from the United States. The Big Mac Index is a famous attempt to simplify PPP. It measures the cost of a Big Mac in many countries (see Figure 7.14). There are many other predictors of PPP, such as trade-weighted baskets, that are effective for forecasting.

Absolute purchasing power parity does not take inflation into account. For instance, the price of a Big Mac is higher in Norway than Brazil, but Brazil has a higher inflation rate. Relative purchasing power parity makes the adjustment by comparing two countries' inflation rates and taking the difference into account. It could be that price increases of the Big Mac were due to inflation, as opposed to other factors (Figure 7.14).

While, theoretically, PPP is a powerful tool, it does have its shortcomings. Richard Meese and Kenneth Rogoff conducted a study that showed that PPP is not an accurate forecasting tool in the short run (Meese and Rogoff 1983). Even economists will concede that PPP is better as a long-term predictor of currency exchange rates because it can take up to several years for consumer prices to converge.

FIGURE 7.14 Big Mac Index

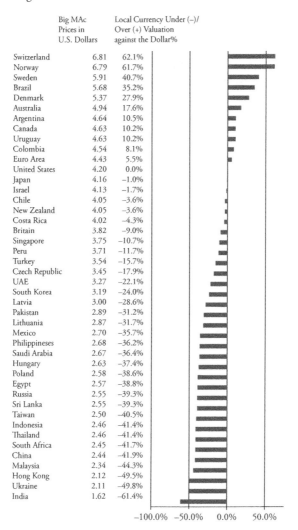

	Big MAc Prices in U.S. Dollars	Local Currency Under (−)/ Over (+) Valuation against the Dollar%
Switzerland	6.81	62.1%
Norway	6.79	61.7%
Sweden	5.91	40.7%
Brazil	5.68	35.2%
Denmark	5.37	27.9%
Australia	4.94	17.6%
Argentina	4.64	10.5%
Canada	4.63	10.2%
Uruguay	4.63	10.2%
Colombia	4.54	8.1%
Euro Area	4.43	5.5%
United States	4.20	0.0%
Japan	4.16	−1.0%
Israel	4.13	−1.7%
Chile	4.05	−3.6%
New Zealand	4.05	−3.6%
Costa Rica	4.02	−4.3%
Britain	3.82	−9.0%
Singapore	3.75	−10.7%
Peru	3.71	−11.7%
Turkey	3.54	−15.7%
Czech Republic	3.45	−17.9%
UAE	3.27	−22.1%
South Korea	3.19	−24.0%
Latvia	3.00	−28.6%
Pakistan	2.89	−31.2%
Lithuania	2.87	−31.7%
Mexico	2.70	−35.7%
Philippineses	2.68	−36.2%
Saudi Arabia	2.67	−36.4%
Hungary	2.63	−37.4%
Poland	2.58	−38.6%
Egypt	2.57	−38.8%
Russia	2.55	−39.3%
Sri Lanka	2.55	−39.3%
Taiwan	2.50	−40.5%
Indonesia	2.46	−41.4%
Thailand	2.46	−41.4%
South Africa	2.45	−41.7%
China	2.44	−41.9%
Malaysia	2.34	−44.3%
Hong Kong	2.12	−49.5%
Ukraine	2.11	−49.8%
India	1.62	−61.4%

−100.0% −50.0% 0.0% 50.0%

Source: McDonald's, Economist, January 12, 2012.

GDP per Capita

GDP per capita is calculated by dividing the gross domestic product of a country by the average population. This measure will be more accurate if it is also adjusted for PPP because it adjusts for inflation and cost-of-living standards.

Observing GDP per capita allows one to see how wealthy a country is relative to another country. Measuring annual rate of change of GDP per capita is equally important (see Table 7.5). This gives us a sense of whether the country's citizens are becoming richer and more productive or not. Incorporating this factor into one's process can be useful in longer-term currency strategies. As a country becomes richer and productivity rises, foreign investment flows into the country, which, over time, will strengthen the local currency, according to the Balassa-Samuelson effect. Based on this measure

TABLE 7.5   GDP per Capita by Country and Region

	World Bank	
	GDP per Capita (PPP Adjusted)	GDP per Capita (Annual Growth)
Americas	**2012**	**2012**
United States	49,965	1.5%
Canada	42,533	0.6%
Mexico	16,731	2.7%
Brazil	11,909	0.0%
Argentina*	17,554	7.9%
Europe		
United Kingdom	36,901	−0.5%
Germany	40,901	0.6%
France	36,104	−0.5%
Italy	33,111	−2.7%
Spain	32,682	−1.5%
Turkey	18,348	0.9%
Asia		
Japan	35,178	2.2%
China	9,233	7.3%
South Korea	30,801	1.6%
Singapore	61,803	−1.1%
Australia	44,598	1.8%
Hong Kong	51,946	0.3%

*Data for Argentina as of 2011.
Source: Bloomberg and World Bank.

alone, the Singapore dollar (SGD) is the most attractive candidate, because Singapore has both the highest GDP per capita and the highest annual growth rate.

Carry Indicators for Currency Valuation

Carry is a critical component in currency valuation. In currencies, carry is the return one makes on holding a currency, assuming that the exchange rate is held constant. Carry strategies are typically executed by borrowing in lower-yielding currencies like Japanese yen, U.S. dollars, and British pounds and buying higher-yielding currencies like Australian dollars, New Zealand dollars, Brazilian reals, Turkish lira, and other currencies in emerging markets.

OIS Differential

One way to predict effective carry is to look at the respective policy rates of two countries. For example, if one U.S. dollar were equal to one Australian dollar and someone told you that currency would be fixed for six months, you would want to hold Australian dollars since the yield on the currency relative to the Australian dollar is greater (see Figure 7.15). Carry is the interest rate differential between two currencies or a basket of currencies. Many carry strategies involve funding or borrowing in U.S. dollars and Japanese yen to buy higher-yielding currencies like the New Zealand dollar and Australian dollar. The carry trade is a very crowded trade, which means that in large risk off markets such as 2008, the strategy suffers big losses.

LIBOR Differentials

LIBOR is an unsecured borrowing rate that banks charge each other. It is arguably one of the most important rates in the world. LIBOR can also be defined as LIBOR = Fed Funds + (LIBOR − Fed Funds) as is the case with the United States, where Fed Funds is the risk-free component and LIBOR − Fed Funds is effectively a credit (risk) component. By using a relative measure where spreads are taken, one can get a good sense of the direction of the currency, meaning that the interest rate differential drives demand for a currency. Figure 7.16 shows the front contract in LIBOR and EURIBOR.

FIGURE 7.15   Australian Dollar/U.S. Dollar versus the RBA Rate/Fed Funds Effective Spread

Source: Bloomberg.

FIGURE 7.16   Euro/U.S. Dollar versus Front Eurodollar/EURIBOR Spread

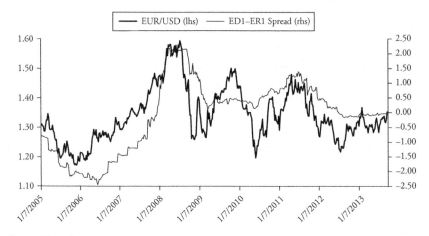

Source: Bloomberg.

Risk-Adjusted Carry

Risk-adjusted carry not only takes carry and LIBOR differential into account, but also adjusts for volatility. Risk-adjusted carry tends to outperform standard carry trades and is useful in a cross-currency analysis.

Table 7.6 looks at high-yielding currencies against lower-yielding currencies. Within each group, one would ideally want the highest carry-to-risk ratio. For instance, the New Zealand dollar (NZD) against the euro (EUR)

TABLE 7.6 Carry-to-Risk Ratios on Carry Currencies

	3M Carry (LIBOR)	30D Volatility	Carry-to-Risk Ratio
AUD/USD	2.7%	8.8%	**0.31x**
AUD/EUR	2.8%	9.2%	0.31x
AUD/JPY	2.8%	14.3%	0.20x
AUD/GBP	2.4%	8.7%	0.28x
NZD/USD	2.6%	11.8%	0.22x
NZD/EUR	2.7%	10.4%	**0.26x**
NZD/JPY	2.7%	15.6%	0.17x
NZD/GBP	2.3%	10.7%	0.22x
USD/BRL	8.5%	16.5%	**0.51x**
EUR/BRL	8.6%	20.3%	0.42x
JPY/BRL	8.6%	22.2%	0.38x
GBP/BRL	8.2%	20.3%	0.40x
USD/ZAR	4.9%	14.5%	0.34x
EUR/ZAR	5.0%	13.8%	**0.36x**
JPY/ZAR	5.0%	18.0%	0.28x
GBP/ZAR	4.6%	15.6%	0.30x
USD/RUB	6.1%	8.6%	0.71x
EUR/RUB	6.2%	6.2%	**1.00x**
JPY/RUB	6.2%	13.2%	0.47x
GBP/RUB	5.8%	7.0%	0.83x

Note: Rates and historical volatility are subject to change.
Source: Bloomberg. Data as of September 2013.

has the highest carry-to-risk ratio amongst other New Zealand crosses, making it more attractive as a carry trade in a basket. The volatility and carry components are always in flux so it is important to make adjustments in one's trading to account for changes.

For carry trades, finding the carry-to-risk ratio is useful and so is comparing all the currency pairs on a relative basis. Measuring the standard error of the sample and finding the most attractive pairs on the whole is helpful in mean-reverting carry strategies. Running a regression can also help optimize returns.

Bloomberg Shortcuts

FX Essentials

FXIP <GO>	Bloomberg FX information portal
FX <GO>	Electronic trading menu
WCR <GO>	World currency rates
XDSH <GO>	Custom real-time FX market views
XCRV <GO>	Chart and compare FX term structures
WCRS <GO>	Rank best and worst performing currencies
FXTF <GO>	Search for currency data and tickers
FXFC <GO>	FX rate forecasts
FXCT <GO>	Calculate FX carry trades
FXFB <GO>	Create a forward rate bias strategy
FXTP <GO>	Analyze FX trader performance

FX Spot/Forward Market Monitors

BFIX <GO>	Spot and forward fixing rates
FXFR <GO>	Monitor spot/forward exchange rates

Calculators

FRD <GO>	Calculate forward exchange rates
FXFM <GO>	FX rate forecast model
FXFA <GO>	Analyze implied interest rates and NDFs
FFRC <GO>	Futures-implied currency forward rates
FXIA <GO>	Locate FX arbitrage opportunities
FXCC <GO>	Calculate the cost of carry
FXCT <GO>	Carry trade indices
MRA <GO>	Create multiple regression matrices
CORR <GO>	Create correlation matrices
FXCA <GO>	Currency conversion calculator

FX Derivatives and Volatility

FXDV <GO>	FX options/volatility menu
OVML <GO>	Price multi-leg foreign exchange options for currency/ precious metals pairs

OVRA \<GO>	Option valuation risk analysis
OVDV \<GO>	Specify FX volatility surfaces
WVOL \<GO>	Customizable list of implied volatilities
VOLC \<GO>	Implied vs. realized volatilities and FX rates
XODF \<GO>	Defaults for OVML, OVDV, VOLC, and VCAL
OVGE \<GO>	Generic option valuation

Summary

The aim of this chapter is to provide the reader with a basic foundation for analyzing currency markets and foreign exchange. It also begins to explore the different markets traded and the basics of currency regimes. Additionally, it provides a number of important valuation techniques for currency market modeling.

CHAPTER 8

Equities

This chapter provides an overview of equity indices, equity derivatives, and model valuation techniques. Model valuation techniques are performed on a macro level and are designed to provide a general sense of value in the stock market as a whole. Trading equities can take many forms, from value investing to long/short strategies to event-driven trading. In macro, a trader should understand equity in terms of market behavior in the country he or she is trading, the sectors that make up those indices, and correlation risk.

Equity Indices Overview

An equity index measures a country's equity performance using a specific basket of stocks. For example, the S&P 500 is a basket of 500 stocks, while the Dow Jones Industrial Average is only 30 blue chip stocks. Table 8.1 shows major equity indices by region:

These indices can be traded directionally or as a relative value trade where one goes long one index and shorts another index. It is important to know the beta, correlation coefficient, volatility, and return of these indices. Additionally, different indices have different exposures, so the Bovespa is more likely to be affected by commodities than the NIFTY, while the S&P 500 has more financial exposure than the Nasdaq, which is more technology-weighted.

The construction of equity indices can also vary. Price-weighted indices only take into consideration the price of each stock. The problem with price-weighted indices is that they ignore the market capitalization of the companies in the index and can be strongly affected by the move of one company.

TABLE 8.1   Equity Indices by Region

United States	Europe	Asia Ex-Japan	Japan	Emerging Markets
S&P 500	Euro Stoxx 50	Shanghai Comp	Nikkei	Bovespa
Nasdaq	DAX	Hang Seng	Topix	NIFTY
DJIA	CAC 40	KOSPI	JASDAQ	Micex & RTS
Russell 2000	FTSE 100	ASX 200		Mexico IPC
Wilshire 5000	FTSE MIB	NZX 50		TOP 40 & JALSH
	IBEX 35			BIST 30 & 100
	AEX			Jakarta Comp

The S&P 500 is weighted based on the market capitalization of the individual components.[1] For instance, Apple had a strong move in early 2012, which accounted for more than 10 percent of the overall performance in the S&P 500. There are many methodologies, so it is useful to know the weighting structure of each index in order to accurately interpret its meaning.

The MSCI World Index is a collection of over 1,600 global stocks intended to track global equity performance. It includes more than 20 countries. MSCI also has the MSCI Emerging Markets Index (MXEF <Index>), which is designed to track emerging market equity performance.[2] These are just a few of the countless number of equity indices; what follows is an outline of the basic concepts and tools used to interpret them.

Taking a Top-Down Macro Approach

Many macro traders take a top-down approach to trading equities (see Figure 8.1). They start with a global view, narrow that view to the countries that will outperform and then select the best companies within that country and sector. The idea behind using a top-down approach is that if the investor has a knack for knowing where the next hot trade will be, he or she will typically see the most reward from buying the single stock equities in the country and sector that he or she thinks will move in price. Since the index is diversified and has many stocks in many industries, the investor may want to limit exposure to a small number of the stocks that best reflect his or her view.

---

[1] "Market Indices," SEC, www.sec.gov/answers/indices.htm.
[2] "MSCI World Index," MSCI, www.msci.com/resources/factsheets/index_fact_sheet/msci-world-index.pdf.

FIGURE 8.1 A Top-Down Approach

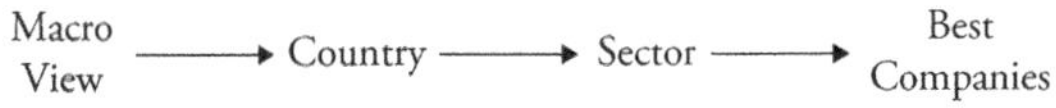

$$\text{Macro View} \longrightarrow \text{Country} \longrightarrow \text{Sector} \longrightarrow \text{Best Companies}$$

Stock Baskets

Stock baskets are a way of buying a number of stocks that are grouped together. The groups of stocks are known as "baskets." These are desirable because they can hedge the risk associated with buying a specific single stock by diversifying and ameliorating idiosyncratic risk. For example, at the end of June and the beginning of July 2012, fears of a drought during the silking process caused the price of corn to move more than 20 percent. Someone bullish on the agricultural sector in the United States who missed the strong corn move could express his or her view through fertilizer companies, as there is a strong (but not exact) correlation to corn prices. Since the fertilizer stocks didn't move as much as corn, if the investor was bullish the sector, it may have made sense to create a basket to get diversification and catch the second leg of the move.

It can be dangerous to pick an outright stock because a macro trader's expertise is not in single stocks. A trader would be exposed to significant risk if he or she picked a single name instead of a basket of stocks in the sector. Since the prices of each stock are different, it is appropriate to weight the stocks by notional and then back in to the amount of shares necessary to meet the notional requirement. In Figure 8.2, energy stocks were chosen because of their relationship to crude oil (WTI), but the stocks in a sector can be chosen for various macro reasons. Relative value stock baskets tend to be of long/short equity, where the research process is dictated by various factors and fundamental analysis.

Sector Rotation

Sector rotation is a term used for different cyclical patterns that occur in the stock market during various economic regimes. A sector is a group of stocks that represents companies in a similar business. For instance, companies like ExxonMobil, Chevron, and ConocoPhillips would all fall into the "energy" sector. Traders must periodically examine the different sectors to see which ones are more likely to outperform in a particular economic cycle. If a country was in a recession, one would want to scale back on the industrial sector and go long consumer staples, with stocks like Procter & Gamble and Coca-Cola. Conversely, if a country were in a period of growth, one would want to be long in industrials, as the country will likely be using resources to

FIGURE 8.2   Absolute Price Chart of WTI Relative to Individual Energy Stocks

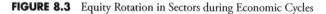

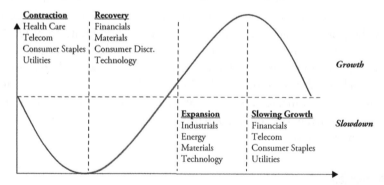

Source: Bloomberg.

FIGURE 8.3   Equity Rotation in Sectors during Economic Cycles

build and develop. Figure 8.3 shows which sectors tend to outperform in the different economic cycles. In order to best position one's equity portfolio, it is critical to know whether or not the economy is in contraction, recovery, expansion, or slowing growth.

Equity Derivatives

Equity derivatives are a class of derivatives that derive their value from an underlying equity security. Since their value is derived from an underlier, the derivatives fluctuate with changes in the underlying asset's equity. Equity derivatives broadly include futures, options, and swaps, a few of which are described in the sections that follow. For purposes of this chapter, we will provide introductions to exchange traded funds (ETFs), American depositary receipts (ADRs), the Volatility Index (VIX), variance swaps, and dividend swaps.

Exchange Traded Funds (ETFs)

Exchange traded funds, better known as ETFs, are one of the fastest-growing products in finance. They give investors a fast, cheap way to get exposures without having to buy a basket separately, which can increase transaction costs. They are listed on exchanges and trade like stocks, but allow investors to track performance of assets. Examples include stocks, indices, commodities, foreign exchange, fixed income, levered funds, and volatility. Additionally, retail investors find ETFs attractive since there is a broad selection of indices without mutual fund fees, although it is important to know that ETFs do charge fees. Read the prospectus to determine what fees will be incurred. See Table 8.2 for some ETFs that are widely traded by category.

TABLE 8.2 ETFs by Category

Countries—Developed	Description
SPY	S&P 500
QQQ	Nasdaq
DIA	DJIA
IWM	Russell 2000
EFA	MSCI
EWA	Australia
EWC	Canada
EWQ	France
EWG	Germany
EWI	Italy
EWJ	Japan
EWN	Netherlands
EWP	Spain
EWU	United Kingdom

TABLE 8.2 *Continued*

Countries—Emerging	Description
FXI	China
EWZ	Brazil
EEM	MSCI Emerging Markets
EWW	Mexico
EWS	Singapore
EWM	Malaysia
EWY	South Korea
EWT	Taiwan
EZA	South Africa
RSX	Russia
INDA	India

U.S. Sectors	Description
XLY	Consumer Discretionary
XLP	Consumer Staples
XLE	Energy
XLF	Financial
XLV	Health Care
XLI	Industrials
XLB	Materials
XLK	Technology
XLU	Utilities
XME	Metals and Mining
GDX	Gold Miners
IYR	Real Estate
XHB	Home Builders
XRT	Retail

U.S. Fixed Income	Description
SHY	1–3-Year Treasuries
IEI	3–7-Year Treasuries
IEF	7–10-Year Treasuries
TLH	10–20-Year Treasuries
TLT	20+-Year Treasuries
MBB	MBS
LQD	Investment-Grade Corporates
HYG	High-Yield Corporates
JNK	High-Yield Bond
BOND	PIMCO Total Return
PCY	Emerging Markets Sovereigns

Commodities	Description
GLD	Gold
SLV	Silver
USO	Oil
UNG	Natural Gas
DBA	Agriculture
DBC	Commodities Index

Currencies	Description
FXA	Australian Dollar
FXB	British Pound
FXC	Canadian Dollar
FXY	Japanese Yen
FXE	Euro
FXF	Swiss Franc
FXM	Mexican Peso
UUP	U.S. Dollar Index

ETFs are formed through a process called creation/redemption. Using gold (GLD) as an example, if an investor bought one million shares trading at $150, then State Street, which manages the ETF, will buy 100,000 ounces of gold (assuming the price of one ounce of gold is $1,500; $150 × 1 million shares = $150 million notional, which is then divided by $1,500 = 100,000 ounces). The process by which State Street buys 100,000 ounces of gold is referred to as the creation process. The investor not only owns the GLD ETF, but also has a claim on a respective amount of gold. If the same investor then chooses to sell all of his or her GLD shares, then State Street would sell the 100,000 ounces of gold back, a process known as redemption. If the investor is a big enough shareholder, some ETFs allow the investor to ask for the physical asset, but each ETF is different. Again, read the prospectus for the specifics of each one.

ETFs also allow investors to buy a basket of equities in foreign countries and sectors very easily. If a particular investor wants to be long energy names but isn't sure what stock is optimal and wants diversification, he or she can buy the Energy Select SPDR ETF (XLE). The ETF for Brazil (EWZ) allows investors to get exposure to stocks in Brazil. Although with many ETFs the return profile is very similar to indices, it is very important to know the makeup of each ETF. For example, the Bovespa and EWZ clearly have a very high correlation. However, the Bovespa contains less Petrobras while the ETF EWZ has had as much as 15 percent Petrobras. While this may not make a large difference on the whole, if the country index has a lower weight in energy than the ETF, the ETF has more risk. Investors also like ETFs because they have a very liquid market to trade options, but it is important for the investor to be aware of the underlying risks involved with options.

American Depository Receipts (ADRs)

American depositary receipts (ADRs) are products that trade like a stock, meaning that the depository bank has ownership in a non-U.S. stock, holds it, and then lists the equity on a U.S. exchange in U.S. dollars. ADRs have become increasingly popular. Investors like single stock equities in foreign countries and it is also convenient to trade them in the United States and in U.S. dollars. However, ADRs are subject to foreign exchange risk; since the shares held are bought locally, they are converted into U.S. dollars, which in turn affects the price listed in the United States.

Examples of large ADRs in the United States include:

Petrobras (Symbol: PBR, Brazil)
British Petroleum (Symbol: BP, United Kingdom)

Cemex (Symbol: CX, Mexico)
Nokia (Symbol: NOK, Finland)
Gazprom (Symbol: OGZPY, Russia)
Alcatel-Lucent (Symbol: ALU, France)

The Volatility Index (VIX)

The Volatility Index (VIX) trades using the S&P 500 as its underlying reference and is extrapolated by using various strikes of implied volatility one month out. The VIX monitors the change in implied volatility of the S&P 500. It is negatively correlated with equity returns, because volatility usually rises when equities fall (see Figure 8.4). During large market selloffs, the VIX can move from the mid-teens to 30 in a matter of days and, as a result, VIX options make tremendous hedges. Many traders use the VIX as an asymmetric hedge, particularly in options.

VIX spot (VIX <INDEX>) is monitored on a daily basis as a relative comparison to equity performance. One can also trade VIX futures and VIX options; however, both should be used with extreme caution because there is the potential for large losses if one is not familiar with the product. VIX futures typically trade in contango and one can trade the futures outright or do basis trades (buying one future and selling another month's futures contract), with the idea that the basis tightens or widens in addition to collecting carry. When the market experiences a sharp selloff and VIX spot spikes higher, the VIX futures typically trade in backwardation in anticipation of VIX spot eventually coming down. VIX options have become very liquid, and are another option for taking a view or using the VIX as a hedge. Users of options, especially VIX options, should have an options background before using them. VIX options are effectively the implied volatility of the particular part of the VIX curve one is trading; it can be thought of as the volatility of volatility, or derivative of a derivative. More specifically, it is a stronger view on kurtosis and skew, and can move very aggressively in either direction (see Figure 8.5).

Other volatility indices include:

V2X Index—Euro Stoxx 500 Volatility Index
VXN Index—Nasdaq Volatility Index
VXD Index—DJIA Volatility Index
RVX Index—Russell 2000 Volatility Index
GVZ Index—Gold Volatility Index
OVX Index—Crude Oil Volatility Index

FIGURE 8.4   VIX Annualized Average Daily Closing and Correlation to the S&P 500

VIX Average Daily Closing Value
For Daily Returns of VIX versus S&P 500

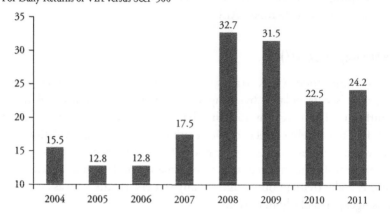

Negative Correlations
For Daily Returns of VIX versus S&P 500

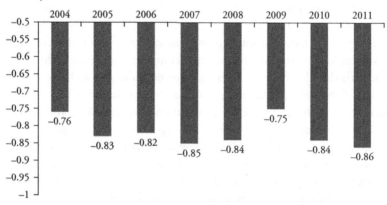

Source: CBOE and Bloomberg.

Variance Swaps

Variance swaps are OTC products that allow investors to get pure variance exposure. Just like being long volatility or long the VIX, variance swaps provide a hedge to long equity portfolios. The problem with options is that volatility is not the only variable and the investor is subject to interest rate, dividend risk, and other risks. Additionally, if investors want volatility protection with options, they must delta hedge, which is cumbersome and can be costly. Another advantage of variance swaps is that they take realized volatility into account. When you buy an option you are implicitly paying for the

FIGURE 8.5 Historical Chart of the VIX Index (Spot)

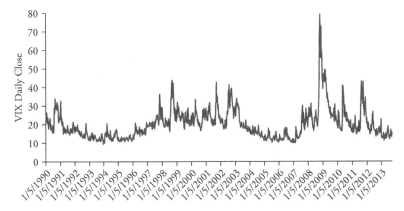

Source: Bloomberg.

implied volatility, which is usually higher than realized volatility. Variance swaps are priced with realized volatility, which gives the buyer slightly more edge in most market conditions. The biggest disadvantages of variance swaps is that they are OTC and require margin, and when you make money on the trade with the intention to unwind, dealers take a very generous spread, particularly when the trade works in your favor.

The biggest consideration that one needs to keep in mind with variance swaps is that the payoff structure has convexity and is nonlinear. If an investor is long variance, he or she will benefit from gains and losses relative to realized volatility (see Figure 8.6).

FIGURE 8.6 Payoff Structure of a Long Variance Swap Position

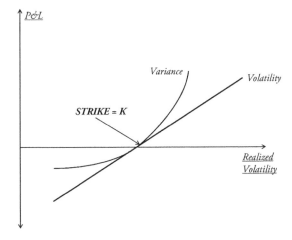

Volatility is measured in relative terms by the $\sqrt{252}$, which is equal to 15.87 or roughly 16 vol is equivalent to a 1 percent daily move. If the volatility level is at 24, this means that the average expected daily move is 1.5% (rounding 15.87 to 16; 24/16 =1.5%).

If a variance swap is being quoted at 24, this implies that the realized daily volatility will be around 1.5 percent. Variance swaps are quoted by strike (or reference realized volatility), vega notional, variance units, and maturity. The strike, or "K," is the reference volatility strike. Let's assume that the investor wants to go long the variance swap with a strike 24, a vega notional of 1,000,000, and the contract realizes 29 volatility. This contract has 20,833 variance units $(1,000,000/(2 \times 24))$ and the payoff is $5,520,833 [$(29^2 - 24^2) \times 20,833$)]. Instead of a realized volatility of 29, if one substitutes different realized volatilities, one can quickly see the nonlinear payoff that variance swaps offer.

$$\text{Variance Units} = \frac{\text{Vega Notional}}{\text{Strike} \times 2}$$

$$\text{Payoff} = (\text{Realized Volatility}^2 - \text{Strike}^2) \times \text{Variance Units}$$

Dividend Swaps

A dividend swap, or div swap, is an OTC or exchange-traded product that allows one to take a view on dividends of an index (for example, S&P 500 and Euro Stoxx 50) to be higher, or lower, than a fixed amount. Dividend swaps on the S&P 500 trade OTC while on Euro Stoxx 50 they trade in listed futures and options.

If one wanted to take a view on the S&P 500 dividend thinking they would go higher, they would use $31.00 as their fix (assuming that's the current market rate). The OTC market is pricing in that the dollar amount of dividends will be $31.00 on the S&P 500 in 2014, so if the S&P 500 at the time of the trade was at 1,350, then the implied dividend yield would be would be 2.3% (= 31/1,350). Further, the contract would be set from December 31, 2013, until December 31, 2014, and div swaps typically trade in baskets of 100,000 in the OTC market. So, one would quote the market as saying that they want 500,000 baskets of the 2014 div swap paying $31. Let's assume that the investor is correct, and that suddenly GDP growth expectations skyrocket and the market moves to $36. The P&L payoff structure would be: $(36.00 - 31.00) \times 500,000 = $2,500,000 + P&L. BNP Paribas has a great screenshot for div swaps on the S&P 500 with BPDV

<GO> 6 on Bloomberg. Div swaps trade on an exchange for the Euro Stoxx 50 in Europe. DEDA <Index> CT allows one to see the prices on div swaps for the SX5E.

Valuation Techniques for Equities

Equity trading has many valuation approaches. These can be done on an index or single stock level and, while each approach is unique, they do overlap in many regards and they often give the same signals. The following sections will provide a brief description of each of these techniques and how using them in combination can provide insight into the relative performance value of the stock market.

Price-to-Book Value (P/B)

Price-to-book value (P/B) is a measure for value in the stock market. The higher the numerator (price) moves relative to the denominator (book value), the less value there is in the stock market. P/B is one of the measures many people use in their models to get a sense of whether the stock market is overbought or oversold. If the price moves exorbitantly high relative to the book value (as in the 1999–2000 technology boom), it is clear that these are periods where the market may be overbought and due for a correction. Conversely, during the financial crisis in 2008, P/B was trading on the S&P 500 around 1.5, which indicated that the S&P was oversold and a value buy. A P/B greater than 2.5× is generally thought to be overbought, and a P/B lower than 1.5× is oversold (see Figure 8.7). Price to Book is often brought up in Graham and Dodd as a measure of value. James Tobin developed the Q Ratio, which looks at the market value of a stock market and compares it to the replacement cost/asset value and gives it a score between 0 and 1. As the Q Ratio approaches 0, it is oversold, and at 1 is overbought. In times of inflation, the Book Value may not reflect the replacement costs as well as the Q Ratio.

Price-to-Dividend

The price-to-dividend ratio is the price of the stock, or stock index, divided by the annual dividend. Price-to-dividend tells you how many dollars someone is willing to spend to receive $1 of dividend. For instance, a price-to-dividend yield of 40 means that an investor is willing to pay $40 for $1 of

FIGURE 8.7   S&P 500 Historical Price/Book Value

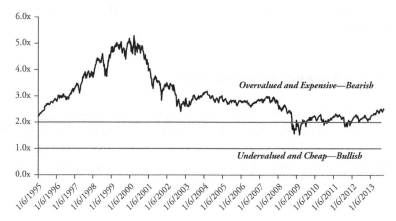

Source: Bloomberg.

FIGURE 8.8   S&P 500 Historical Dividend Yield

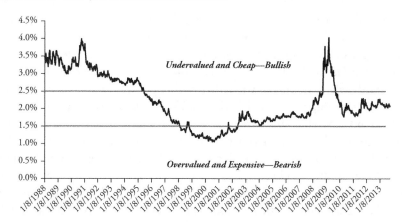

Note: Dividend is for the last twelve months (LTM).
Source: Bloomberg.

dividends. The reciprocal of the price-to-dividend ratio is the dividend yield, which is dividend/price. Both are equally useful measures, so the ratio one uses is simply a matter of preference. In the prior example, $1/$40 = 2.5%. A holder of a stock or index generally has a bullish view, so a nice feature of the dividend yield is that the investor is getting paid while they wait (long carry) (see Figure 8.8).

Price-to-Earnings Ratio (P/E)

The price-to-earnings ratio (P/E) is the price investors are willing to pay for each $1 of earnings. It is probably the most watched equity ratio. It measures the price of the stock index, or single stock, divided by the earnings per share (EPS). One of the great qualities of the P/E ratio is that it is one of the best techniques for comparable analysis in equities. One can compare the P/E ratios of emerging markets to developed markets and even go much further to break down a sector and look at the single stocks to determine which names are more expensive or less expensive relative to their peers. The reciprocal of the P/E ratio is the earnings yield (see Figure 8.9).

On a single-stock level, one of the flaws of the P/E ratio is that it does not take leverage into account. In a booming economic period, a company with more debt will likely have a higher EPS, but more risk of bankruptcy during a down period. One can look at the enterprise value to earnings before interest, taxes, depreciation, and amortization (EBITDA), which takes net debt into account in the interest of creating an "apples to apples" comparison. Others believe that since the recent 2008 downturn, many managers opt to buy back stock, which is accretive, even when it is suboptimal (for example, price-to-book value is too high) to boost EPS, hence making the P/E ratio artificially low and lacking substance. Whether or not this is true or false will only be revealed in time. However, few can deny that this is one of the oldest, most basic measures of equity value, and still a very valuable tool.

FIGURE 8.9   S&P 500 Historical Price/Earnings Ratio

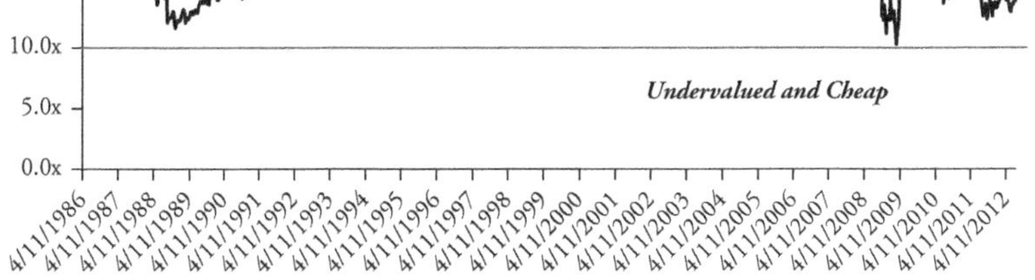

Note: EPS is 12 months trailing.
Source: Bloomberg.

Forward P/E is equally as important, if not more important, than current P/E ratio. It is calculated by taking the current price divided by expected EPS for the next year and uses an average of analysts who have forecasted earnings on a single stock or index. Companies are expected to grow over time, and hence, most of the time, forward EPS estimates are higher than current EPS for stock indices. What is important when looking at the forward P/E ratio is the change in analyst expectations for EPS and the overall EPS growth year after year.

Price-to-Free Cash Flow

Free cash flow is the cash a company or index has remaining from operations after it has paid out to maintain or grow its asset base (better known as capital expenditures). This is a valuable tool in corporate finance because the cash flow statement of any company has cash flow from operations, financing and investing. Cash flow from operations net of capital expenditures gives some-one the general sense of how the business operations are generating cash. There are several ways to derive free cash flow; however, the simplest calculation is:

Free Cash Flow = Cash Flow from Operations – Capital Expenditures (Capex)

Price-to-free cash flow is a measure of return that investors receive on the shares that they own. Many value investors who subscribe to the Graham and Dodd approach to value investing use this as one of their top screens for evaluating which stocks are cheap and which stocks are expensive. The lower the price-to-free cash flow, the cheaper the stock/stock index is considered to be (see Figure 8.10). The reciprocal of price-to-free cash flow is the free cash flow yield, which is more attractive the higher it is.

Stock Market Capitalization as a Percentage of GDP

Stock market capitalization as a percentage of GDP is useful for trying to locate potential bubbles. The higher the number deviations above 100 per-cent, the more worrisome it is. When the rise is very quick this can be the makings of a bubble-like equity market and should be watched with caution. Japan's stock market capitalization as a percent of GDP reached over 150 percent in 1989 during the peak, only to fall below 100 percent in 1990, after which it did not reach above 100 percent for over a decade. Figure 8.11 shows U.S. stock market capitalization as a percentage of GDP.

Commodity Prices

Commodity prices are a great measure of breadth of a bull market in stocks, GDP growth, and inflation expectations. Rising commodity prices eventually

FIGURE 8.10 S&P 500 Historical Free Cash Flow Yield

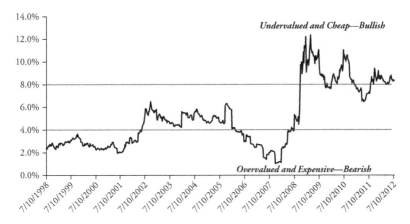

Note: Bloomberg historical calculation underestimates capital expenditures, which means that the free cash flow yield is likely overstated. Also, free cash flow per share is calculated based on the last 12 months.
Source: Bloomberg.

FIGURE 8.11 U.S. Historical Stock Market Capitalization as a Percentage of GDP

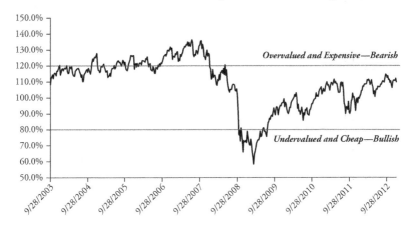

Source: Bloomberg.

become inflationary for an economy, which is typically met by a central bank tightening, like a hike or selling of open market operations, which have bearish implications. Building in price changes in year-over-year change in commodity prices is a useful tool for pricing potential overbought and oversold scenarios. For instance, in 1987 and 2007, the year-over-year change in commodity prices was above the mean range, meaning there were bearish, inflationary pressures, followed by the markets selling off significantly in both observations (see Figure 8.12).

Markit CDX High Yield Index

The CDX High Yield Five-Year Index (see Figure 8.13) is the CDS spread in basis points on high-yielding securities. It has a high correlation to the VIX, which makes sense because when there is a low VIX, investors have more risk appetite and perceive default risks to be lower. As the VIX rises, the S&P 500 tends to fall, which can result from market fears. One would observe that the two are inversely related. When the stock market falls, higher yielding corporates tend to get sold, and, as a result, the price falls and yield rises. In tandem, as the yield rises, the CDX High Yield Index rises and is a good inverse corollary to equity price moves.

Purchasing Manager's Index (PMI)

Purchasing manager's index (PMI) is a survey of purchasing managers and is used as a leading indicator of how the economy is performing. For most countries, it is an indicator with a score of 0 to 100 (few are –50 to 50). Since it is a leading indicator, sharp slope changes and deviations from the midpoint (above or below 50) provide strong signals and often lead equity

FIGURE 8.12 CRB Index Historical Year-over-Year Change

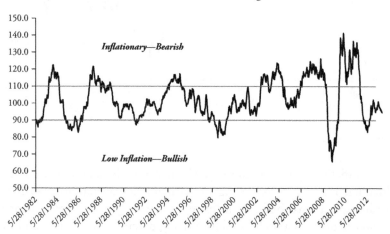

Source: Bloomberg.

FIGURE 8.13 Five-Year CDX High Yield Index

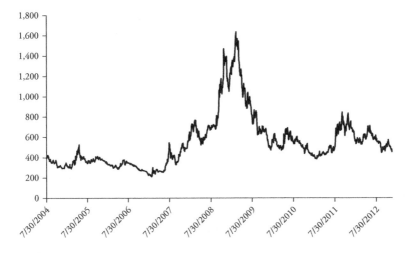

Note: Index is CDX.NA.HY
Sources: Bloomberg, JP Morgan, and Markit.

FIGURE 8.14 Historical Chart of ISM Manufacturing PMI

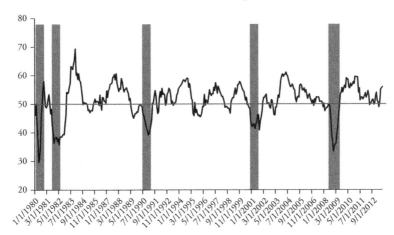

Note: Shaded regions indicate recessions.
Source: Bloomberg.

rallies and selloffs (see Figure 8.14). Modeling in PMIs is a common practice and a useful indicator as well. It's also interesting to note that when the ISM (the name for the U.S. PMI) goes below 50, the United States typically enters recession.

Dry Bulk Index

The Baltic Dry Index (BDIY <Index>), commonly known as the Dry Bulk Index, is a composite of the Baltic Capesize, Panamax, Handysize, and Supramax indices, which provide prices for shipping raw material dry bulk and trades on the Baltic exchange. Dry bulk shipping consists of shipping cargo containing coal, ore, grains, and other raw materials. Since raw materials generally are a good leading indicator, monitoring changes in the Dry Bulk Index is helpful. Figure 8.15 shows a historical chart of the Dry Bulk Index.

The amount of ships available is fixed (i.e., supply is fixed), because it can take up to 10 years for a large ship to be built. Demand for shipping tends to be inelastic in that it is unaffected by the change in price, meaning that whoever is shipping materials is not price sensitive, as is the case with buying crude oil. Dry bulk shipping moves mostly raw materials. Since raw materials are generally sensitive to changes in demand, they serve as a great leading indicator. Since one must ship raw materials, watching shipping prices gives one a sense for demand for raw materials. Adding in a factor that monitors the Dry Bulk Index is useful in predicting market extremes.

FIGURE 8.15 Historical Price Chart of the Baltic Dry Index

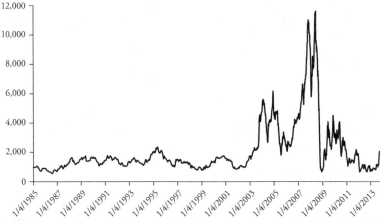

Source: Bloomberg.

Trading Index or ARMS Index

The Trading Index, more commonly known as the TRIN Index or ARMS Index, is a technical sentiment indicator that gives one a sense of whether the market is overbought or oversold (see Figure 8.16). The ARMS Index measures in the numerator advancers over decliners and the denominator advancer's volume over decliner's volume. When the index trades above 1, that is considered bearish and if the index trades below 1, that is more bullish. To smooth out the volatility of the index, it does help to use a moving average. The purpose of the ARMS Index is to gauge how extended either extreme is and also to help timing.

$$\text{ARMS Index} = \left(\frac{\# \text{ of Advancing Issues}}{\# \text{ of Declining Issues}} \right) / \left(\frac{\text{Advancers Volume}}{\text{Decliners Volume}} \right)$$

Consumer Confidence

In the United States, consumption accounts for more than 70 percent of GDP and, as a result, consumer confidence is an indicator used to gauge how optimistic consumers are about the state of the economy; the higher

FIGURE 8.16 Historical Chart of ARMS Index with 100-Day Smoothing

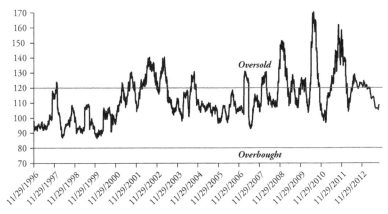

Note: 100-day average smoothing to remove volatility.
Source: Bloomberg.

the optimism, the higher the indicator and the more likely consumers are to spend (see Figure 8.17). The opposite is true if consumers are less certain of economic conditions. Some of the questions on the survey inquire about planned purchases like homes, automobiles and major appliances, and vacation intentions. The Consumer Confidence Index provides a valuable insight into the minds of consumer optimism, which in turn likely translates to a change in consumption and ultimately GDP, which affects equity performance.

Australian Dollar Volatility

The Australian dollar is one of the main risk on currencies because Australia is a large commodity exporter and because of the Australian dollar's reliance on Asian economies. As a result, monitoring the Aussie dollar is a useful endeavor because it can act as a barometer for overall equity performance. Since the Aussie often moves in tandem with equity prices, it is helpful to monitor implied volatility on the Australian dollar.

Building in a factor that takes three-month AUD/USD implied volatility into account is helpful and gives almost the same indication as the VIX since the two are highly correlated and the inverse of the S&P 500 performance (see Figure 8.18). Specifically, factoring in the rate of change is the most useful approach, since in times of stress the rate of change in three-month AUD/USD implied volatility shifts suddenly and aggressively. Given the choice, using the

FIGURE 8.17   Conference Board Consumer Confidence Index

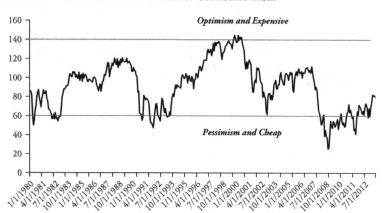

Sources: Conference Board and Bloomberg.

FIGURE 8.18 Australian Dollar Three-Month At-the-Money Volatility versus the VIX Index

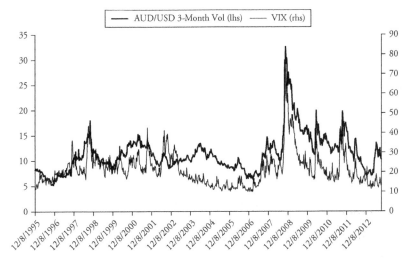

Source: Bloomberg.

VIX is a more effective factor. However, using the two combined on an absolute basis does smooth out any error and provides a more useful measure.

Bloomberg Shortcuts

Equity Market Surveillance

WEI <GO>	World Equity Indices
WEIF <GO>	World Equity Indices Futures
IMOV <GO>	Equity Index/Industry Group Movers
IMAP <GO>	Price Movements across Industries
MOST <GO>	Most Active Stocks

Top-Down Analysis

EA <GO>	Earnings Season Results
FLNG <GO>	Search for 13F Filings
GRR <GO>	Group Ranked Returns
RRG <GO>	Relative Rotation Graph
BI <GO>	Bloomberg Industries
RES <GO>	All Research

Equity Idea Generation

EQS <GO>	Equity Screening
EQBT <GO>	Equity Back-Testing
FSRC <GO>	Fund Screening
FTST <GO>	Factor Back-Tester

M&A and Private Equity

MA <GO>	Mergers and Acquisitions
MARB <GO>	Mergers and Acquisition Arbitrage
PE <GO>	Private Equity Search

Company & Security Analysis

DES <GO>	Company Description
MGMT <GO>	Top Executives and Board Members
CF <GO>	Company Filings
CN <GO>	Company News and Research
BRC <GO>	Single Company Research
ANR <GO>	Analyst Recommendations
FA <GO>	Financial Analysis
GUID <GO>	Bloomberg Guidance
ERN <GO>	Company Earnings
EE <GO>	Earnings Estimates
BDVD <GO>	Bloomberg Dividend Projections
DVD <GO>	Dividend/Split Information
COMP <GO>	Comparative Returns
RV <GO>	Custom Peer Group Analysis
CAST <GO>	Capital Structure
DDIS <GO>	Debt Distribution
SI <GO>	Short Interest
SPLC <GO>	Supply Chain
HDS <GO>	Top Holders
OWN <GO>	Holdings: Ownership
EVT <GO>	Events Calendar
BQ <GO>	Bloomberg Quote

Corporate Calendars

EVTS <GO>	Corporate Events Calendar
ACDR <GO>	Events Calendar
CACT <GO>	Corporate and Municipal Actions

Derivatives

OMON <GO>	Options Monitor
OMST <GO>	Most Active Options

Summary

The goal of this chapter is to serve as a reference for equities, including equity indices, equity derivatives and model valuation techniques. These are important concepts in global macro and the valuation techniques provide a useful way of observing and analyzing value in the stock market as a whole. Equity trading takes many different forms and dozens of books have been written on this topic alone. This chapter is intended to impart the general concept that, in order to trade equity, one should have background knowledge of the country one is trading, the sectors that make up those indices, and correlation risk.

CHAPTER 9

Fixed Income

In order to understand global macro, it is essential to have a basic knowledge of the fixed income market. Bank credit and debt capital markets are the lifeblood of the financial system. The fixed income universe is vast, and this chapter aims to provide the reader with an understanding of LIBOR, swaps, fed funds, overnight index swaps, and FRAs. The chapter also covers fixed income futures, TIPS, sovereign credit, and credit default swaps. Given the depth of fixed income, we will not cover every product. This chapter is designed to equip you with the necessary background to be a successful global macro trader. Figure 9.1 shows the basic construct of the fixed income universe.

Funding/Money Markets

Money markets allow the flow of short-term capital between lenders and borrowers. Capital markets are financial markets generally categorized by the buying and selling of equity and fixed income securities, while money markets generally refers to debt securities maturing in one year or less. Money market instruments generally are safe and the principal is viewed to be safe, though some credit risk exists, as was evident during the 2008 financial crisis. Money market instruments are usually issued in units of $1 million or more and maturities are generally under one year. There is a large secondary market for most money market instruments, which makes them liquid. The money market includes short-term credit market instruments, futures market instruments, and the Federal Reserve's discount window. Many

FIGURE 9.1   Basic Fixed Income Universe: Overview

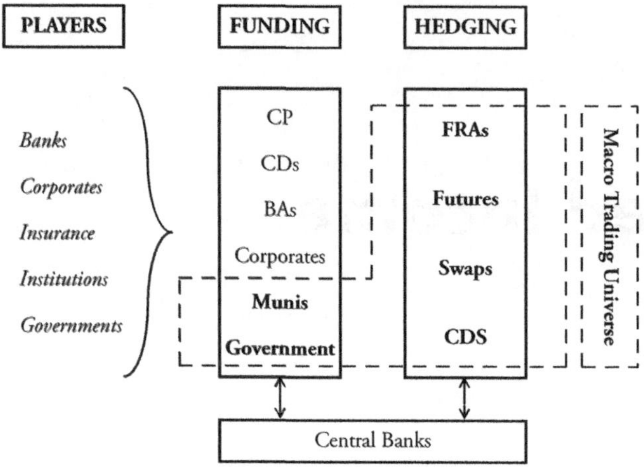

Note: Bold with Dashed line Represents Macro Trading Universe.

market instruments offer retail investors a slightly higher return and rather than purchasing individual securities, many retail customers purchase money market funds to get diversification and liquidity. There are several types of money market instruments and the following sections introduce commercial paper, Treasury securities, government agencies, municipal securities, banker's acceptances, time deposits, interbank loans, and repurchase agreements.

Commercial Paper

Commercial paper is an unsecured, short-term debt obligation of a corporation and banks. Most has a maturity of between 90 and 270 days, since it can avoid registering with the Securities and Exchange Commission (SEC) if the security has a maturity of less than 270 days. Commercial paper is used for short-term financing needs such as financing accounts receivables, inventories, and short-term liabilities. The advantage for corporations to issue commercial paper is that they receive lower rates than they would receive if they borrow directly from banks.

Treasury Securities

The U.S. Treasury, and state and local governments, raise significant amounts of capital in the money market. The Treasury raises funds in the money market by selling U.S. Treasury bills (T-bills), which are short-term obligations of the U.S. government short-term obligations, while state and local governments raise funds through the municipal market. T-bills are sold in regular auctions to help finance budget deficits and refinance maturing T-bills. Additionally, the U.S. Treasury issues T-bills to smooth out uneven tax receipts; so, for instance, when tax receipts are in a seasonal low, the U.S. Treasury will issue additional T-bills until the tax receipts are received. Treasury bills are the largest of all the money market instruments by volume, since the U.S. government is considered to be the risk-free rate.

As a brief history:

> Treasury bills were first authorized by Congress in 1929. After experimenting with a number of bill maturities, the Treasury in 1937 settled on the exclusive issue of three-month bills. In December 1958 these were supplemented with six-month bills in the regular weekly auctions. In 1959 the Treasury began to auction one-year bills on a quarterly basis. The quarterly auction of one-year bills was replaced in August 1963 by an auction occurring every four weeks. The Treasury in September 1966 added a nine-month maturity to the auction occurring every four weeks but the sale of this maturity was discontinued in late 1972. Since then, the only regular bill offerings have been the offerings of three- and six-month bills every week and the offerings of one-year bills every four weeks. The Treasury has increased the size of its auctions as new money has been needed to meet enlarged federal borrowing requirements.[1]

Treasury Inflation-Protected Securities (TIPS)

Treasury inflation-protected securities (TIPS) were introduced in 1997 as way to index to inflation in order to not suffer the negative effects of inflation. They are a form of U.S. government debt. TIPS are typically issued on a quarterly basis, with 5-year, 10-year, and 30-year maturities.

Auctions

> 5-year TIPS—April, *August, *December
> 10-year TIPS—January, *March, *May, July, *September, *November
> 30-year TIPS—February, *June, *October

---

*This is a reopening. In a reopening, we sell an additional amount of a previously issued security. The reopened security has the same maturity date and interest rate as the original security. However, as compared to the original security, the reopened security has a different issue date and usually a different purchase price.

---

[1] "Instruments of the Money Market," The Federal Reserve Bank of Richmond. 1993. www .richmondfed.org/publications/research/special_reports/instruments_of_the_money_market.

TIPS pay interest every six months. The interest rate is a fixed rate determined at auction. Though the rate is fixed, interest payments vary because the rate is applied to the adjusted principal. Specifically, the amount of each interest payment is determined by multiplying the adjusted principal by one-half the interest rate.[2]

TIPS are indexed to CPI-U NSA (consumer price index for urban consumers), giving investors a way to index to inflation and diversify their U.S. debt exposure. CPI-U includes food and energy, which are the most volatile components of CPI and, as a result, short-end TIPS trade like food and energy (CPURNSA<Index>). They accrue inflation (or deflation) on a daily basis. TIPS allow investors to take a view on real rates or inflation.

Nominal Rate (U.S. Treasuries) = Real Rate + Implied Inflation

Another great feature of TIPS is that they have a price floor, such that at maturity, you get the greater of the par value ($100), or the inflation-adjusted principal (> $100). This floor does not apply to coupon payments. For instance, if CPI is 5 percent for a year, then the TIPS will trade at 105. Conversely, if CPI is –2 percent, then the floor is still 100 (although 98 would be used to calculate the interest rate).

Index Ratio

There is a three-month lag between the CPI-U NSA and the index reference calculation. Further, since the figure is monthly, there is a daily interpolation that needs to be done to make this adjustment.

Let's walk through a sample calculation, using March 1, 2012, as a reference (see Figure 9.2):

- CPI-U NSA reference for March 1, 2012, we will use December 2011 CPI-U NSA = 225.672
- CPI-U NSA reference for April 1, 2012, we will use January 2012 CPI-U NSA = 226.665

Now assume a March 16, 2012, settle. The calculation for "Reference Index on Settlement" is as follows:

---

[2] Treasury Direct

$$Reference\ Index = \left(Prior\ Period\ NSA\ CPI \right) + \left(\frac{Day - 1}{30} \right)$$
$$\times \left(Current\ Period\ NSA\ CPI - Prior\ Period\ NSA\ CPI \right)$$
$$= \left(225.672 \right) + \left(\frac{16 - 1}{30} \right)\left(226.665 - 225.672 \right) = 226.169$$

Looking at the TIIJan14 (YA <GO>), the Base Index = 184.774, so 226.169/184.774 = 1.224

The result:

1. Multiply your original principal (100) times the index ratio, which equals your inflation-adjusted principal ($100 \times 1.224 = 122.4$).
2. Multiply your inflation-adjusted principal by half the stated coupon-rate on your security (i.e., 2 percent). The resulting number is your semiannual interest payment.[3]

Breakevens

Breakeven inflation rate (breakevens, for short) is a product that gives exposure to the inflation rate alone by backing into the implied inflation rate from

FIGURE 9.2   Inflation-Indexed Yield Analysis Bloomberg Screenshot

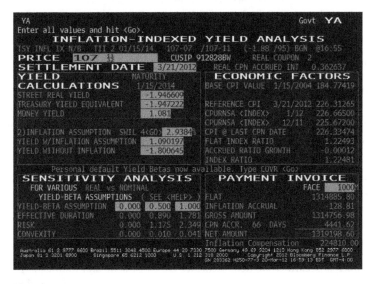

Source: Bloomberg.

---

[3] Federal Reserve Bank of New York.

TIPS. This helps back into the market perception of real rates by combining the nominal and market expected inflation rate.

Nominal Rates – Inflation = Real Rates*
(Treasuries) – (Breakevens) = Real Rates

---

*This is a simplified version of the Fisher Equation.

USGGBE02 <Index> = 2-Year Breakeven
USGGBE05 <Index> = 5-Year Breakeven
USGGBE10 <Index> = 10-Year Breakeven
USGGBE30 <Index> = 30-Year Breakeven

The following table from April 2, 2012, shows that the market has priced in negative real rates for the next 10 years:

	Nominal	–	Inflation	=	Real
2 Years	0.3229		2.0798		–1.7569
5 Years	1.008		2.0795		–1.0715
10 Years	2.182		2.3695		–0.1875

Note: Nominal is yield on U.S. fixed income and inflation is breakeven rate for the specified date.

Government Agencies

Government agencies and government-sponsored enterprises (GSEs) are large borrowers in the U.S. money markets. These includes Fannie Mae and Freddie Mac, which focus on housing, and Sallie Mae, which focuses on student lending. GSEs began with the Federal Farm Credit Banks in 1916, with a focus on agricultural financing. GSEs have become substantial money-market borrowers showing well over $10 trillion in size on the Federal Reserve Flow of Funds Accounts (Z.1).

Municipal Securities

Municipal securities are debt securities issued by state and municipal governments and the special districts and statutory authorities they establish. States and municipalities borrow to finance their own expenditures, to provide funds to some tax-exempt entities such as colleges and nonprofit hospitals, and, to a limited degree, to provide funds to private firms and individuals. State and local governments can borrow at favorable rates because the interest income received by holders of most municipal securities is exempt from federal taxes.[4]

Market participants generally call municipal securities short-term if they have maturities of less than three years or if they have features that shorten their effective maturities to less than three years. The municipal market includes several short-term financing vehicles. Notes such as bond anticipation notes, tax anticipation notes, and revenue anticipation notes provide funds for short periods and are repaid from the proceeds of bond issues, taxes, or revenue-producing projects. Tax-exempt commercial paper and variable-rate demand obligations enable state and municipal issuers to fund long-term projects at short-term rates.[5]

Banker's Acceptance

In the 1970s, banker's acceptances (BAs) were a major source for firms to raise short-term funds in money markets. A banker's acceptance is a promissory note issued by a firm to a bank in exchange for a short-term loan, which the bank then resells at a discount, similar to a T-bill. BAs generally have a maturity of between 30 and 180 days.

There are several differences between commercial paper and banker's acceptances. BAs do not bear interest, and like a T-bill or zero-coupon trade at a discount and then are redeemed at maturity at face value. They are generally linked to the sale or storage of a good, like exports, where the proceeds will be received in a couple months. Lastly, investors rely more on the credit risk of the guarantor bank, rather the underlying issuing company. When BAs were heavily traded, banks were able to borrow at a lower borrowing cost than most companies, so businesses were able to take advantage of bank's lower borrowing costs. However, in the past two decades this borrowing differential has disappeared so companies can borrow at the same rate or better than most banks, so the BA market has shrunk as a result.

Time Deposits

Time deposits, which are also commonly referred to as certificates of deposits or CDs, are bank deposits that cannot be withdrawn without a penalty before

---

[4] "Instruments of the Money Market," The Federal Reserve Bank of Richmond.
[5] Ibid.

a specified maturity date. Time deposits range from 30 days to five years in maturity. However, those that are one year or less are considered money market instruments.

Interbank Loans

Interbank loans refers to a market where banks loan capital to one another. Many interbank loans are done overnight or for maturities of one week or less. This can also help banks manage their end-of-day balances. These loans are done at a specified interbank rate and many banks have their borrowing rate linked to LIBOR, which is discussed later in the chapter.

Repurchase Agreements

A final way banks can raise funds is through repurchase agreements or "repos." A repo is a sale of securities with a simultaneous agreement by the seller to repurchase them at a later date, which is usually done overnight. For the lender or the buyer of the securities, this transaction is often called a "reverse repo." Most repo transactions involve U.S. government securities or GSEs. Repos are classified as money market instruments and are critical to short-term funding.

London Interbank Offered Rate (LIBOR)

London Interbank Offered Rate (LIBOR) is perhaps the most important rate in global financial markets. As defined by the British Bankers' Association:

> LIBOR is the rate at which an individual Contributor Panel bank could borrow funds, were it to do so by asking for and then accepting interbank offers in reason market size, just prior to 11:00 A.M. London time.[6]

LIBOR serves in many ways as the initial funding rate in front-end rates, with three-month LIBOR being the dominant gauge. It is also an unsecured deposit rate that trades offshore and allows banks to bypass certain regulations. LIBOR is not directly tradable, but drives the Eurodollars futures market, which is the most actively traded futures market in the world based on contact volume.

The British Bankers' Association (BBA) calculates the USD LIBOR rate by surveying 16 banks each morning in London about their three-month borrowing rate. The BBA then sorts the survey greatest to smallest and eliminates

---

[6] British Bankers' Association.

both the upper and lower quartile. Once this is done, the BBA then takes an arithmetic average of the remaining rates from the survey (Burghardt 2003). To view this on the Bloomberg terminal, go to BBAM <GO> or BBAL <GO>.

Eurodollar Futures

Eurodollar deposits are time deposits at banks outside the Fed's jurisdiction. Over time, this function has developed into a driving force in money markets. Consequently, Eurodollar futures contracts are the most heavily traded futures contracts in the world, driven by the wholesale funding market. Banks also use Eurodollar futures to extend and shorten the weighted average maturities of their short-term liabilities. A Eurodollar futures contract is a contract on three-month LIBOR spanning three months from the initial date (for example, June 2014 is a contract for three-month LIBOR from June 2014 to September 2014). Each futures contract is $1,000,000 notional, or par-amount. Market participants use Eurodollars to hedge their LIBOR exposure and short-term rates. ED1 <Comdty> on Bloomberg for the Futures Contracts.

$$Value = \$1,000,000 \times \left(1 + r\frac{90}{360}days\right)$$

For every 1-bps change, the future change in interest earned is $25.

Futures Specifications

Contract Size: $1,000,000
Price: 100 – 3-Month LIBOR Yield
 Ex. U.S. 3-Month LIBOR = .50
 100 – 0.50 = 99.50
Tick Value = 1 basis point = 1 Tick. The value of 1 Tick is $25.
Months = March (H), June (M), September (U), December (Z)
 Cash Settlement
Last Day = second day before the third Wednesday (IMM date)[7]

---

[7]CME Group, "Eurodollar Futures: The Basics," September 2011, www.cmegroup.com/trading/interest-rates/files/eurodollar-futures-reference-guide.pdf.

Color = White (Year 1), Red (Year 2), Green (Year 3), Blue (Year 4), Gold
(Year 5), Purple (Year 6), Orange (Year 7), Pink (Year 8), Silver (Year 9),
and Copper (Year 10)

Interest Rate Swaps

Interest rate swaps are derivatives that allow an investor to exchange one
set of interest payments for another. The most common interest rate swaps
are fixed-for-floating swaps, where the investor or hedger has the choice to
receive a fixed rate and pay a floating rate, or pay a fixed rate and receive a
floating rate. If someone is a "receiver" of rates, that means the person believes
the floating portion will drop. Conversely, if a trader is a "payer" of rates, then
he or she believes the rate of that tenure will rise. The bulk of investors who
trade interest rate swaps are merely trying to hedge their interest rate exposure
and lock in a particular spread. In the United States, future LIBOR expectations drive swap curve, and while most trade OTC, increasingly they will be
become exchange traded.

USSW (Tenure) <Index> United States
EUSA (Tenure) <Index> Europe
BPSW (Tenure) <Index> UK
SWSF (Tenure) <Index> Switzerland
CDSW (Tenure) <Index> Canada

Federal (Fed) Funds

Federal funds, or Fed funds, are unsecured loans of reserve balances that
depository institutions make to one another. The rates at which these
transactions occur are called the Fed Funds rates. The most common duration
or term for Fed funds transaction is overnight, though longer-term deals can
be arranged. The Federal Open Market Committee (FOMC) sets a target level
for the Fed funds rate, which is its primary tool for implementing monetary
policy.[8] The Federal Reserve mandates that banks keep 10 percent of their
demand deposits as reserves (i.e. the reserve requirement).[9] Any reserves kept

---

[8] Federal Reserve Bank of New York.
[9] Federal Reserve

at the Fed in excess of the reserve requirement are considered excess reserves. Even though the FOMC targets the Fed funds rate, at the end of the day it is a market rate determined by banks. The Federal funds effective rate (Fed effective) fixing is set by the Fed and is typically released around 8 A.M. EST. This can be found on Bloomberg with FEDL01 <Index>. The Fed effective serves as a reference rate for other front-end products such OIS.

In the advent of the financial crisis and quantitative easing asset purchases, the Fed has flooded banks with additional reserves. This has caused the Fed effective rate to trade below the Fed funds target rate. Furthermore, the Fed pays interest on excess reserves (IOER). Since the supply of reserves at the Fed is so high, the Fed effective and IOER are below the Fed funds rate. As of December 2008, the Fed funds target has been 0.00 to 0.25 percent, which makes it zero-bound (i.e., the FOMC cannot take rates any lower). Since the FOMC will be limited in what it can do, the FOMC can control IOER as a measure to control money policy if the economy worsens and, while unlikely, could even make IOER negative. Additionally, banks pay FDIC insurance premiums on their reserve balances at the Fed, which reduces the net IOER earned.

One can trade the Fed funds futures contract on the Chicago Mercantile Exchange (CME). Fed fund futures fix according to the Fed effective. For example, if FFH4 (Fed Funds Mar14 Contract) trades at 99.79, then the market is pricing in 0.21 for the Fed effective (100-99.97). Table 9.1 shows the contract specifications from the CME.

Overnight Indexed Swaps (OIS)

An overnight index swap (OIS) is a fixed-for-floating interest swap that is indexed against an overnight rate (which, in the United States, is the Fed effective). They are great tools to hedge or speculate in central bank action and typically have a maturity of less than two years. Both notional and maturity are flexible and the OIS is the geometrically averaged difference between interest accrued on the floating leg and the interest accrued on the fixed leg.

The advantages to OIS include the ability to customize dates (under two years) and take central bank policy views, and that it is less volatile than LIBOR (especially in periods of uncertainty). Some disadvantages to OIS are that it has had little liquidity in the past two years, and that multiple fixings can be hard to monitor and has a wide bid/offer depending on the OIS traded.

United States: The Fed funds effective rate is the overnight rate in the United States and settles T + 2.

TABLE 9.1 30-Day Fed Funds Futures Specifications

Underlying Unit	Interest on Fed funds having a face value of $5,000,000 for one month calculated on a 30-day basis at a rate equal to the average overnight Fed funds rate for the contract month.
Price Quote	100 minus the average daily Fed funds overnight rate for the delivery month (e.g., a 7.5% rate equals 92.75).
Tick Size (minimum fluctuation)	Nearest expiring contract month: One-quarter of one basis point (0.0025), or $10.4175 per contract (1/4 of 1/100 of one percent of $5 million on a 30-day basis, rounded up to the nearest cent per contract). All other contract months: One-half of one basis point (0.005), or $20,835 per contract.
Contract Months	First 36 calendar months.
Last Trading Day	Last business day of the delivery month. Trading in expiring contracts closes at 4:00 P.M. on the last trading day.
Final Settlement	Expiring contracts are cash settled against the average daily Fed funds overnight rate for the delivery month, rounded to the nearest one-tenth of one basis point. Final settlement occurs on the first business day following the last trading day. The daily Fed funds overnight rate is calculated and reported by the Federal Reserve Bank of New York.
Settlement Procedure	Daily Fed funds Settlement Procedures (PDF)
Position Limits	Current Position Limits
Block Minimum	Block Trading Minimums
All or None Minimum	All or None Minimums
Rulebook Chapter	CBOT Chapter 22
Trading Hours (All times listed are Central Time)	OPEN OUTCRY MON – FRI: 7:20 A.M. – 2:00 P.M. CME GLOBEX MON – FRI: 5:00 P.M. – 4:00 P.M.
Ticker Symbol	OPEN OUTCRY FF

Europe: The Euro Overnight Index Average (EONIA) is the effective overnight rate for the euro and is computed by the European Central Bank. It is computed as a weighted average of all overnight, unsecured lending transactions undertaken in the interbank market, initiated within the euro area by the contributing banks. Settles T + 2.[10]

---

[10] European Banking Federation. EURIOBR-EBF.

England: The Sterling Overnight Index Average (SONIA) benchmarks the cost of funds in the overnight British pound sterling market and provides a methodology for fixing overnight indexed swaps. It was introduced by the Wholesale Markets Brokers' Association (WMBA) in March 1997 and is the weighted-average rate to four decimal places of all unsecured sterling overnight cash transactions brokered in London.[11]

Switzerland: Tomorrow/Next OIS (TOIS) is the interbank overnight rate for the Swiss Franc. Settles T + 2.

For example, as of March 2012, the Bank of England bank rate was 0.50 percent. The December 2012 MPC Central Bank Meeting OIS is 0.48/0.52. The middle of market is 0.50, which implies that the market had priced no action by the Bank of England by December 2012. If, for instance, market dynamics changed favorably and the MPC Central Bank OIS was, for instance 0.625, that means the market was pricing in a 50 percent chance for a hike. (One hike is 0.25, back of the envelope calculation is 0.625 − 0.50 = 0.125, 0.125/0.25 = 50%.)

LIBOR-OIS Spread

LIBOR-OIS is a great tool to gauge market stress and crisis. LIBOR is an unsecured lending rate amongst banks, while OIS or Fed effective is usually a daily rate that is compounded. Typically this spread will widen during periods of crisis. During the 2008 financial crisis and Lehman fiasco, LIBOR-OIS spreads skyrocketed because institutions effectively stopped trusting each other since loaning money for longer periods of time is a greater credit risk. European banks were short dollar funding, and because LIBOR is unsecured, they demanded more for dollar lending (Figure 9.3).

During the ongoing European crisis, many people have been long this chart. A widening of the U.S. LIBOR/OIS spread does not automatically indicate a crisis situation; rather it simply acts as a useful barometer for credit risk. In the case of the European crisis, it was never definite that this spread would widen because LIBOR is affected by many other factors. But because it frequently does signify a period of crisis, it is a useful tool for monitoring pressure on funding markets.

---

[11] British Bankers' Association.

FIGURE 9.3   Historical Chart of LIBOR-OIS Spread

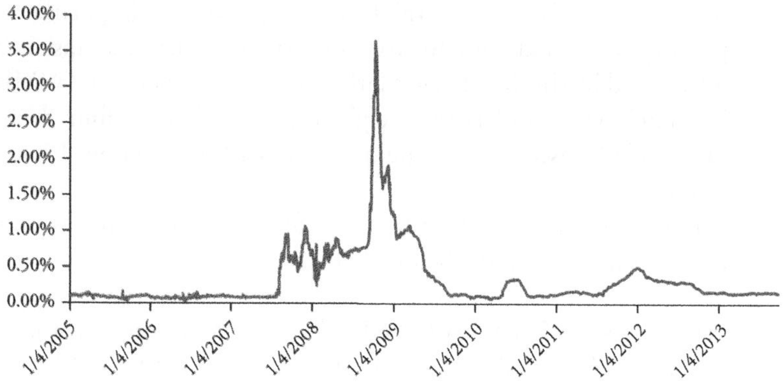

Source: Bloomberg.

Forward Rate Agreements (FRAs)

A forward rate agreement (FRA) is an exchange of prespecified reference rates (LIBOR in the United States) for a fixed floating rate. FRAs are more customized than Eurodollars, allowing the trader to pick specific dates and have several other advantages. Eurodollars, on the other hand, are bound by their quarterly IMM expiry, so one must trade the particular dates of the contract. Eurodollars also lack convexity.

FRAs have fixing, settle, and maturity dates.

- The fixing date is the date of the trade.
- The settle date is the start of the contract.
- The maturity date is the conclusion of the contract.

Example: 3*6 over 15th

Assume we are in March 2013.
3 refers to the months forward (June 2013)
6 refers to the maturity date (September 2013)
The 15th refers to the day of the month for the settle and maturity months (June 15, 2013, and September 15, 2013).
This is equivalent to 3-month forward 3 month.
(*Note:* There are many substrategies and runs in FRAs—this is merely intended to give a quick overview.)

U.S. Fixed Income Futures

U.S. fixed income futures are standardized futures contracts that allow one to trade various maturities in U.S. fixed income (2-yr, 5-yr, 10-yr, 30-year, and ultra-long). See Figure 9.4.

Trading futures allows for leverage, since one needs to post only initial margin and then the variation or "maintenance" margin based on the daily change of the futures price. Futures like the S&P 500 are cash settled, but Treasury bond and note futures are physically settled, which lends to the concept of cheapest-to-deliver. This means that as the futures expire, depending on what the price of the futures contract does, certain physical Treasuries are more advantageous to deliver. Furthermore, to avoid the hassle of "physical delivery," most traders roll their positions, meaning that they close the front contract and initiate the same position on the next contract on the curve.

Treasuries have term premium, which implies a positive sloping yield curve, which means that the futures curve on Treasuries is usually in backwardation (see Figure 9.5), meaning that the front contracts trade at a higher price than the further out contracts. This is unique to Treasury futures in that most futures trade above the underlier, due to carrying costs and storage costs. Underlying instruments generally have a higher interest rate than short-term financing costs.

FIGURE 9.4 Market Pricing Factors on U.S. Fixed Income Yield Curve

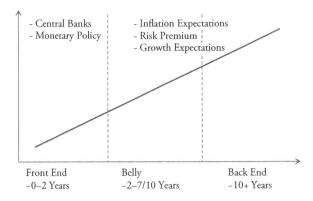

FIGURE 9.5   Bloomberg Screenshot of U.S. Fixed Income Strip

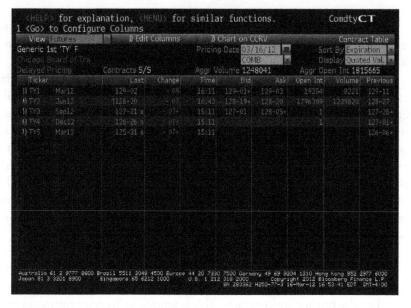

Source: Bloomberg LP.

Contract Specifications:

Contract Size: $200,000 (2-Year) and $100,000 (5-Year, 10-Year, 15+Year, and 25+Year)

Contracts:

	Tick Size	Tick Value
2-Year = TU1 <Comdty>	¼	$15.625
5-Year = FV1 <Comdty>	¼	$7.8125
0-Year = TY1 <Comdty>	½ (+)	$15.625
15+Year = US1 <Comdty>	01	$31.25
25+Year = WN1 <Comdty>	01	$31.25

Months: March (H), June (M), September (U), December (Z)

Physical Settlement

It is important to understand the difference between the dirty price and clean price. The dirty price adds accrued interest while the clean price (quoted price) does not include accrued interest.

For Germany, Schatz cover ~2-Year maturity (DU1 <Comdty>), bobl's are 4.5 to 5.5 years to maturity (OE1 <Comdty>) and the bunds are 8.5 to 10.5 years to maturity (RX1 <Comdty>). Gilts and JGBs are also a big market, but are not applicable in this text. Each one of these markets has unique characteristics and contract sizes.

Types of Expressions

Flatteners and Steepeners

Flatteners and steepeners allow traders to take different parts of the curve and trade them based on a view that they have on the spread (done DV01 neutral). One example is the U.S. 10-Year–U.S. 2-Year (2s 10s). For example, if a trader thought that 2's 10's would trade lower than 185, he or she would put on a flattener. Conversely, if they thought it would go above 185 bps, they would put on a steepener. 2's 10's can be a very good indicator for Fed activity as well (see Figure 9.6).

If one believes that rates will rise more on the front end (short-term rate) than back end (longer-term rate) they are hoping for a bear flattener. If they

FIGURE 9.6   Historical Chart of U.S. 2s/10s Flattener

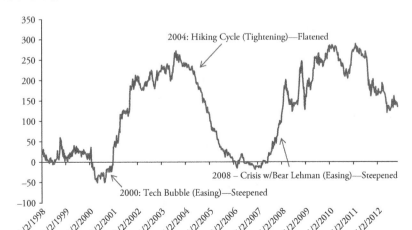

Source: Bloomberg.

FIGURE 9.7   Bear and Bull Flatteners

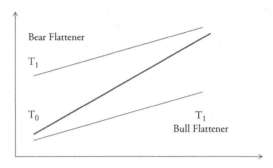

believe that longer-term rates will decrease more than short-term rates, they are doing a bull flattener trade (see Figure 9.7).

Carry and Rolldown

When trading steepeners, flatteners, and parts of the curve, traders must be mindful of carry and rolldown. Since each leg has a different rate, the investor is obligated to make whole on the interest differential being DV01 neutral (carry). By going long or short a Treasury, you have a carry component and at the end of each month or quarter. You must roll your contracts or fixed income security to have the same exact maturity as the profile of the original trade (rolldown).

Sovereign Credit

A sovereign, according to the International Swaps and Derivatives Association (ISDA) 2003 definition, is any state, political subdivision, or government, or any agency, instrumentality, ministry, department, or other authority (including the central bank) thereof. Simply put, when someone thinks of U.S. government debt, they are thinking of sovereign debt.

Note: This can be found with DDIS<GO> on Bloomberg

When thinking about issuance and looking at Greece: Though the Hellenic Republic is the issuer, every country has multiple issuers. In Greece's case, Hellenic Republic Government Bond, Hellenic Republic Government International Bond, Hellenic Republic Treasury Bond, and Hellenic Railways Organization SA are just some of the issuers. The debt is also issued in four different currencies: euros, U.S. dollars, Swiss francs, and Japanese yen, though Euro-denominated debt represents over 95 percent of total debt with roughly €300 billion outstanding.[12]

Sovereign Curve

A nice way to quickly see how a particular curve is behaving on Bloomberg is to use the PX function plus two-letter country code. For example, Portugal is PXPO <GO>. This allows the user to see the price bid/ask in the first two columns. The next two columns represent the bid/ask on yield. This is very useful on a day-to-day process check, because in the fifth column, the user can see the change on day from February 2012 (see Figure 9.8).

Curve Inversion

If you look closely at the Portuguese curve, you will notice that the five-year yield is several percentage points higher. This is referred to as an "inverted curve" which, further out in the yield curve, typically means that the market is pricing in default risk. (If it is closer to the front end and not as steep, this just means that cuts are likely. This is a gauge typically used to predict recessions.)

FIGURE 9.8 Portuguese Government Bonds Screenshot

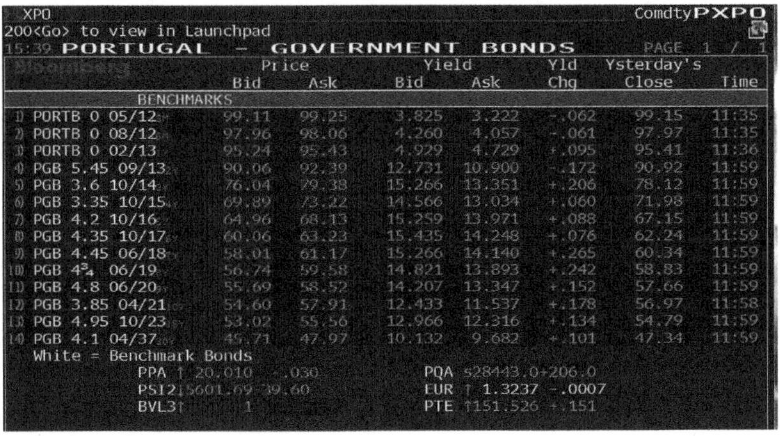
XPO Comdty PXPO
200<Go> to view in Launchpad
15:39 PORTUGAL – GOVERNMENT BONDS PAGE 1 / 1

	Price Bid	Price Ask	Yield Bid	Yield Ask	Yld Chg	Ysterday's Close	Time
BENCHMARKS							
1) PORTB 0 05/12	99.11	99.25	3.825	3.222	-.062	99.15	11:35
2) PORTB 0 08/12	97.96	98.06	4.260	4.057	-.061	97.97	11:35
3) PORTB 0 02/13	95.24	95.43	4.929	4.729	+.095	95.41	11:36
4) PGB 5.45 09/13	90.06	92.39	12.731	10.900	-.172	90.92	11:59
5) PGB 3.6 10/14	76.04	79.38	15.266	13.351	+.206	78.12	11:59
6) PGB 3.35 10/15	69.89	73.22	14.566	13.034	+.060	71.98	11:59
7) PGB 4.2 10/16	64.96	68.13	15.259	13.971	+.088	67.15	11:59
8) PGB 4.35 10/17	60.06	63.23	15.435	14.248	+.076	62.24	11:59
9) PGB 4.45 06/18	58.01	61.17	15.266	14.140	+.265	60.34	11:59
10) PGB 4¾ 06/19	56.74	59.58	14.821	13.893	+.242	58.83	11:59
11) PGB 4.8 06/20	55.69	58.52	14.207	13.347	+.152	57.66	11:59
12) PGB 3.85 04/21	54.60	57.91	12.433	11.537	+.178	56.97	11:58
13) PGB 4.95 10/23	53.02	55.56	12.966	12.316	+.134	54.79	11:59
14) PGB 4.1 04/37	45.71	47.97	10.132	9.682	+.101	47.34	11:59

White = Benchmark Bonds
PPA ↑ 20.010 -.030 PQA s28443.0+206.0
PSI2↓5601.69 39.60 EUR ↑ 1.3237 -.0007
BVL3↑ 1 PTE ↑151.526 +.151

Source: Bloomberg LP.

[12] Bloomberg.

Here are some examples of other countries in Europe that have experienced curve inversions recently:

PXGR <GO> Greece
PXSP <GO> Spain
PXIT <GO> Italy
PXBE <GO> Belgium

Credit Default Swaps (CDS)

(*Note:* Each region in the world has certain peculiarities, so this section is intended to provide a loose definition of the topic. For further details, please refer to ISDA and the broker-dealer of choice.)

The easiest way to think of credit default swaps is in terms of insurance. For example, a homeowner pays an insurance company a premium to insure against arson, robbery, natural disaster, and so on, so that if the house burns down, the homeowner is entitled to receive an amount near the original value of the home.

Taking this homeowner example further, let's assume the house is based in California, is worth $500,000, and the insurance cost is 1 percent a year ($5,000). If there was a breakout of wildfires in the area, would the insurance company still charge 1 percent to insure the same home? It's likely the insurance premiums would rise to reflect the new risk. CDS works in the same way. The main features of CDS are that you do not metaphorically need to own the house—more than one person can "insure" you against the event of your house burning down. This part of CDS, where notional CDS exceeds the notional of the reference obligation (in this example, California) has come under scrutiny, and rightfully so. Lastly, imagine if the insurance company that sold you the policy on your home was no longer in business; you might have to bear the full loss of your home in the event of a fire. In CDS terms, this is referred to as credit risk—AIG is a perfect example of this credit risk, which ultimately led to the U.S. government bailing them out.

Short credit risk = Paying the spread = Buyer of credit protection
Long credit risk = Receiving the spread = Seller of credit protection

The CDS premium is quoted at an annual spread, but paid quarterly. So 100 bps spread means that 25 bps is paid per quarter by the protection buyer, usually in March, June, September, and December.

The Basic Parameters for CDS Contracts

1. Reference Obligation
2. Notional Amount
3. Spread
4. Maturity

Credit Events

A viable credit event trigger is an event that triggers the CDS. When this occurs, the protection buyer stops paying the premium and delivers the reference bond to the protection seller. Then the protection seller makes the protection buyer whole by transferring par (100).

CDS is an OTC contract, which means each contract is unique—but these two credit events are characteristic of most:

1. Failure to Pay: This means that sovereign stops making interest payments.
2. Restructuring: This means that the sovereign postpones, reduces, or defers its obligations. There is one big difference between sovereign and corporate CDS. CDS is not automatically triggered during a restructuring event and both protection buyer and seller have a right (but not an obligation) to trigger the CDS.

Credit Risk

Credit risk, also referred to as counterparty risk, is the risk that the party on the other side of your trade will not make good on their obligations.

FIGURE 9.9 Cash Flow during Life of CDS and Physical Settlement during Default

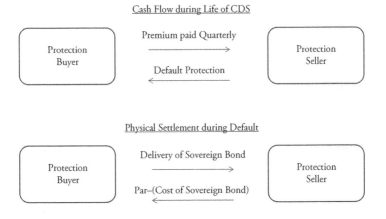

Credit risk is a critical concept that was reinforced during the 2008 Lehman bankruptcy and first brought to light during the collapse of LTCM.

In Table 9.2, JP Morgan's Five-Year CDS is lowest, which implies more safety (that's the market price of safety). All else being equal, if all four banks give the same price, you would want to trade with JP Morgan since the market deems them less risky.

Reference Entities

While in normal and social dialogue we refer to name of the country (e.g., Greece), that name does not necessarily represent the legal entity in terms

TABLE 9.2   Five-Year CDS

Bank of America	196	bps
Citigroup	181	bps
Goldman Sachs	218	bps
JP Morgan	90	bps

Source: Bloomberg and Market as of 3/21/2012.

TABLE 9.3   European Country with Respective Reference Entity

Country	Reference Entity
Austria	Republic of Austria
Belgium	Kingdom of Belgium
Cyprus	Republic of Cyprus
Finland	Republic of Finland
France	French Republic
Germany	Federal Republic of Germany
Greece	Hellenic Republic
Ireland	Republic of Ireland
Italy	Republic of Italy
Malta	Republic of Malta
The Netherlands	Kingdom of the Netherlands
Portugal	Portuguese Republic
Spain	Kingdom of Spain
UK	United Kingdom of Great Britain and Northern Ireland

TABLE 9.4 Sample of Sovereign Defaults from 1998 to 2006

Year	Country	Total Defaulted Debt ($ millions)	Comments
November 1998	Pakistan	$1,627	Pakistan missed an interest payment but cured the default subsequently within the grace period (within four days). Shortly thereafter, it defaulted again and resolved that default via a distressed exchange, which was completed in 1999.
August 1998	Russia	$72,709	Missed payments first on local currency Treasury obligations. Later a debt service moratorium was extended to foreign currency obligations issued in Russia but mostly held by foreign investors. Subsequently, failed to pay principal on MINFIN III foreign currency bonds. Debts were restructured in August 1999 and February 2000.
September 1998	Ukraine	$1,271	Moratorium on debt service for bearer bonds owned by anonymous entities. Only those entities willing to identify themselves and convert to local currency accounts were eligible for debt repayments, which amounted to a distressed exchange.
July 1998	Venezuela	$270	Defaulted on domestic currency bonds in 1998, although the default was cured within a short period of time.
August 1999	Ecuador	$6,604	Missed payment was followed by a distressed exchange; over 90 percent of bonds were restructured.
September 2000	Peru	$4,870	Peru missed payment on its Brady Bonds but subsequently paid approximately $80 million in interest payments to cure the default, within a 30-day period.
January 2000	Ukraine	$1,064	Defaulted on DM-denominated Eurobonds in February 2000 and defaulted on USD-denominated bonds in January 2000. Offered to exchange bonds with longer term and lower coupon. The conversion was accepted by a majority of bondholders.
November 2001	Argentina	$82,268	Declared it would miss payment on foreign debt in November 2001. Actual payment missed on January 3, 2002. Debt was restructured through a distressed exchange offering where the bondholders received haircuts of approximately 70 percent.

(Continued)

TABLE 9.4 *Continued*

Year	Country	Total Defaulted Debt ($ millions)	Comments
June 2001	Moldova	$145	Missed payment on the bond in June 2001 but cured default shortly thereafter. Afterward, it began gradually buying back its bonds, but in June 2002, after having bought back about 50 percent of its bonds, it defaulted again on remaining $70 million of its outstanding issue.
April 2003	Uruguay	$5,744	Contagion from Argentina debt crisis on 2001 led to currency crisis in Uruguay. To restore debt sustainability, Uruguay completed a distressed exchange with bondholders that led to extension of maturity by five years.
April 2005	Dominican Republic	$1,622	After several grace period defaults (missed payments cured within the grace period), the country executed an exchange offer in which old bonds were swapped for new bonds with a five-year maturity extension, but the same coupon and principal.
December 2006	Belize	$242	Belize announced distressed exchange of its external bonds for new bonds due in 2029 with a face value of U.S.$546.8. The new bonds are denominated in U.S. dollars and provide for step-up coupons that have been set at 4.25 percent per annum for the first three years after issuance. When the collective action clause in one of Belize's existing bonds is taken into account, the total amount covered by this financial restructuring represents 98.1 percent of the eligible claims.

Source: Moody's. Sovereign Default and Recovery Rates, 1983–2006, June 2007.

of sovereign debt. We refer to this as a reference entity (e.g., Greece is the Hellenic Republic). This is also useful because if you trade the underlying bonds, these double as their reference entities used by the credit default swaps.

Recovery Rates on Sovereign Issuers

The severity of expected loss on sovereign credit is 1 minus the recovery rate, which is usually assumed to be 40 percent. If you bought a sovereign credit for $100 and there was a default, you would expect to get $40 back and lose $60 of the investment. While industry standards like this are useful in a practical way, it also helps to see historical defaults to get a better sense of what often happens in practice (see Figure 9.10).

One can see that though the average is 55 percent of this data set, it has 24 percent standard deviation, which is not enough evidence to dispute the standard 40 percent assumed recovery rate.

Why Trade Sovereign CDS?

Buying CDS protection offers a very attractive risk/reward profile. For instance, on a notional of $10,000,000, with a 100 bps spread, the investor pays $100,000 per year with almost unlimited upside (up to $10,000,000). We refer to this as an "asymmetric payoff," which is the crux of Nassim Taleb's black swan strategy. Additionally, more often than not, CDS is purchased to hedge a long fixed income position, which can include an index, sovereign, or corporate bonds, to minimize risk and the spread between the underlying fixed income instrument and CDS contract. This is referred to as "basis."

Exchange Traded Funds (ETFs)

Fixed income ETFs are a fast and excellent way to gain exposure to various diversified fixed income portfolios. Fixed income ETFs aim to replicate an underlying bond index or category, which usually consists of large, diversified,

FIGURE 9.10 Recovery Rates on Defaulted Sovereign Bond Issuers

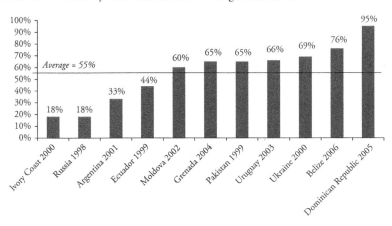

Source: Moody's. Sovereign Default and Recovery Rates, 1983–2006, June 2007.

TABLE 9.5 Sample of Various Fixed Income ETFs

Symbol	Description
SHY <Equity>	iShares 1–3 Year Treasury Bonds
IEF <Equity>	iShares 7–10 Year Treasury Bonds
TLT <Equity>	iShares 20+ Year Treasury Bonds
TBT <Equity>	ProShares UltraShort 20+ Year Treasuries
AGG <Equity>	iShares Core Total Aggregate U.S. Bonds
LQD <Equity>	iShares iBoxx $ Investment Grade Corporate Bonds
TIP <Equity>	iShares TIPS Bond
MBB <Equity>	iShares MBS
MUB <Equity>	iShares National AMT-Free Municipal Bonds
LQD <Equity>	iShares iBoxx $ Investment Grade Corporate Bonds
PCY <Equity>	PowerShares Emerging Markets Sovereign Debt
HYG <Equity>	iShares iBoxx $ High Yield Corporate Bonds
JNK <Equity>	SPDR Barclays High Yield Bonds
BKLN <Equity>	PowerShares Senior Loan Portfolio

and liquid bonds. The objective is to help the fixed income ETF be more liquid, active, and transparent. In addition to these advantages, they provide both sophisticated and retail investors a quick and easy way to enter markets that they may not have had access to ordinarily. Table 9.5 provides a list of fixed income ETFs that are commonly used and represent a broad range of products.

Bloomberg Shortcuts

Fixed Income and Government Agency Current Markets

WB <GO>	Display/Analyze/Compare Bond Data
WBF <GO>	Monitor World Bond Futures
WS <GO>	Monitor World Interest Rate Swap Matrices
FIT <GO>	Navigate the Fixed Income Markets
USSW <GO>	Monitor Various Economic Data

AUCR <GO>	Find Global Government Auction results
PXAM <GO>	Monitor Bloomberg Generic Agency Pricing
NIM2 <GO>	Access U.S. Agencies New Issue Monitor
MSM <GO>	Matrix of Spreads to U.S. Treasuries
TACT <GO>	TRACE Reported Volume
BTMM <GO>	Treasuries and Money Markets
CMW <GO>	Credit Market Watch Charts
CSDR <GO>	Access Sovereign Debt Ratings

Finding Securities

SRCH <GO>	Search Bloomberg's Fixed Income Database
AXES <GO>	Search Dealers' AXES Pages
RMGR <GO>	Monitor Incoming RUNS Lists

Multi-Security Analysis/List Management

BLRV <GO>	Bond Relative Value Monitor
HS <GO>	Graph Historical Price Spreads
SS <GO>	Compare Spread/Risk/Proceeds Differentials
RUNS <GO>	Create and Send Custom Run Sheets
WANT <GO>	Access a Menu of Bids Wanted Functions
SW <GO>	Calculate the Swap for Two Bonds
BFLY <GO>	Calculate Butterfly/Barbell Analysis

Security and Issuer Analysis

BQ <GO>	Bloomberg Quote
DES <GO>	Company's Fundamentals/Financials
YA <GO>	Calculate Yield Analysis
YAS <GO>	Yield and Spread Analysis
YTC <GO>	Calculate Yields to Call
ASW <GO>	Calculate Relative Value of Asset Swaps
OAS1 <GO>	Option-Adjusted Spread Analysis
AOAS <GO>	OAS for Callable Benchmark Agencies
HZ1 <GO>	Gauge Total Return Horizon
RV <GO>	Run Custom Peer Group Analyses
CN <GO>	Display Company News and Research
COC <GO>	Analyze Cost of Carry
COV <GO>	Covenant/Default Information
CRPR <GO>	Analyze an Issuer's Credit Profile
AGGD <GO>	Search for Institutional Exposure

| CBS <GO> | Display a List of Comparable Bonds |
| CRVD <GO> | Assess Relative Value of an Issuer's Bonds |

Hedge Analysis

TED <GO>	Calculate Euro-Future Strip Hedge Scenarios
FYH <GO>	Futures Hedging
PDH1 <GO>	Position Duration Hedging
HGBD <GO>	Hedge a Bullet Bond in the CDS Market
HGCS <GO>	Analyze Single Name CDS or Index CDS Curve Trades

Money Markets and Repo Money Market Overview

MMR <GO>	Money Market Rate Monitor
BTMM <GO>	Euro Treasury and Money Market
ER EMU <GO>	Euro Composite Rates
EBF <GO>	Euribor, EONIA Fixings
BBAM <GO>	Official BBA Libor Fixings
GGR1 <GO>	T-Bills Rates for Various Countries
BBC <GO>	Currency Markets Monitor Screens
WIR <GO>	Interest Rate Futures

Money Market Rates Forecast

BYFC <GO>	Money Markets Analysts Forecast
WIRP <GO>	Interest Rate Implied Probability
FFIP <GO>	Federal Funds Implied Probability

Money Market News

| NI MMK <GO> | Money Markets News |
| NI FX <GO> | Interest Rate/Money Market/FX news |

Pricing/Analysis

GA1 <GO>	Forward Rate from Two Deposit Rates
FXFA <GO>	Arbitrage Opportunities for Deposit Rates
FRD <GO>	FX Forward Calculator
EUSF <GO>	Euro Synthetic FRAs
SA <GO>	Global Synthetic FRAs
BC3 <GO>	CP/CD Calculator
FXCT <GO>	Carry Trade History

Repo

RRRA <GO>	Repo/Reverse Repo Analysis
BSR <GO>	Buy/Sell Back Repo Analysis
FPA <GO>	Bond Forward Price Analysis
COC <GO>	Cost of Carry for a Bond
FE5 <GO>	Cross-Currency Repo Calculator

Interest Rate Swaps, Swaptions and Structured Notes Rates, Forecasts, Inflation

BYFC <GO>	Interest Rates Yield Forecasts
ILBE <GO>	Display Fastest and Slowest Rates of Inflation
ILBI <GO>	Find and Analyze Inflation Indices
SLIQ <GO>	Display Short-Term Borrowing Rates
TLIQ <GO>	Display Graph of Debt Securities

Broad Markets

USSW <GO>	Monitor Various Economic Data
BBTI <GO>	Electronic Trading for IRS
SSRC <GO>	Monitor Swap Rates, FRAs, Swaptions and Cap/Floor Volatilities, and More
IRSB <GO>	Monitor Global Interest Rate Swap Rates
ILBM <GO>	Monitor Inflation Swaps Prices
ISDA <GO>	Display ISDA Fixes for Interest Rate Swaps Worldwide
WB <GO>	Display/Analyze/Compare Bond Data
WS <GO>	Monitor World Interest Rate Swap Matrices

Calculators

SWPM <GO>	Create/Manage and Store, Mark-to-Market Options on Interest Rate Swaps
SWPM_ASW <GO>	Perform Asset-Swap Valuation on Corporate Bonds
HG IRS <GO>	Hedge Your Bond with an Interest Rate Swap
HG FYH <GO>	Hedge Your Bond/Swap with Weighted Bond Futures
VOLM <GO>	Calculate Interest Rate Volatility
XFWC <GO>	Multiple Forward Rates Calculator

Other Tools

YCRV <GO>	Perform Yield Curve Analysis
FWCM <GO>	Matrix of Forward Swap Rates and Spreads

FWCV <GO>   Analyze Historical and Custom Forward Rates
HSA <GO>   Display Historical Spread Analysis
SA <GO>   Access a Euro Strip Analysis Menu
FRD <GO>   Calculate Spot/Forward Exchange Rates
XIRS <GO>   Portfolio Interest Rate Swap Monitor
IRDL <GO>   Display Interest Rate Swaps
NSV <GO>   ATM Normal Swaption Volatility Data

Structured Notes

STNT <GO>   Structured Products Main Menu
SND <GO>   Structured Products Definitions
SWPM_YAF <GO> Price and Analyze Floating Range Accrual Notes
SWPM <GO>   Create/Manage   and   Store,   Mark-to-Market
                   Options on Interest Rate Swaps
YASN <GO>   Price a Selected Structured Note
SRCH <GO>   Search Tool for Structured Notes

Menus and Defaults

IRSM <GO>   Access the Fixed Income Derivatives Menu
WWCC <GO>   View the Worldwide Credit Crunch Menu
SWDF <GO>   Set Interest Rate Swap Curve Contributor Defaults
IRDD <GO>   Displays Interest Rate Swap Descriptions
SWIL <GO>   Display/Update Inflation Swap Curves/CPI Values
ET <GO>   Electronic Trading Main Menu

Credit Default Swaps Single Name

CDSW <GO>   Credit Default Swap Valuation
CRDV <GO>   Credit Derivatives Menu
CDS <GO>   Single Name Lookup
CDTK <GO>   CDS Ticker Lookup
QCDS <GO>   Quick CDS Valuation and Horizon
CDSV <GO>   CDS Curve Lookup
FWCS <GO>   Forward Curve Analysis
HGCS <GO>   CDS Curve Trade Valuation

Index

CDSW <GO>   Credit Default Swap Valuation
CRDV <GO>   Credit Derivatives Menu

CDSI \<GO>	Credit Index Lookup
CDX \<GO>	Credit Index Monitors
CDIA \<GO>	Credit Index Analysis
MEMC \<GO>	Credit Index Members
CINS \<GO>	Credit Index Constituent Search

Structured Credit

CDST \<GO>	Synthetic CDO tranche valuation
CDOT \<GO>	Credit Index Tranche Data
CDSO \<GO>	Credit Default Swaption valuation
CIX \<GO>	Customized Index Construction
CORR \<GO>	Customized Correlation Matrix
XCOR \<GO>	Correlation Spreadsheet

Market Overview

GCDS \<GO>	Historical CDS Comparison
CMOV \<GO>	CDS Biggest Movers
CDEQ \<GO>	Credit versus Equity Monitor
CEHA \<GO>	CDS Scenario and Horizon Analysis
WCDS \<GO>	World CDS Pricing

Capital Structure/Ratings

CAST \<GO>	Capital Structure
ECCG \<GO>	Credit versus Equity Analysis
GV \<GO>	Credit versus Equity Volume Analysis
ISSD \<GO>	Issuer's Financial Operations
DDIS \<GO>	Issuer's Debt Maturity Profile
CRPR \<GO>	Current/Historical Credit Ratings
RATC \<GO>	Issuer Credit Ratings Revisions

Bond Relative Value

CRVD \<GO>	CDS versus Cash Basis
VCDS \<GO>	Bond Valuation from CDS
HGBD \<GO>	Bond Hedge Analysis
HS \<GO>	Two-Security Historical Spread and Correlation Analysis

Pricing and Defaults

| IMGR \<GO> | Fixed Income RUNS Manager |

QMGR \<GO\>	Fixed Income Quote Detail
CDSL \<GO\>	Saved CDS Securities
CDSD \<GO\>	CDS Pricing Defaults

Education/Reference

SNAC \<GO\>	ISDA Standardization Portal

Summary

The goal of this chapter is to provide a reference guide for the fixed income market. Understanding global macro requires knowledge of the fundamentals of fixed income, such as money markets, LIBOR, Eurodollar futures, Fed funds, OIS, U.S. fixed income futures, trading strategies, and TIPS. Again, fixed income is a term that encompasses a vast number of topics, so this chapter does not intend to act as an extensive source of information regarding fixed income, but rather to provide as an introduction for global macro traders.

CHAPTER 10

Commodities

In the context of global macro trading, the term commodity refers to goods that have little to no product differentiation and are fungible, or easy to replace. For example, it makes little difference whether the copper pipes in one's house come from Chile or Peru, since basic elements are the same no matter where they originated. The definition of economics is rooted in the allocation of scarce resources, and commodities are the most basic form of economics in global macro trading.

Having an understanding of supply and demand forces is a core component of macro trading. These forces are affected by factors like global growth and weather droughts, which can cause a dearth of a particular agricultural end product (like corn or wheat). Additionally, the composition of players in commodities is different from the other three product groups, and it has its own market conventions. For example, producers and companies like Glencore Xstrata and Vitol own physical assets in many commodities, so they have a big advantage against a talented macro trader, since they often see supply and demand dynamics unfold before traditional speculators. Additionally, in some markets like natural gas, producers like Chesapeake do not want to take price risk and, as a result, hedge a lot of their exposure in the back end of the futures curve.

Commodities are the most volatile of the four product groups, so while it's possible to make money in a short period of time without understanding the basic drivers, this can be detrimental over the long term. Knowing that a particular country is a top producer in a commodity is valuable when issues of political risk arise in unstable areas. Commodity prices, in their most basic form, are a function of supply and demand, so any change in either side of the equation can cause a change in price.

The goal of this chapter is to provide the reader with an overview of energy, precious metals, industrial metals and agricultural commodities. Understanding the supply and demand drivers, as well as the producers and consumers, is of the utmost importance in trading any commodity. Otherwise, one is trading blindly without any compass. This chapter will provide beginners with an expansive overview of commodities, and for the experts, it will serve as a great resource and refresher.

Supply Drivers

Each individual commodity has its own supply drivers. Understanding the basic concepts of the supply drivers is critical for trading and understanding how commodity prices are driven. Listed below are big-picture factors that affect supply.

- **Reserves:** Saudi Arabia has the largest oil reserves in the world (excluding the Venezuelan Orinoco belt). If one of the fields in Ghawar (the biggest oil field in the world) suddenly discovered additional reserves, that would mean that their supply of oil would hold steady and potentially increase. However, if their oil fields become less attainable for some reason, the supply of crude oil would be squeezed. The same relationship applies to gold. For decades, South Africa was the largest producer of gold, but over time their reserves were depleted. Had other countries not discovered enough gold to offset that depletion, the price of gold would likely be higher than it is today.
- **Production:** Not only are commodity reserves critical, but the ability to produce, or mine, is just as important, especially in the short run. In early 2011, when Libya was attempting to overthrow its dictator Mu'ammar Gadhafi, its production was disturbed. This disruption caused the price of crude oil to move higher. Ironically enough, since the fall of Gadhafi, Libya has not been able to restore old production levels. In another example, the Ivory Coast exports roughly 30 percent of the world's cocoa. After an election in the last decade, there was a battle between opposition parties over who should become the new ruler. This caused a military offensive on both sides where cocoa exports were banned in a ploy to reallocate funding in the election. This ban caused cocoa prices to soar.
- **Acreage:** In agriculture, the profitability of a crop tends to push acreage production to the most profitable crop. This can mean that the less profitable crop has less supply and the more profitable crop has more supply,

which can actually have an opposite effect on price if there is a supply shortage. Government programs also affect the supply production of crops. For instance, in ethanol, there are particular subsidies provided to corn growers that affect what they plant on their acres.

- **Yield:** Yield is determined by type of soil, weather conditions, and fertilizer costs. For instance, more than 90 percent of soybeans are genetically modified and do not require pesticides, which can increase yield. This subtle change does have an impact over time, and soybean crops have taken the place of many wheat crops in past years.

- **Weather:** Agriculture is also sensitive to unexpected weather changes and virtually no crop is immune. Understanding the timelines of seasonal weather to the extent that they can be predicted is of the utmost importance in dealing with agriculture. For instance, in Brazil in 1997, there were severe droughts and frost that drastically hampered coffee bean output, causing the price of coffee to more than double.

Demand Drivers

Demand drivers are the end users of commodities. Their role in commodity trading is just as crucial as supply drivers. Listed below are the big picture demand drivers that affect commodities over time. Keep in mind that each individual commodity has its own demand drivers.

- **Population Growth:** The biggest long-term factor in commodities is population growth. The United Nations estimates that the current world population stands at 7 billion and will grow to over 9 billion by 2050. That means that the global population will increase by 25 percent over the next 30 years, which will continue to increase the demand for food and commodities as well. Long-term players in the commodities market are awaiting the inevitable population increase, which will translate into more demand for all commodities.

- **Standard of Living:** As emerging markets like China, India, and others get richer and command a bigger piece of the global GDP pie, they will demand more and more commodities. For example, as China develops its infrastructure, it continues to need more copper and energy to grow. As its citizens get richer, they will eat more crops and livestock, which, in turn, means that their livestock will need more agricultural commodities, and so on. Likewise, watches and jewelry account for more than 10 percent of Swiss exports, and they continue to see double-digit growth due in large part to demand from China. As the Chinese get richer they're also demanding more precious metals in addition to these other commodities.

- **Alternative Energy:** Since 1996, use of corn as an input into ethanol in the United States has risen by more than 10 times. As the world becomes larger and its need for energy grows, there will constantly be new innovations to use alternative energy. While the demand for crude oil or coal may decrease, other commodities quickly fill the demand void, such as the use of more natural gas as a cleaner, cheaper option.

Ending Stock

Ending stock is the concept of building inventory, and is just as integral a part of commodities as supply and demand. Ending stocks can also adversely affect the price of the underlying commodity. Many agricultural commodities have only one or two planting cycles per year. However, demand for commodities is continuous 365 days a year. Even though corn may be harvested in the United States in late fall and early winter, people still demand corn for all its various uses throughout the year. Ending stock effectively measures the inventory of a particular commodity. Ending stock that is stored becomes a part of the supply as it is drawn. This can be referred to as beginning balance, which is similar across many accounting concepts (Figure 10.1).

Contango and Backwardation

Contango refers to near-term futures contracts that are traded cheaper than further-futures contracts. Contango exists due to factors like storage and transportation costs. For instance, when gold is held in a vault, the owner loses opportunity cost of capital and also incurs the storage costs. This in turn gets passed on to the futures price.

FIGURE 10.1 Supply and Demand with Ending Stock

Backwardation occurs when the near-term futures trade at a premium to further-dated futures contracts. Backwardation can occur when there is a supply shortage. When the Ivory Coast, the largest exporter of cocoa, experienced political distress and the resulting stoppage of cocoa exports, the near-term supply was extremely constrained. If anyone wanted cocoa during the export ban, they would have had to pay a hefty premium. However, in time, when the Ivory Coast settled down and began to export cocoa again, one would expect the price to be much lower. This is one example of backwardation and how it can cause the front-end contract to trade at a premium. In agriculture, right before the harvest comes, and the ending stock is depleted, meaning that in the short run supply will likely be tight, the front-end contract will likely trade at a premium just before the next harvest. Thus, if someone wants the corn immediately, they would need to pay a premium, as opposed to paying a lower price at the new harvest.

The shape of the futures curve can be simple or complex. Figure 10.2 is more complex, in that it exhibits both the properties of contango and backwardation. When corn is first harvested and supply is at its zenith, the price of that month in futures would be expected to be low relative to later in the crop cycle year. Cost of carry and storage costs are incurred, which creates contango. As the year progresses and the stock is depleted, the supply begins to run thinner, and more front-dated contracts trade at premium just prior to harvest since supply is tighter, causing backwardation. These complex patterns are what cause the shape of many commodity curves to have both contango and backwardation.

FIGURE 10.2 Corn Futures Strip

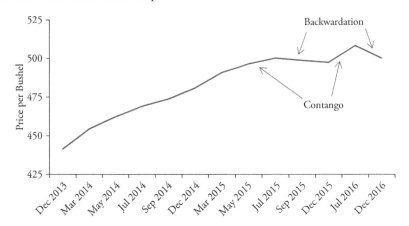

Source: Bloomberg. As of September 30, 2013.

FIGURE 10.3 CRB Index Historical Price Chart

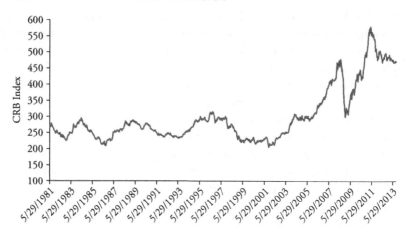

Source: Bloomberg.

CRB Index

The Commodity Research Bureau (CRB) Index is intended to represent the price of a broad range of commodities. The index is composed of 22 commodities and dates back to the 1950s[1] (see Figure 10.3). It provides investors a relative way to see the price changes of commodities over time.

Investors looking for a basket of commodities to trade in an easier fashion can trade the Deutsche Bank Agriculture ETF, DBA <Equity>, which is composed of corn, soybeans, sugar, cattle, coffee, cocoa, and more agricultural commodities. Additionally, Deutsche Bank has a commodities fund, DBC<Equity>, which includes energy, precious metals, agriculture, and industrial metals. The only caution with DBC is that more than 50 percent of the index is energy weighted.[2]

Return and Volatility

Commodities have a higher volatility than foreign exchange, equities, and fixed income. Additionally, returns for commodities have been higher. While the

---

[1] Jefferies CRB Index.
[2] Deutsche Bank Funds.

TABLE 10.1   Commodity Risks and Returns, 1970–2006
Annualized Monthly Returns (Continuously Compounded)

	Average Return	Volatility	Equity	Bonds	Cash	GSCI
Equity	10.39	15.20	1.00	0.24	–0.03	–0.04
Bonds	8.42	10.34		1.00	0.06	–0.04
Cash	5.82	0.82			1.00	–0.02
S&P GSCI™	10.89	18.50				1.00

Source: Goldman Sachs, Commodities as an Asset Class, July 28, 2007.

high volatility of commodities can turn some people off, it has an attractive Sharpe ratio as a relative comparison and, prior to the 2008 financial crisis, had a negative correlation. Table 10.1 compares returns for equities, bonds, cash, and the S&P GSCI (Goldman Sachs Commodity Index).

Energy

Global energy usage has increased by over 50 percent over the last 25 years and is likely to continue increasing at a similar rate as more emerging markets grow in population and wealth. The most used energy source is oil, accounting for 33 percent of total energy demand in 2012. Coal, which is not environmentally friendly, is the second most common energy source, globally accounting for 30 percent of demand. It is followed by natural gas, which used 24 percent of global energy demand.[3] Both oil and natural gas are liquid futures contracts that are critical pieces of the commodity pie, collectively accounting for more than 50 percent of global use of energy. In this section, we cover the oil and natural gas markets. Given the strong demand for energy, biofuels like ethanol have increased in demand and now affect agricultural markets like corn and sugar.

Oil

Crude oil, or petroleum, is a complex mixture of hydrocarbons that are found in the Earth's crust. The word "petroleum" originated from the Latin word

---

[3] "BP Statistical Review of World Energy June 2012." BP. June 2012. www.bp.com/assets/ bp_internet/globalbp/globalbp_uk_english/reports_and_publications/statistical_energy_ review_2011/STAGING/local_assets/pdf/statistical_review_of_world_energy_full_ report_2012.pdf.

petra (rock) and *oleum* (oil). The first commercial drilling of oil began with Edwin Drake in 1859 in Pennsylvania. Combustion, the process of breaking down the hydrocarbons, releases energy that is used for many purposes around the world. Crude oil is the raw material that is used to make gasoline, kerosene, and liquefied petroleum gases (LPGs). Gasoline is used in cars, trucks, and other types of transportation, while kerosene is used for diesel, and heating oil is used for heating buildings, airplanes, buses, and trains. See Figure 10.4 for a chart showing historical crude oil prices.

Types of Oil

The quality of oil varies from region to region and even from field to field. There are over a hundred different types of crude oil. The two measures used in determining the quality of crude oil are sulfur content and API gravity. The most valuable crudes are ones that have a high specific gravity with low sulfur. API gravity measures the weight of crude relative to water. The higher the API gravity (measured in degrees), the lighter the crude. An extreme example

FIGURE 10.4   Historical Chart of Crude Oil Prices

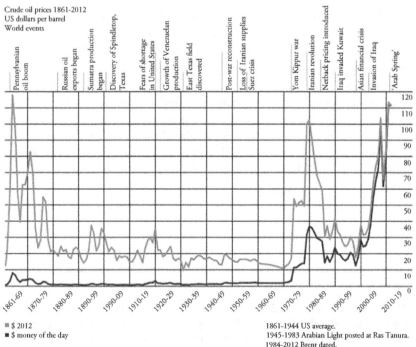

Source: BP Statistical Review of World Energy, June 2012.

would be oil sands from Canada, where one would expect the crude to have a low API gravity (making it heavier and less desirable). If the API gravity is less than 10, it sinks in water. When observing the API gravity of crude oil, the API gravity crudes of 25 or lower are called "heavy" (less desirable), and those of 35 or higher are called "light." Furthermore, oil having a low sulfur content is considered sweet while high sulfur content is sour. The most desired crude oil is light, sweet crude and the least desired is heavy sour crude.

Figure 10.5 illustrates some of the more important crude oils and their relative API gravity and sulfur content, graphically comparing global grades. West Texas Intermediate (WTI) and Brent Crude Oil are high quality since they are light, sweet. Crudes from Mexico and Venezuela, for instance, are not as high quality, so all else being equal, they trade at a lower price.

Producers

Saudi Arabia is the largest producer of oil and second largest exporter, while Russia is the second largest producer and world's largest exporter (see Table 10.2). The United States, on the other hand, is third by production, and the world's largest importer, representing 19 percent of oil imports (see Table 10.3). Of the top 10 producers, five are OPEC members, and all OPEC production constitutes over 35 percent of production.

FIGURE 10.5   Global Crude Grades

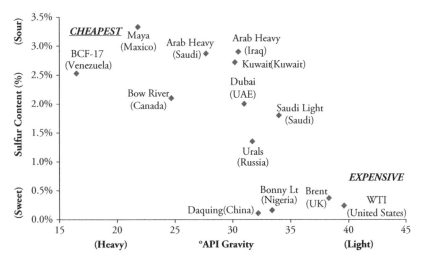

Source: EIA.

TABLE 10.2 Global Top 10 Oil Producers and Consumers

OIL (thousand barrels daily)	2008	2009	2010	2011	2012
Production					
1 Saudi Arabia	10,663	9,663	10,075	11,144	11,530
2 Russia	9,950	10,139	10,365	10,510	10,643
3 United States	6,783	7,263	7,552	7,868	8,905
4 China	3,814	3,805	4,077	4,074	4,155
5 Canada	3,207	3,202	3,332	3,526	3,741
6 Iran	4,396	4,249	4,356	4,358	3,680
7 UAE	3,026	2,723	2,895	3,319	3,380
8 Kuwait	2,786	2,511	2,536	2,880	3,127
9 Iraq	2,428	2,452	2,490	2,801	3,115
10 Mexico	3,165	2,978	2,959	2,940	2,911
Other	32,714	32,276	32,635	30,790	30,965
Total Supply	**82,932**	**81,261**	**83,272**	**84,210**	**86,152**
Consumption					
1 United States	19,490	18,769	19,134	18,949	18,555
2 China	7,947	8,229	9,272	9,750	10,221
3 Japan	4,882	4,429	4,473	4,465	4,714
4 India	3,077	3,237	3,319	3,488	3,652
5 Russia	2,862	2,772	2,892	3,089	3,174
6 Saudi Arabia	2,378	2,592	2,790	2,835	2,935
7 Brazil	2,439	2,467	2,676	2,740	2,805
8 Korea	2,308	2,339	2,370	2,394	2,458
9 Germany	2,502	2,409	2,445	2,369	2,358
10 Canada	2,315	2,195	2,316	2,404	2,412
Other	35,852	35,626	36,146	36,396	36,490
Total Demand	**86,052**	**85,064**	**87,833**	**88,879**	**89,774**
Imbalance (Supply – Demand)	–3,120	–3,803	–4,561	–4,669	–3,622

Sources: EIA and BP Statistical Review.

TABLE 10.3 Global Top 10 Oil Exporters and Importers

OIL (thousand barrels daily)

	Exports	2012		Imports	2012	
1	Middle East	19,699	35.6%	Europe	12,488	22.6%
2	FSU*	8,597	15.5%	United States	10,587	19.1%
3	Asia Pacific	6,109	11.0%	Japan	4,743	8.6%
4	West Africa	4,564	8.3%	Rest of World	27,496	49.7%
5	South and Central America	3,834	6.9%			
6	Canada	3,056	5.5%			
7	United States	2,680	4.8%			
8	North Africa	2,604	4.7%			
9	Europe	2,174	3.9%			
10	Mexico	1,366	2.5%			
	Rest of World	631	1.1%			
		55,314			55,314	

*FSU = former Soviet Union

Consumers

The United States is the largest consumer of oil in the world, consuming almost 19 million barrels of oil a day. That number almost doubles China, which is the second largest consumer of oil. China became the second largest consumer in 2005, more than doubling its demand since 2001 and averaging 7 percent annual demand growth over that period. The United States, by comparison, has declined slightly. All BRIC countries have shown growth in consumption and all four are in the top 10 for oil consumption.

National Oil Companies

A national oil company (NOC) is a majority state-owned oil company. Sadly, the biggest oil companies in the world are NOCs and members of OPEC, which helps them maintain collusion on oil prices. An international oil company (IOC) is typically a publicly listed, Western integrated oil company like ExxonMobil, British Petroleum (BP), or Royal Dutch Shell. The biggest

IOCs are Saudi Aramco, the National Iranian Oil Company (NIOC), Iraq National Oil Company (INOC), Kuwait Oil Company (KOC), and Petróleos de Venezuela SA (PDVSA). They are very important to understand because they are members of OPEC and also have political risk.

Saudi Aramco

Saudi Aramco is considered the largest company in the entire world, but since they are private they do not often get the media attention the size would normally garner. Not only does it have the largest value of any company in the world, but it also has the largest reserve of oil in the world, equating to roughly one-sixth of global reserves. Founded in 1933, Saudi Aramco started with concessions and joint ventures with U.S. oil companies, Chevron and Standard Oil (which is now ExxonMobil). Saudi Aramco has a production capacity of 12.5 million bbl/d and reserves of 266 billion barrels.[4]

NIOC

The National Iranian Oil Company (NIOC) was established in 1948, and was nationalized from the Anglo-Iranian Oil Company (which is now British Petroleum). There has been flip-flopping between the IOCs and NOCs for years. During a coup d'état in 1953, most of the oil in Iran was once again in control of the IOC's, which was then reversed in 1979 by a revolution, sending it back into the hands of the NIOC. Today, NIOC is the second largest NOC (excluding PDVSA Orinoco Belt). Clearly, with the political risk and current Khamenei/Rouhani regime, there are many risks to production. NIOC has a capacity of 3.5 million bbl/d and reserves of 157 billion barrels.[5]

PDVSA

Petróleos de Venezuela SA (PDVSA) was founded in 1975 by the Organic Law that Reserves the Industry and Commerce in Hydrocarbons to the State (LOREICH), which instantly nationalized the local oil industry. The Orinoco Belt find in Venezuela could contain a couple hundred billion barrels of oil, though it is mostly tar sands, which are less desirable. In the 1990s, PDVSA opened its oil industry to IOCs since it lacked the expertise to get this type

---

[4] Saudi Aramco, EIA, BP Statistical Review, and Bloomberg. As of September 2013 and December 2012, respectively.

[5] The Foreign Trade Regime of the Islamic Republic of Iran. Ministry of Commerce 2009, EIA, NIOC, BP Statistical Review, and Bloomberg. As of September 2013 and December 2012, respectively.

of oil, though the PDVSA still owns the majority investment. PDVSA has the world's largest reserves when the Orinoco Belt is included. PDVSA has capacity of 2.9 million bbl/d and reserves of 298 billion barrels.[6]

INOC

The Iraq National Oil Company (INOC) started in 1966, though the Iraq Petroleum Company was created beforehand. Over time, the INOC nationalized oil assets during the rule of Saddam Hussein. The 2003 Iraq War brought down Saddam Hussein and to this day it is still not fully clear which IOCs will dominate oil production and what the country's political stability will be. INOC has capacity of 3.3 million bbl/d and reserves of 150 billion barrels.[7]

KOC

The Kuwait Oil Company (KOC) was founded in 1934 with a 50%/50% venture between Anglo-Persian Oil Company (British Petroleum) and Gulf Oil Corporation (which is now Chevron). In 1938, oil was found in commercial quantities in the Burgan Field, and in 1975 the Kuwait government took 100 percent ownership and nationalized the venture. In 1991, Saddam Hussein invaded Kuwait in an attempt to take KOC's oil fields in the Gulf War. KOC has capacity of 3.3 million bbl/d and reserves of 102 billion barrels.[8]

OPEC[9]

The Organization of the Petroleum Exporting Countries (OPEC) is a permanent, intergovernmental organization, created at the Baghdad Conference on September 10–14, 1960, by Iran, Iraq, Kuwait, Saudi Arabia, and Venezuela. OPEC is the single most important influence on the supply of global oil, accounting for more than 35 percent of global production and more than 70 percent of global reserves. OPEC is headquartered in Vienna, Austria.

OPEC works as a collusive organization where the member states agree on production allocations, thereby controlling the world price of oil and supply. Table 10.4 highlights the quotas for each country, how much they

---

[6] PDVSA, EIA, BP Statistical Review, and Bloomberg. As of September 2013 and December 2012, respectively.
[7] INOC, EIA, BP Statistical Review, and Bloomberg. As of September 2013 and December 2012, respectively.
[8] PDVSA, EIA, BP Statistical Review, and Bloomberg. As of September 2013 and December 2012, respectively.
[9] OPEC. As of September 2013 and December 2012, respectively.

TABLE 10.4 OPEC Production and Quota Table

OPEC Countries (million barrels daily)	Dec-11 Quota*	Production Sep-13	Production Capacity Sep-13	% of OPEC Production Capacity	Spare Capacity	Spare Capacity (% of OPEC)	Reserves Dec-12	Total Global Oil Reserves	Reserves as % of OPEC
Saudi Arabia	8.05	10.00	12.50	34%	2.50	45%	265.9		16%
Iran	3.34	2.60	3.50	10%	0.90	16%	157.0		9%
Iraq	N/A	3.30	3.30	9%	0.00	0%	150.0		9%
UAE	2.22	2.90	2.80	8%	−0.10	−2%	97.8		6%
Kuwait	2.22	3.00	3.30	9%	0.30	5%	101.5		6%
Qatar	0.73	0.72	0.78	2%	0.06	1%	23.9		1%
Nigeria	1.67	2.15	2.40	7%	0.25	5%	37.2		2%
Libya	1.47	0.30	1.55	4%	1.25	23%	48.0		3%
Algeria	1.20	1.15	1.20	3%	0.05	1%	12.2		1%
Venezuela	1.99	2.69	2.90	8%	0.21	4%	297.6		18%
Angola	1.52	1.74	1.87	5%	0.13	2%	12.7		1%
Ecuador	0.43	0.53	0.53	1%	0.00	0%	8.2		0%
Total	24.85	31.08	36.63	100%	5.55	100%	1,211.9	1,668.9	73%

*As of September 2013 the OPEC-12 Quota is 30 million barrels daily.
Sources: IEA, EIA, LMIU, GTIS, BP Statistical Review, Wood Mackenzie Platt's Oilgram, *Petroleum Intelligence Weekly, Petroleum Economist Africa Oil and Gas Monitor, Energy Day,* and *Oil and Gas Journal.*

produce, and other critical figures that help traders determine the tightness in oil supply. OPEC is the marginal supplier of crude oil, and Saudi Arabia has the largest spare capacity of any country in the world. In the event that there is a global shortage or supply shock, OPEC is the marginal supplier since they hold most of the reserves. This is called "The Call on OPEC," which usually means that Saudi Arabia increases its production since they have the largest spare capacity.

OPEC has 12 member countries. The five founding members, Iran, Iraq, Kuwait, Saudi Arabia, and Venezuela, formed the organization in 1960. Qatar joined in 1961, Libya joined in 1962, the UAE joined in 1967, Algeria joined in 1969, Nigeria joined in 1971, and Angola and Ecuador joined in 2007 (Ecuador had originally joined OPEC in 1973 but left in 1992). The nations of Indonesia and Gabon were once OPEC members, but withdrew in 1994 and 2009, respectively.

OPEC's objective is to "coordinate and unify petroleum policies among Member Countries, in order to secure fair and stable prices for petroleum producers; an efficient, economic, and regular supply of petroleum to consuming nations; and a fair return on capital to those investing in the industry." The Oil and Energy Ministers of the OPEC member countries meet at least twice a year and regulate the production quotas of each country to control the supply of oil. Since OPEC countries control the lion's share of global oil, they can control supply by colluding, which in turn keeps prices higher than they would be under a noncolluding environment.

Benchmark Crude Oil Prices and Trading

Figure 10.5 highlights the different grades and types of crude oil, but a macro trader can't easily trade all of them individually. Benchmark crudes are the types of crude oil that are the most liquid and are exchange traded. They are West Texas Intermediate and Brent Crude.

WTI Crude Oil (WTI)

West Texas Intermediate, known as WTI, is the benchmark for U.S. crude oil. It is a light, sweet oil and a higher-grade crude oil than Brent Crude (see Figure 10.5). Since WTI is very high quality, it is most often refined into gasoline. Further, WTI crude is delivered to Cushing, Oklahoma, which is the hub for U.S. crude oil. Because the United States demands so much oil, WTI is used primarily to feed U.S. demand rather than for exports. Figure 10.6 shows the historical price chart of WTI crude.

FIGURE 10.6   Historical Price Chart of WTI Crude Front Contract

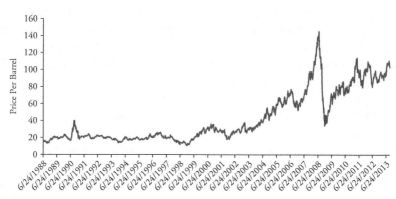

Source: Bloomberg.

WTI Crude Oil trades on the CME (via the NYMEX) under the futures symbol CL1 <Comdty> for the front contract. One contract is equal to 1,000 barrels of oil, so if the price of WTI is $100 per barrel, then the notional is $100,000. Options are very liquid on these markets. There is an ETF under the symbol USO <Equity>, which tracks the price of the WTI contract. Caution should be taken with this ETF because it is subject to contango and futures rolls, so investors may not get the same return they would see in the futures market depending on the duration of the trade and fees paid.

Brent Crude Oil

Brent Crude was originally sourced from multiple oil fields in the North Sea, and is used to price more than half of the world's internationally traded crude oil. Brent is a light, sweet crude, though it is not as high a grade as WTI. Brent can be refined into products like heating oil and gasoline. It is currently experiencing depletion issues that will not likely be resolved since little new reserves have been found. The critical factor to keep in mind with Brent Crude is that it is most averse to supply shocks as a result of seaborne supply disruptions (pirates, tensions in the Middle East, etc.). Figure 10.7 shows the historical price chart of Brent Crude.

Brent Crude trades on the ICE under the futures symbol CO1 <Comdty> for the front contract. One contract is equal to 1,000 barrels of oil, so if the price of Brent is $100 per barrel, then the notional is $100,000. Options are very liquid on these markets. The Brent Crude futures contract is deliverable to Sullom Voe, an island north of Scotland.

FIGURE 10.7 Historical Price Chart of Brent Crude Front Contract

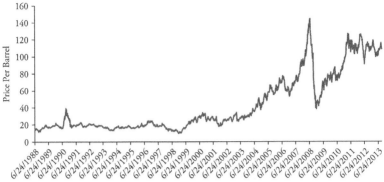

Source: Bloomberg.

WTI–Brent Spread

Even though Brent Crude is a slightly lower grade crude oil than WTI, in recent years it has traded at a premium to WTI. Part of the reason is that the North Sea has experienced depletion, and Brent Crude is the marginal barrel of oil that gets shipped to emerging markets like China and India from the Middle East. This causes demand for Brent to be more aggressive than for WTI. Additionally, on the supply side, pipelines in Cushing, Oklahoma, are not as efficient and cause a supply buildup, which drives prices lower. Brent Crude is also more sustainable to supply shocks on the front end as a result of Middle East tensions, such as in Iran, Libya, or other countries in the region. All these factors have given Brent Crude a premium over WTI even though it is slightly a lower grade. Figure 10.8 shows a historical price chart of the WTI–Brent spread.

PADDs

The United States is divided into five PADDs, which stands for Petroleum Administration for Defense Districts. Originally, this was created on December 2, 1942, during World War II and called the Petroleum Administration for War (PAW). It was intended to organize the distribution of petroleum products. While the PAW was abolished on May 3, 1946, the same districts were later reinstated on October 3, 1950, under the name Petroleum Administration for Defense and again abolished April 23, 1954, concluding the end of the Korean War. It was later taken over by the

FIGURE 10.8   Historical Price Chart of WTI–Brent Spread Front Contract

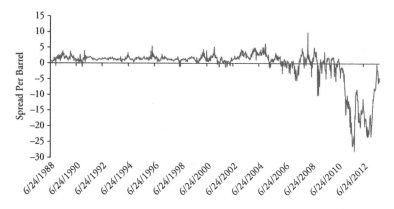

FIGURE 10.9   PADD Map

Source: U.S. Energy Information Administration.

U.S. Department of the Interior's Oil and Gas Division and the same five districts stand today (see Figure 10.9).[10]

Understanding supply for crude in PADD II and III is most important for crude prices and the crack spread, since that is where most refiners in the United States are located. Heating oil demand mostly arises from PADD I, so monitoring demand in that region is critical to heating oil prices.

---

[10]EIA, U.S. National Archives, and Bloomberg.

Chokepoints

Total world crude oil consumption as of 2012 is 90 million barrels per day (bbl/d), with more than half of that being moved by tankers on water. By volume of oil shipped, the Strait of Hormuz and the Strait of Malacca are the two of the world's most strategic chokepoints. Chokepoints are critical, because these are areas that can affect the supply, which in turn affects the price of crude oil. Recently, in a political maneuever, Iran has threatened to interfere with the Strait of Hormuz, so one can see how having an understanding of chokepoints is critical in crude oil trading.[11]

Strait of Hormuz

The Strait of Hormuz is the most important chokepoint since it is the largest by flow (17 million bbl/d in 2011, which is about 20 percent of global traded oil and 35 percent of seaborne oil). It is located between Iran and Oman in the Persian Gulf and interference has escalated recently due to the political tension in that area. There has been question as to whether Iran is enriching uranium for weapons and, in order to combat military threats, Iran has threatened to close off the Strait of Hormuz if Israel or another country attacks it. More than 85 percent of the oil that leaves heads to Asian countries like Indonesia, China, and Japan, where China represents a bulk of the demand. Figure 10.10 shows the chokepoint at the Strait of Hormuz.

The Strait of Malacca

The Strait of Malacca is the second largest chokepoint, connecting the Indian and Pacific Ocean. It is important because it is the shortest route from the Middle East to Asia, and is specifically important to growing Asian economies, such as China. It is located between Singapore, Malaysia, and Indonesia and supplies 14 million bbl/d. The Strait of Malacca has been subject to piracy attacks. However, the U.S. Navy and others have been policing the area more in order to decrease these incidences. Figure 10.11 shows the map of the Strait of Malacca.

Mandab Strait and Suez Canal

Mandab Strait has 3 million bbl/d pass through it, and is situated near Djibouti, Eritrea, and Yemen. Recently, extremist Somali pirates have been attacking tankers in many violent raids. The Suez Canal is situated in Egypt and has traffic of 2 million bbl/d. The pirating has been a recurring problem in this area. Figure 10.12 shows where the Mandab Strait is geographically.

---

[11] EIA.

FIGURE 10.10   Map of Strait of Hormuz

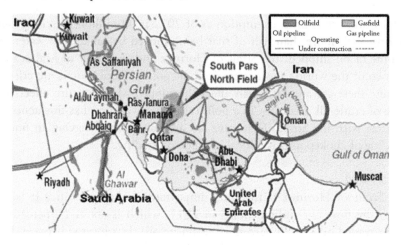

Source: U.S. Energy Information Administration.

FIGURE 10.11   Map of Strait of Malacca

Source: U.S. Energy Information Administration.

Pipelines

Pipelines are the only practical way to transport large volumes of oil. The costs of transporting oil over long distances would be too expensive without pipelines. The world's longest pipeline is the Druzhba pipeline (or the "Friendship Pipeline"), which is over 2,300 miles long and carries up to 1.4 million bbl/d

FIGURE 10.12 Map of Mandab Strait

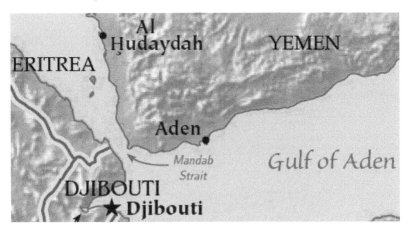

Source: U.S. Energy Information Administration.

(Figure 10.13). It runs from eastern Russia to Germany, Poland, Hungary, and Croatia. Russia uses this pipeline strategically and has built alliances with neighboring countries, like Ukraine, in order to get discounts on their gas.

Keystone and Keystone XL Pipeline

The Keystone Pipeline is a pipeline that spans from Alberta, Canada, over the oil sands to Patoka, Illinois (refineries), and Cushing, Oklahoma. Cushing is the hub for WTI and crude in the United States. Cushing is problematic in that there is a huge supply buildup, which is a main driver behind why WTI has been trading at a discount to Brent even though it is a slightly higher grade. To combat this supply buildup, a very controversial project known as "Keystone XL" has been proposed (Figure 10.14) to build additional pipelines from Canada and from Cushing to Texas and Louisiana, which would stop the excessive supply buildup and also make seaborne trade easier for WTI.

The current capacity of Keystone is roughly 400,000 bbl/d, and with the addition of Keystone XL it would add another 600,000 bbl/d, helping to carry 1 million bbl/d and likely collapsing the WTI–Brent Spread.

Crack Spread

Refining is a process that converts crude oil into more usable products. Crude oil is a string of long and complex hydrocarbons, and the process of refining

FIGURE 10.13 Druzhba Pipeline

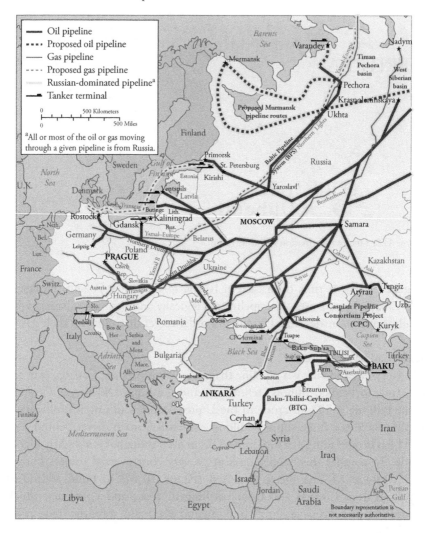

Source: U.S. Energy Information Administration.

breaks these hydrocarbons down into more homogeneous usable products. The gasoline (reformulated gasoline blendstock for oxygen blending, or "RBOB") you use in your car is a result of refining crude oil into RBOB. The refining margin is called the crack spread, which is the spread between the raw materials (crude oil) and the finished product (e.g., gasoline and heating oil) that can be sold by refiners. When the crack spread is high,

FIGURE 10.14 Keystone and Keystone XL Proposal

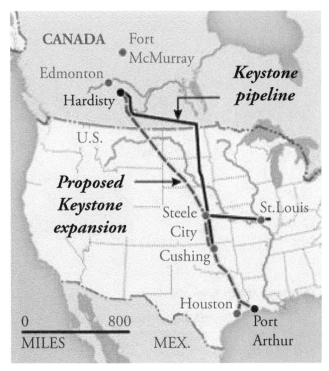

Source: Laris Karklis, "Keystone XL Pipeline Map," *Washington Post*, June 22, 2012; updated January 31, 2014.

refiners like Valero, Tesoro, and Sunoco do very well, and conversely when the crack spread narrows, or even becomes negative, margins get significantly squeezed, causing refiners to slow production. A very common crack spread to monitor is the WTI Cushing/New York Harbor RBOB and heating oil spread, shown in Figure 10.15.

Because gasoline production is almost double that of heating oil, the 3:2:1 crack spread is the most popular (see Figure 10.16); in other words, 3 crude oil futures versus 2 gasoline futures (RBOB) and 1 heating oil (HO) futures contract. The other common crack spreads are 2:1:1 and 5:3:2. CRKS <GO> is the screen that shows Bloomberg's main crack spreads. Factors that can affect the crack spread are supply buildups in Cushing (or other factors that affect the price of WTI), driving demand for gasoline, refinery shutdowns, and hurricanes, which can cause refinery and supply

FIGURE 10.15 WTI Cushing/New York Harbor RBOB and Heating Oil Crack Spread
Historical Price Chart

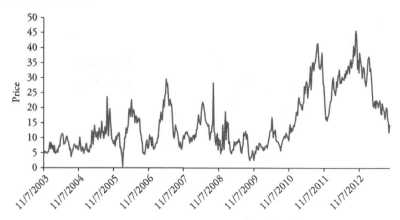

Source: Bloomberg.

FIGURE 10.16 Sample of 3:2:1 Crack Spread

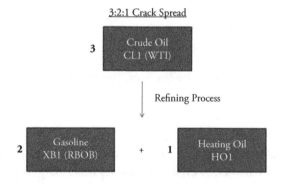

shutdowns. Something worth noting is that heating oil futures contracts
(HO) have changed contract specifications to a new grade and quality speci-
fication of the Colonial Pipeline's Fungible Grade 61 for ultra-low-sulfur
diesel (ULSD), beginning with the May 2013 HO delivery month (which is
a cleaner heating oil).

The calculation of the crack spread is pretty straightforward except for a
few small nuances. Gasoline and heating oil are pricing in cents per gallon,
while crude oil is priced in dollars per barrel. One barrel equals 42 gallons, so
it must be adjusted from cents to dollars and gallons to barrels.

Example: 3:2:1 Crack Spread[12]

WTI = $ 83.23

Gasoline = 265.68 ¢

Heating Oil = 262.79 ¢

265.68 × 2 × 0.42 + 262.79 × 1 × 0.42 =$333.54

$83.23 × 3 = $249.69

$333.54 − $249.69 = $83.85 (crack spread for 3 barrels of oil)

$83.85/3 = $27.95

$27.95 is the theoretical crack spread per barrel

Natural Gas

In its purest state, natural gas is primarily composed of methane and is color-less, odorless, and a highly flammable hydrocarbon, which gives off energy when burned. Natural gas is created from organic matter trapped in pockets of the Earth's crust. It it is the cleanest and safest fossil fuel.

Figure 10.17 shows where natural gas is typically found in the Earth's crust. It also shows what is commonly referred to as vertical drilling, which was the old way of extracting natural gas. Extraction needed to be precise and it became costly since new drills needed to be installed even in close proximi-ties. This resulted in the development of horizontal drilling, which allows the vertical drill, once underground, to have a connecting drill that can be angled at 90° to allow the whole surface area to be extracted in a more time-efficient and cost-effective way.[13]

Shale

Shale is a type of rock that is a recent big development in the U.S. natural gas market. Shale gas refers to natural gas reserves that are trapped inside shale and need special drilling and processing. Many estimates claim that by the year 2020, it will account for 50 percent of U.S. supply. It also has envi-ronmental implications—there is an ongoing argument as to whether or not shale gas is safe or if it harms the environment, which is why the EPA takes this issue very seriously.

---

[12] Bloomberg and NYMEX. Prices as of June 1, 2012.

[13] EIA and NaturalGas.org.

FIGURE 10.17   Natural Gas Drilling

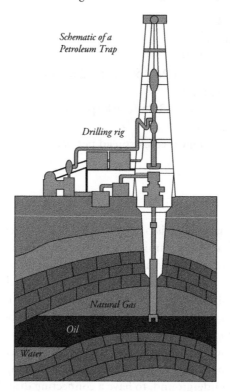

Source: U.S. Energy Information Administration.

Flaring

Flaring is the process of burning unwanted natural gas. The abundance of natural gas in the United States, and flaring of it, is one of the biggest drivers for the consistent bear market seen in natural gas prices in recent years. Furthermore, the United States has inefficient regulations whereby there are times when a producer must mandatorily explore for natural gas even when there is no demand, resulting in increased flaring. There are times when the driller wins the contract, and often they are not allowed to sit on reserves and must begin drilling regardless if there is an end user or not.

LNG

When natural gas is cooled to –260°F it changes into a liquid form, known as liquefied natural gas (LNG). LNG is useful in transporting natural gas and for importing and exporting natural gas. It takes 600 times less space than in its gaseous state, making it attractive for international trade.

Uses

Natural gas is most attractive as an energy source because it is considered to be much cleaner than other typical fossil fuels, producing 30 to 50 percent less carbon dioxide than gasoline or coal. Natural gas can be used in power generation in electricity. Additionally, fuel cell technology is looking to become more cost-effective, in order to allow natural gas to be used more. Natural gas can also be used in transportation, and many metropolitan cities have tried to take the lead in using buses that run on natural gas.

Natural gas is also used to make ammonia, which is used in fertilizer. As a result, U.S. and Canadian fertilizer and agricultural companies have a competitive advantage in the agricultural business. Since, natural gas is the cheapest in North America, their input costs are cheaper than global competitors, which then gets passed on in the supply chain.

Production

The United States and Russia are the two largest producers of natural gas, accounting for 38 percent of global production (see Table 10.5). Gazprom controls a majority of Russia's natural gas production, while in the United States, Chesapeake, Devon Energy, Apache, Anadarko, Occidental Petroleum, ExxonMobil, and Conoco make up a bulk of the production. In the United States, Louisiana, New Mexico, Oklahoma, Texas, Wyoming, and the Gulf of Mexico account for more than 70 percent of production. Russia, Iran, Turkmenistan, and Qatar have more than half the world's proven natural gas reserves.[14]

Conventions

Gas is priced in U.S. dollars per million British thermal unit (MMBtu). A Btu is the quantity of heat required to raise the temperature of one pound of water by one degree Fahrenheit. Physical volume is measured in Mcf, which is one thousand cubic feet—roughly equivalent to 1 MMBtu.

---

[14] EIA and Naturalgas.org.

TABLE 10.5 Global Top 10 Natural Gas Producers and Consumers

Natural Gas (billion cubic meters)	2008	2009	2010	2011	2012	
Production						
United States	571	584	604	649	681	20.3%
Russia	602	528	589	607	592	17.6%
Iran	116	131	146	152	161	4.8%
Qatar	77	89	117	145	157	4.7%
Canada	177	164	160	160	157	4.7%
Norway	99	105	108	102	115	3.4%
China	80	85	95	103	107	3.2%
Saudi Arabia	80	79	88	92	103	3.1%
Algeria	86	80	80	83	82	2.4%
Indonesia	70	72	82	76	71	2.1%
Other	1,096	1,053	1,124	1,124	1,139	33.9%
Total Supply	3,054	2,969	3,192	3,291	3,364	
Consumption						
United States	659	649	682	691	722	21.8%
Russia	416	390	414	425	416	13.2%
Iran	119	131	145	154	156	4.8%
China	81	90	107	131	144	4.1%
Japan	94	87	95	106	117	3.3%
Saudi Arabia	80	79	88	92	103	3.3%
Canada	96	95	95	101	101	3.1%
UK	99	91	99	83	78	2.5%
Germany	81	78	83	75	75	2.2%
Italy	78	72	76	71	69	2.2%
Other	1,207	1,183	1,293	1,306	1,334	40.0%
Total Demand	3,012	2,944	3,176	3,232	3,314	
(Supply – Demand)	43	25	16	59	50	

Sources: EIA and BP Statistical Review of World Energy, June 2013.

FIGURE 10.18 Historical Price Chart of Natural Gas Front Contract

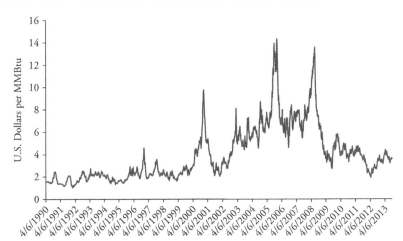

Source: Bloomberg.

Natural gas futures, NG1 <Comdty> (front month) trade on the NYMEX. One contract is 10,000 million British thermal units (Btu's) for delivery in Henry Hub in Louisiana, which is where the contract gets its name. The front end of the futures curve is predominantly a speculators' market, while longer-term futures is more of a producers' market, in which the companies involved in the natural gas market hedge their exposures (see Figure 10.18). For retail investors, there is an ETF under the symbol UNG <Equity>, which tracks the price of the Henry Hub futures contract. Caution should be taken with this ETF because it is subject to contango and futures rolls, so investors may not get the same return they would see in the futures market.

Precious Metals

Precious metals are a classification of metals that are considered to be rare and of economic value. They have recently gained significant attention because real rates are historically low and have been negative in many countries. Also, the unprecedented increase in central bank balance sheets has some questioning the intrinsic value of fiat money. Precious metals have always provided global macro traders with important information. Gold and silver tend to react more to economic conditions and central bank policy, whereas precious metals like

FIGURE 10.19   Historical Price Chart of Gold

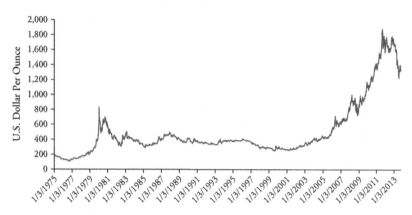

Source: Bloomberg.

platinum have different drivers, such as catalytic converters in automobiles, which are largely driven by an increase in emerging market demand. Having an understanding of each precious metal can be very helpful to a trader in currency markets.

Gold

Gold's atomic number is 79 and its atomic symbol is AU, for *aurum*, the Latin word for gold. It was first mined in ancient Egypt and first used in coins in what is now considered Turkey around 640 BC. Gold is a dense, yellow precious metal, malleable and ductile. All of these factors perhaps contributed to its use as a store of value, since it is easier to make into coins and doesn't erode or tarnish. The use of gold in jewelry accounts for more than 40 percent of demand and gold as an investment is the second biggest driver of demand. Under the Bretton Woods system, global foreign exchange effectively fixed the gold standard until 1971, when the U.S. dollar was no longer fixed to gold. While gold is a precious metal and a commodity, it has gained popularity as a form of currency because faith has been lost in fiat currencies (see Figure 10.19).

Central banks are one of the biggest players in the gold market, holding 31,920 tonnes as of October 2013. The United States is the largest holder, with 8,134 tonnes making up 73 percent of its total reserves (see Table 10.6). In total, the average gold-to-reserve ratio for all central banks is less than

TABLE 10.6 Central Banks Gold as a Percent of Reserves

		Tons	% of Reserves
1.	United States	8,133.5	73.0%
2.	Germany	3,390.6	69.8%
3.	Italy	2,451.8	68.4%
4.	France	2,435.4	67.6%
5.	China	1,054.1	1.3%
6.	Switzerland	1,040.1	9.0%
7.	Russia	1,015.5	8.9%
8.	Japan	765.2	2.7%
9.	Netherlands	612.5	55.8%
10.	India	557.7	8.8%

Source: World Gold Council, as of October 2013.

20 percent, and for China it is only 1.3 percent, which means that China will likely be a huge buyer of gold for many years to come, though this behavior has not emerged yet. In 2011, central banks bought 457 tonnes, which is the highest since 1964 and in 2012 bought 535 tonnes. A bulk of this demand came from emerging markets wanting to diversify as a result of their building reserves, as well as increased worry over sovereign credit risk and fiat money.

For most of the twentieth century, South Africa was the largest producer of gold, but due to depletion of mines and labor unrest, China has overtaken it as the leading producer of gold. China, the United States, Australia, and South Africa collectively account for more than 40 percent of global gold production. India, which is the largest consumer of gold, demanded over 500 tonnes for jewelry and 300 tonnes for investment in 2011, of which 50 percent is used for weddings (Table 10.7).

Recent Events and Considerations on Real Rates

In May 1999, Gordon Brown, who at the time was UK chancellor and later became prime minister, decided to sell almost half of the United Kingdom's gold reserves. At the time, gold was trading at 20-year lows and the UK

TABLE 10.7 Global Gold Supply and Demand Table

Gold (tons)	2010	2011	2012
Supply			
Mine Supply	2,523.2	2,846.9	2,827.7
Recycled Gold	1,640.7	1,668.5	1,625.6
Total Supply	4,163.9	4,515.4	4,453.3
Demand			
Jewelry	2,016.8	1,972.1	1,908.1
Technology	466.4	452.9	428.2
Bar and Coin Demand	1,199.8	1,515.4	1,255.6
Central Bank Net Purchases[1]	–	456.8	534.6
ETFs	367.7	185.1	279.0
OTC Flow	113.2	−66.9	47.8
Total Demand	4,163.9	4,515.4	4,453.3

[1]Excludes Delta Hedging of Central Bank options. 2010 data not available.
Sources: World Gold Council. Gold Demand Trends Full Year Report, Thomson GFMS, and LBMA.

Treasury started selling from July 1999 to March 2002. The UK sold 395 of their nearly 715 tonnes when the program started, representing a 55 percent depletion of gold reserves. Over the 17 gold auctions conducted, the approximate price received for the gold sold was $275 per ounce. This horrendous timing by Gordon Brown is referred to as the *Brown Bottom*.[15]

Another interesting concept with gold is real interest rates. In the paper *Gibson's Paradox and the Gold Standard*, Larry Summers (who later became U.S. Secretary of the Treasury) concludes that during periods of negative real interest rates, people prefer gold to fiat currency because they will seek to preserve their purchasing power. Conversely, in periods when real interest rates are positive, parties prefer fiat currency since it is deemed to increase purchasing power. The negative real interest rate experience in the United States is one of the big drivers in gold's increase in value—as real rates became more positive, gold prices fell (Barsky and Summers 1988).

---

[15]Bank of England.

To many, gold has become a store of value (money) and can be quoted with the symbol XAU <Curncy>. Gold can be traded through the ETF GLD <Equity>, which is managed by State Street. Its popularity has grown due to its ease for retail investors to trade, ability to trade small notional, and the current liquid options market. GLD trades at 1/10th the value of the price of one ounce of gold, so if spot gold were trading at $1,500/ounce, GLD would trade close to $150 per share. Listed options are very liquid on both the ETF and futures contract. Additionally, gold futures (GC), which trade on the Comex, are also very liquid and trade at a contract size of 100 troy ounces, so if the price of gold is trading at $1,500/ounce, one contract is $150,000 notional. Physical gold is also an option but many investors prefer the traded instruments since they are more liquid in the sense that the physical often incurs a wider bid/offer. One advantage to physical gold is that some investors believe that there is a shortage of physical gold and that the ETF market and other derivatives do not actually have the gold backing what is claimed. If this urban myth were true, it would likely only come to light in a catastrophic financial calamity.

Silver

Silver has the atomic number 47 and symbol Ag, which is derived from its Latin name *argentum*. It was first mined 5,000 years ago in what is now the country of Turkey. Silver is usually found near the earth's crust, which makes it easier to mine.

Uses

Silver has the highest electrical conductivity of all metals, but because it is more expensive, copper is more widely used. Silver is a great conductor of heat and reflector of light, which makes it ideal for solar panel use. For many years, photography was one of the biggest demand drivers for silver, but since the dawn of digital cameras, demand for silver for photography continues to shrink. Most silver is used in industrial applications such as batteries, electronics, and machinery. Jewelry and silverware also make up a sizeable portion of silver demand, widely using sterling silver.[16]

Sterling silver gets its name from sixteenth-century England, when 92.5 percent silver was mixed with 7.5 percent of other alloys. Additionally,

---

[16] Silver Institute.

the pound sterling gets its name because it used to be measured against how much deliverable silver could be traded for pound sterling. The Hong Kong dollar was pegged to the silver standard until 1935, when silver prices became very volatile as a result of the Great Depression. Triple 9s refers to 99.9 percent pure silver and quadruple 9s is 99.99 percent pure.

The biggest driver for silver demand is the development of the solar panel market, which uses silver. Over 90 percent of photovoltaic cells rely on quadruple 9 silver (99.99 percent purity). In 2006, solar demand for silver was less than 2 percent and by 2012 it came to represent more than 10 percent of silver demand (see Table 10.8).

Mexico and China account for 47 percent of global production (see Table 10.9). The top five producers, which also include Peru, Australia, and Russia, account for 83 percent of production, making silver production concentrated. The United States and China account for more than one-third of silver's global consumption.

The Hunt Brothers

The Hunt brothers were billionaires from the Texas oil industry. In the 1970s they started to accumulate large amounts of silver, which ultimately led to an attempt to corner the silver market. As a result, in January 1980, the price of silver hit $50 when just two years prior in January 1978, the price of silver was under $5 an ounce (see Figure 10.20). From January until March 1980 the price of silver fell drastically, wiping out a substantial portion of the Hunt brothers' wealth.

Like gold, silver has become a store of value (money) and can be quoted with the symbol XAG <Curncy>. Silver can be traded through the ETF SLV <Equity>. SLV trades at the value of one ounce of silver. Listed options are very liquid on both the ETF and futures contract. Additionally, silver futures (SI), which trade on the Comex, are also very liquid and trade at a contract size of 5,000 troy ounces, so if the price of silver is trading at $25/ounce, one contract is $125,000 notional. Triple 9s silver is the deliverable for the futures contract.

Platinum

Platinum's atomic number is 78, and its atomic symbol is Pt. Platinum got its name from the Spanish word *platina*. Platinum is almost twice has heavy as gold and has a gravity density of 21, compared to 19 for gold. It has many of the attractive attributes of gold, being more ductile, but is significantly more

TABLE 10.8 Global Silver Supply and Demand Table

Silver (millions of ounces)	2002	2003	2004	2005	2006	2007	2008	2009	2010	2011	2012	
Supply												
Mine Production	594.5	597.2	613.6	636.6	641.1	665.9	683.6	716.1	751.4	757.0	787.0	
Government Sales	59.2	88.7	61.9	65.9	78.5	42.5	30.5	15.6	44.2	12.0	7.4	
Old Silver Scrap	197.3	196.0	197.4	201.6	206.0	203.0	200.9	200.0	228.7	258.1	253.9	
Producer Hedging	0.0	0.0	9.6	27.6	0.0	0.0	0.0	0.0	50.4	12.2	0.0	
Net Investment	17.4	0.0	0.0	0.0	0.0	0.0	0.0	0.0	0.0	0.0	0.0	
Total Supply	**868.3**	**881.9**	**882.4**	**931.7**	**925.6**	**911.4**	**915.0**	**931.7**	**1,074.7**	**1,039.4**	**1,048.3**	
Demand												
Fabrication												
Industrial Applications	355.3	368.4	387.4	431.8	454.2	491.1	492.7	405.1	500.0	487.8	465.9	44.4%
Photography	204.3	192.9	178.8	160.3	142.2	117.6	101.3	79.3	72.1	66.1	57.8	5.5%
Jewelry	168.9	179.2	174.8	173.8	166.3	163.5	158.7	159.8	167.4	186.5	185.6	17.7%
Silverware	83.5	83.9	67.2	67.6	61.2	58.6	57.4	59.1	51.2	48.3	44.9	4.3%
Coins and Medals	31.6	35.7	42.4	40.0	39.8	39.7	65.3	78.8	99.4	118.3	92.7	8.8%
Fabrication (Total)	843.5	860.1	850.6	873.6	863.7	870.5	875.3	782.0	890.1	907.1	846.8	
Producer Dehedging	24.8	20.9	0.0	0.0	6.8	24.2	8.5	17.4	0.0	0.0	41.5	
Net Investment	0.0	0.9	31.8	58.1	55.1	16.6	31.2	132.2	184.6	132.3	160.0	
Total Demand	**868.3**	**881.9**	**882.4**	**931.7**	**925.6**	**911.4**	**915.0**	**931.7**	**1,074.7**	**1,039.4**	**1,048.3**	

Source: World Silver Survey 2013 and GFMS.

TABLE 10.9   Global Silver Mine Production

	Silver (millions of ounces)	2012	
	Supply		
	Mine Production		
1.	Mexico	162.2	*27.3%*
2.	China	117.0	*19.7%*
3.	Peru	111.3	*18.7%*
4.	Australia	56.9	*9.6%*
5.	Russia	45.0	*7.6%*
6.	Poland	41.2	*6.9%*
7.	Bolivia	39.7	*6.7%*
8.	Chile	37.0	*6.2%*
9.	United States	32.6	*5.5%*
10.	Argentina	24.1	*4.1%*
	Other	120.0	*20.2%*
	Mine Production (Total)	**787.0**	

Source: World Silver Survey 2013 and GFMS.

FIGURE 10.20   Historical Price Chart of Silver

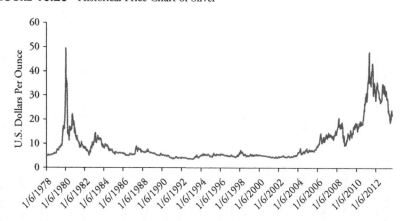

Source: Bloomberg.

FIGURE 10.21 Historical Price Chart of Platinum

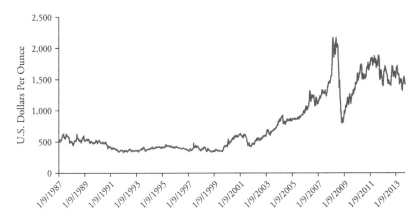

Source: Bloomberg.

rare and is one of the rarest elements on earth. South Africa holds 80 percent of global platinum reserves.

Trading platinum can be thought of as a play on both emerging markets and the automotive industry (see Figure 10.21). Catalytic converters in automobiles account for 38 percent of global demand, and marginal increase in demand has been coming from emerging markets. Following trends in the automobile market is essential for trading platinum (see Table 10.10).

Additionally, 31 percent of global demand comes from jewelry. For example, watches account for roughly 10 percent of Swiss exports and demand is continuing to rise 10 percent or more annually, largely from China.

Platinum futures (PL) are liquid and trade on the Comex at a contract size of 50 troy ounces, so if the price of platinum is trading at $1,500/ounce, one contract is $750,000 notional. Platinum can be traded through ETFs, but these are not as liquid as GLD, SLV, and do not have options. Physical platinum is also an option but not nearly as liquid for investors as gold and silver. Many traders also follow the platinum/gold ratio (see Figure 10.22).

Industrial Metals

Industrial metals, commonly referred to as base metals, are less expensive than precious metals and far more abundant. Industrial metals also oxidize

TABLE 10.10   Global Platinum Supply and Demand Table

Platinum (thousands of ounces)	2006	2007	2008	2009	2010	2011	
South Africa	5,295	5,070	4,515	4,635	4,635	4,855	*74.9%*
Russia	920	915	805	785	825	835	*12.9%*
North America	345	325	325	260	200	350	*5.4%*
Zimbabwe	165	170	180	230	280	340	*5.2%*
Others	105	120	115	115	110	100	*1.5%*
Total Supply	6,830	6,600	5,940	6,025	6,050	6,480	
Autocatalyst	3,905	4,145	3,655	2,185	3,075	3,105	*38.4%*
Jewelry	2,195	2,110	2,060	2,810	2,420	2,480	*30.6%*
Investment	−40	170	555	660	655	460	*5.7%*
Other	1,830	1,845	1,720	1,140	1,755	2,050	*25.3%*
Total Recycling	−1,415	−1,590	−1,830	−1,405	−1,830	−2,045	
Total Demand	6,475	6,680	6,160	5,390	6,075	6,050	
Balance (Supply − Demand)	355	−80	−220	635	−25	430	

Source: Johnson Matthey, Platinum 2012.

FIGURE 10.22   Platinum/Gold Ratio

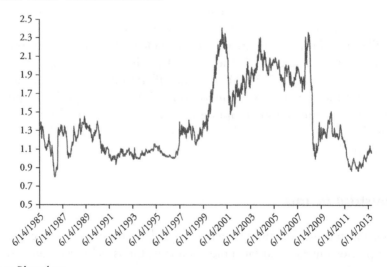

Source: Bloomberg.

and corrode more easily than precious metals. They are used in industrial applications and include the metals copper, aluminum, nickel, lead, and zinc. Since industrial metals are used in many industrial applications, they are generally a good leading indicator for economic growth.

Copper

Copper is atomic number 29 and its chemical symbol is Cu. Its name comes from the Latin word *cuprum*. Copper was first mined as far back as 10,000 years ago and also during the Roman Empire near modern-day Cyprus and Greece. It had been mined prior to that as a by-product of other metals. Copper is one of the best tools available for global macro trading and it is often considered a leading indicator; copper has often been nicknamed "Dr. Copper" or "having a PhD in economics."

Global production of copper is dominated by South America, specifically Chile and Peru (see Table 10.11). China is the second-largest producer, and

TABLE 10.11   Global Top 10 Copper Producers and Consumers

Copper (thousand tons)							
	Mine Production	2012			Consumption	2012	
1.	Chile	5,434	26.8%	1.	China	8,845	43.0%
2.	China	1,490	7.3%	2.	EU-15	2,748	13.4%
3.	Peru	1,299	6.4%	3.	United States	1,760	8.6%
4.	United States	1,195	5.9%	4.	Japan	985	4.8%
5.	Australia	914	4.5%	5.	Korea	723	3.5%
6.	Russia	720	3.6%	6.	Russia	646	3.1%
7.	Zambia	695	3.4%	7.	India	609	3.0%
8.	Canada	580	2.9%	8.	Taiwan	433	2.1%
9.	Congo	561	2.8%	9.	Turkey	428	2.1%
10.	Mexico	500	2.5%	10.	Brazil	426	2.1%
	Others	3,310	16.3%				
	Recycled	3,583	17.7%		Others	2,947	14.3%
		20,280				20,550	

Sources: ICSG, USGS, and the World Copper Bulletin, October 2013.

the largest importer of copper, representing roughly 40 percent of imports. Since China is the second-largest economy and growth engine in the world, copper prices move in sync with China's growth expectations. Copper is considered one of the first inputs into an economy that is urbanizing and undergoing societal development, which plays right into the BRIC story. Chile is the most important player in the copper market, representing more than 40 percent of consumption. Chile nationalized its copper company, Codelco, in 1975 under dictator Augusto Pinochet, and has roughly 11 percent of global reserves. In 2011, 36 percent of Codelco's exports went to China.[17]

Copper is one of the most recycled of all metals. Recycled copper is known as "secondary copper" and is nearly impossible to distinguish from primary copper, which is mined. Global refined copper has surged 300 percent over past decades and represents a sizeable part of the market. Additionally, China keeps large stockpiles of copper as a form of speculation. Many believe this could cause the copper market to experience severe downturns. Hence, China stockpiles and changes should be closely watched.

Copper is used in building construction, which accounts for 33 percent of copper demand, consisting of plumbing, buildings, architecture, and electrical power. Additionally, infrastructure accounts for 15 percent of copper demand, which includes power/utility and telecommunications. Equipment manufacturing makes up 52 percent of demand and includes industrial applications, automotive, consumer products, electronics, and cooling equipment.[18] Visibly following where copper goes, it is evident that copper is a major input into a growing society, which plays into the growth of emerging markets and their need for infrastructure and new constructions.

Copper is traded on the London Metals Exchange (LME) and NYMEX (Figure 10.23), and is liquid on both exchanges. LMCADS03 <Comdty>, which is the LME Copper 3-Month Rolling Forward that trades on the LME, trades in dollars per ton, and each contract is 25 tons. So, if LMCAD03 is trading at $7,500, then the notional is $187,500 ($7,500 × 25) per contract. HG1 <Comdty> is the front futures contract in copper and trades in cents per pound; each contract is 25,000 pounds. So, if HG1 is trading at 350.00 ¢, then the notional is $87,500 (350.00 ¢ × 25,000) per contract. The liquidity on both exchanges is very good, so trading one or the other is a matter of preference and ease of access.

---

[17] Codelco.
[18] The World Copper Factbook 2013.

FIGURE 10.23 Historical Price Chart of Copper Front Contract (NYMEX)

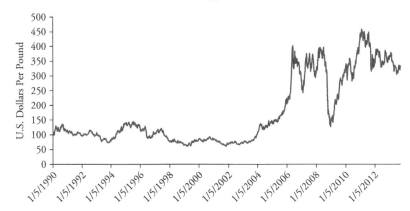

Source: Bloomberg.

Aluminum

Aluminum has the atomic symbol 13 and derives its name from the Latin word *alumen*. It is the most abundant metal in the world, making up almost 9 percent of the Earth's crust. Aluminum is lightweight and does not corrode. It is not found on its own but is combined with other elements, which makes it very difficult to get in pure form as it requires a lot of energy to break apart.

In terms of production and consumption, China is the biggest player, accounting for over 40 percent on both sides (see Table 10.12). Russia is the biggest exporter of aluminum in the world, and the United States, Japan, and Germany are the biggest importers. Interestingly enough, aluminum is one of the few commodities in which China is self-sufficient, meaning supply meets demand.

Once aluminum is separated, it has many uses, because it is a lightweight, very durable, strong, flexible, and recyclable metal. New building constructions use aluminum throughout entire infrastructures. Part of Newton's laws of motion stipulates that Force = Mass × Acceleration. Since, relative to other metals, aluminum is lightweight, it is used in trains and cars. Because the mass is smaller, less force (i.e., energy use) is required to move the object.

Aluminum is traded on the London Metals Exchange (LME) as LMAHDS03 <Comdty>, which is the LME Aluminum 3-Month Rolling Forward. It trades in dollars per ton and each contract is 25 tons. For instance, if LMAHD03 is trading at $2,000, then the notional is $50,000 ($2,500 × 25) per contract (see Figure 10.24).

TABLE 10.12 Global Top 10 Aluminum Exporters and Importers

Aluminum (thousand metric tons)

	Production	2011			Consumption	2011	
1.	China	18,100	40.8%	1.	China	17,629	41.6%
2.	Russia	3,912	8.8%	2.	United States	4,060	9.6%
3.	Canada	2,984	6.7%	3.	Germany	2,103	5.0%
4.	United States	1,986	4.5%	4.	Japan	1,946	4.6%
5.	Australia	1,945	4.4%	5.	India	1,611	3.8%
6.	UAE	1,800	4.1%	6.	Korea	1,233	2.9%
7.	India	1,667	3.8%	7.	Brazil	1,077	2.5%
8.	Brazil	1,440	3.2%	8.	Italy	971	2.3%
9.	Norway	1,122	2.5%	9.	Turkey	870	2.1%
10.	Bahrain	881	2.0%	10.	Russia	685	1.6%
	Others	8,563	19.3%		Others	10,200	24.1%
		44,400				42,386	

Sources: USGS, World Bureau of Metals and Aluminum Minerals Yearbook.

FIGURE 10.24 Historical Price Chart of Aluminum (LME Forward)

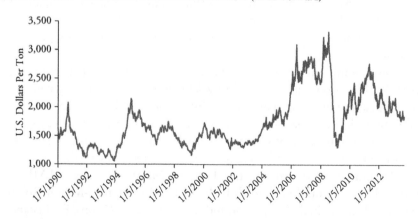

Source: Bloomberg.

Agriculture

Corn and wheat are the biggest grown crops in the world and the United States is the biggest player in the agriculture sector, being either the biggest or amongst the top producers in most agricultural products. In agriculture trading, understanding who the producers are and which factors, like weather, can affect the crop is of the utmost importance. Some of the best agriculture traders have full-time meteorologists on staff so they can predict potential weather changes. While it is impossible to accurately predict this information, the following crops have calendars that help outline which periods of the year are most sensitive.

Corn

Maize originates from the Spanish word *maíz*, and is called corn in the United States. Corn has been used in North and Central America for centuries and has the advantage of being grown in a very diverse climate set (see Figure 10.25). It can be grown at high and low elevations and has relatively

FIGURE 10.25 Corn Planted Acres Map in United States

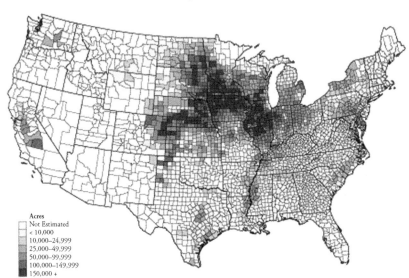

Acres
Not Estimated
< 10,000
10,000–24,999
25,000–49,999
50,000–99,999
100,000–149,999
150,000 +

Source: EIA.

low rainfall requirements. It is also the largest cereal crop. By comparison, corn production for 2011–2012 was 884 million tons, as compared to 697 million tons of wheat.

The United States is the biggest player in the corn market, representing over 35 percent of production and over 30 percent of consumption (see Table 10.13). It is also the largest exporter (see Table 10.14). The western Corn Belt states, Iowa, Illinois, and Nebraska, produce 47 percent of corn in the United States and the eastern Corn Belt states, Indiana and Ohio, produce 11 percent of corn in the United States (see Figure 10.25).[19] Japan is the largest importer of corn, accounting for almost 15 percent of global imports, which is almost twice as much as any other country.

Corn's major uses are livestock feed, ethanol, and food. Ethanol is the new single biggest driving change in the corn market. For the 2012–2013 crop, the United States accounts for 18 percent of exports. By contrast, in 2009–2010, the crop accounted for 54 percent. As global corn demand grows, this will impact corn prices and has been one of the biggest drivers in corn prices (see Figure 10.26). Additionally, as China grows and continues to get richer, its people demand more meat and corn. Demand for corn as feedstock in China grew from 0 percent of total imports in 2007 to over 5 percent of all global imports.

Summer of 2012 Drought

In the summer of 2012, the United States experienced a large drought starting in June and running through August. In the United States, most crops are generally planted during spring months. During the summer months many crops, such as corn, experience their most sensitive periods, when rain and temperature are of the utmost importance. In the summer of 2012, temperatures were at record highs in many planting states with little rainfall. Figure 10.27 shows the crop devastation and drought in that year. This is the worst-case scenario for farmers, as it causes their yields to fall, which in turn decreases the supply forecasts in agriculture and then causes prices to rise dramatically, as they did in this case.

Additionally, when corn, wheat, and soybean prices rise drastically, the cost of feeding livestock increases drastically. This, in turn, typically causes livestock prices in the short run to fall sharply, while later parts of the curve rise. The reason being that, because it becomes too expensive to feed livestock,

---

[19] USDA NASS, Crop Production 2011 Summary, January 12, 2012.

TABLE 10.13 Global Top 10 Corn Producers and Consumers

Corn (thousand metric tons)	2009–10	2010–11	2011–12	2012–13	June 2013–14	
Production						
1. United States	332,549	316,165	313,949	273,832	349,597	36.5%
2. China	163,974	177,245	192,780	205,600	211,000	22.0%
3. Brazil	56,100	57,400	73,000	81,000	72,000	7.5%
4. EU-27	59,147	58,265	68,089	58,539	65,025	6.8%
5. Argentina	10,486	11,919	22,838	20,922	29,000	3.0%
6. Ukraine	25,000	25,200	21,000	26,500	27,000	2.8%
7. India	16,720	21,730	21,760	22,230	22,500	2.4%
8. Mexico	20,374	21,058	18,726	21,500	22,000	2.3%
9. South Africa	9,796	12,043	11,359	13,060	13,800	1.4%
10. Canada	13,420	10,924	12,759	12,200	13,000	1.4%
Others	117,288	121,321	128,111	124,679	132,224	13.8%
Total Supply	**824,854**	**833,270**	**884,371**	**860,062**	**957,146**	

(*Continued*)

TABLE 10.13 Continued

Corn (thousand metric tons)	2009–10	2010–11	2011–12	2012–13	June 2013–14	
Consumption						
1. U.S.	281,615	285,123	279,035	267,601	290,844	31.3%
2. China	165,000	180,000	188,000	207,000	224,000	24.1%
3. EU-27	61,300	64,900	69,200	69,000	70,000	7.5%
4. Brazil	47,000	49,500	50,500	53,000	54,000	5.8%
5. Mexico	30,200	29,500	29,000	27,000	29,000	3.1%
6. India	15,100	18,100	17,200	17,400	18,400	2.0%
7. Japan	16,300	15,700	14,900	14,500	15,500	1.7%
8. Canada	11,868	11,761	11,636	11,900	12,800	1.4%
9. Egypt	12,000	12,500	11,700	11,200	11,200	1.2%
10. Indonesia	8,800	9,800	10,500	10,900	11,100	1.2%
Others	177,312	173,797	199,139	179,811	193,241	20.8%
Total Demand	**826,495**	**850,681**	**880,810**	**869,312**	**930,085**	

Source: USDA. World Corn Production, Consumption, and Stocks. As of September 2013.

240

TABLE 10.14 Global Top 10 Corn Exporters and Importers

Corn (thousand metric tons)	2009–10	2010–11	2011–12	2012–13	June 2013–14
Exports					
1. United States	49,696	45,135	38,428	17,500	32,500
2. Brazil	8,623	11,583	12,674	26,500	20,000
3. Ukraine	5,072	5,008	15,157	13,300	18,000
4. Argentina	16,973	15,198	16,501	23,000	16,000
5. India	1,917	3,376	4,674	4,800	3,500
6. EU-27	1,569	1,096	3,287	1,900	2,500
7. Paraguay	1,359	1,201	2,188	2,400	2,300
8. Russia	427	37	2,027	2,000	2,000
9. Serbia	1,343	2,004	2,331	500	2,000
10. South Africa	1,586	2,839	1,831	2,200	1,900
Others	4,158	4,201	4,655	5,055	4,000
	92,723	**91,678**	**103,753**	**99,155**	**104,700**
Imports					
1. Japan	15,971	15,648	14,892	14,500	15,500
2. Korea	8,461	8,107	7,636	8,500	8,900
3. Mexico	8,298	8,252	11,172	5,500	8,000
4. EU-27	2,758	7,385	6,113	11,300	7,500
5. China	1,296	979	5,231	3,000	7,000
6. Egypt	5,832	5,803	7,154	4,500	5,200
7. Taiwan	4,521	4,134	4,341	4,300	4,300
8. Iran	4,300	3,500	4,000	3,500	4,100
9. Colombia	3,651	3,511	3,209	3,200	3,600
10. Malaysia	3,107	2,809	3,309	3,100	3,400
Others	34,528	31,550	36,696	37,755	37,200
	92,723	**91,678**	**103,753**	**99,155**	**104,700**

Source: USDA. World Corn Trade. As of September 2013.

FIGURE 10.26   Corn Front Contract Historical Price Chart

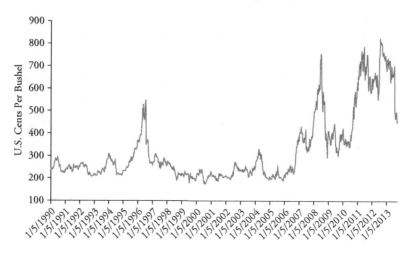

Source: Bloomberg.

FIGURE 10.27   U.S. Seasonal Drought Outlook

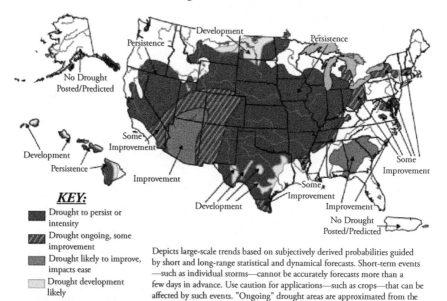

Source: National Oceanic and Atmospheric Administration.

farmers often kill their livestock ahead of schedule. This causes the short-term price to fall, because supply increases. However, the current stock was intended to be used in the future, so because livestock is sold today, supplies will be smaller in the future.

Ethanol

Ethanol, also called *ethyl alcohol,* uses corn as its primary input in the United States, although in Brazil they use sugar. In 2006, ethanol accounted for 4 percent of the U.S. gasoline market, and by 2009 had risen to 8 percent.[20] In 2011, ethanol was 27 percent of total corn demand in the United States, and that number is expected to grow to 35 percent. Ethanol has been the biggest growth driver of demand for corn, as is evident in Figure 10.28.

The U.S. Energy Policy Act of 2005 was created to decrease the dependence on foreign oil. Part of the Act legally mandates and subsidizes more ethanol blended into gasoline. *Gasohol* is the term used to describe gasoline and ethanol mixes of 5 to 25 percent (E5 to E25), and many U.S. states target E10 blend, which ensures that demand for corn via ethanol in the United States is sticky and will continue to grow. Since the 1970s, Brazil has mandated that all gasoline be E20 to E25 blends (20 to 25 percent ethanol). The United States and Brazil account for almost 90 percent of global

FIGURE 10.28 Corn Used for Ethanol Production, 1986–2011 (million bushels)

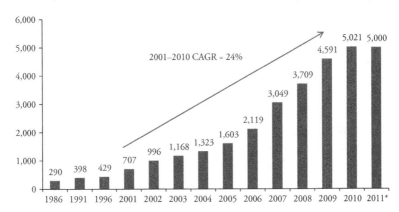

*Crop year ending August 31, 2012. Includes approximately 1.3 billion bushels to be used as distiller's grains for livestock feed. *(Source:* ProExporter Network.) Similar ratios apply for previous years.
Sources: USDA ERS, Feed Outlook, January 13, 2012, and NCGA.

---

[20]USDA Briefing on Bioenergy.

FIGURE 10.29   2011 Top Global Ethanol Producers by Country (in millions of gallons)

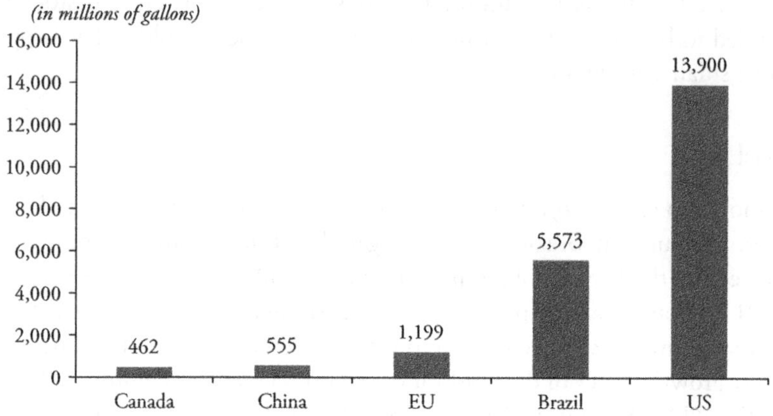

(in millions of gallons)

Source: USDA 2012 Pocket Guide to Ethanol.

ethanol production (see Figure 10.29). The biggest difference between the two countries is that Brazil makes their ethanol from sugar, which is more efficient, while the United States makes their ethanol from corn.

Figure 10.30 shows the crop calendar for corn. Since the United States is the largest producer and exporter of corn, the weather during the silking, beginning in June, is the most critical period to observe. As was the case in the summer of 2012, yields were low because of a drought and this caused corn prices to move significantly higher.

Corn trades with the most volume on the CBOT in Chicago and Dalian Exchange in China. On the CBOT, C 1 <Comdty> is the first contract for corn futures. They are quoted in cents (500 = $5.00) per bushel and the contract size is 5,000 bushels per contract. With corn, one bushel is equivalent to 56 pounds, unlike wheat and soybeans, which equals 60 pounds. One contract in this example would have a notional of $25,000 (500 cents × 5,000 bushels). The contract trades for delivery months March (H), May (K), July (N), September (U), and December (Z).

Wheat

Wheat is believed to have come from the Fertile Crescent near the Nile in what is the modern-day Middle East. Some date wheat back as long as 10,000 years ago, and there has been recent evidence found that it existed more than 20,000 years ago.

FIGURE 10.30 Corn Crop Calendar

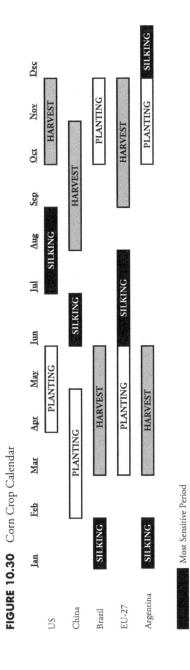

FIGURE 10.31   Wheat Front Contract Historical Price Chart

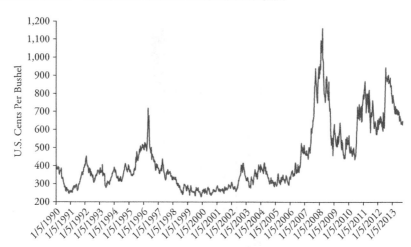

Source: Bloomberg.

Wheat has three classifications: season, gluten content, and color. There are two seasons for wheat, winter and spring. Hard wheat has a high protein (gluten) content while soft wheat has low protein content and is high in starch (sugar). Wheat planted in the spring tends to be hard and wheat planted in the winter tends to be soft. The color of wheat comes in red, white, and amber.

Wheat prices have held their own and will likely continue to do so since it is considered a close substitute to corn (see Figure 10.31). Additional factors that affect wheat prices are adverse changes in weather. For instance, there have been droughts recently in Russia and also export bans by the Russians, which tightened the supply. In February 2008, the United States had low stockpiles; this is a classic case of what happens to commodities when stock gets adversely affected (Figure 10.31). While the United States is the only the fourth-largest producer in the world (see Table 10.15), it is the largest global exporter of wheat (see Table 10.16). Wheat is used to make bread, cakes, flour, noodles, and is an input for beer. It is also frequently used as a feedstock for livestock and starch.

Figure 10.32 shows the wheat crop calendar. The most sensitive time for the wheat planting cycle is during the heading period. Because the United States grows a spring and winter crop, each crop runs on a different calendar from when they are planted all the way to when they are harvested.

TABLE 10.15 Global Top 10 Wheat Producers and Consumers

Wheat (thousand metric tons)	2009–10	2010–11	2011–12	2012–13	June 2013–14	
Production						
1. EU-27	139,720	136,667	138,081	133,049	141,373	20.0%
2. China	115,120	115,180	117,400	121,000	121,000	17.2%
3. India	80,680	80,800	86,870	94,880	92,460	13.1%
4. United States	60,366	60,062	54,413	61,755	57,536	8.2%
5. Russia	61,770	41,508	56,240	37,720	54,000	7.7%
6. Canada	26,950	23,300	25,288	27,205	29,500	4.2%
7. Australia	21,834	27,410	29,905	22,079	25,500	3.6%
8. Pakistan	24,000	23,900	25,000	23,300	24,000	3.4%
9. Ukraine	20,866	16,844	22,324	15,761	21,500	3.0%
10. Turkey	18,450	17,000	18,800	15,500	18,000	2.6%
Others	117,229	109,744	122,847	102,946	120,509	17.1%
Total Supply	686,985	652,415	697,168	655,195	705,378	

(*Continued*)

247

TABLE 10.15 Continued

Wheat (thousand metric tons)	2009–10	2010–11	2011–12	2012–13	June 2013–14	
Consumption						
1. China	107,000	110,500	122,500	125,000	126,500	17.9%
2. EU-27	125,622	122,844	126,875	121,000	122,700	17.4%
3. India	78,150	81,760	81,404	83,841	90,970	12.9%
4. Russia	39,600	38,600	38,000	33,550	36,500	5.2%
5. U.S.	30,977	30,639	32,112	38,341	35,680	5.0%
6. Pakistan	23,000	23,000	23,100	23,900	24,000	3.4%
7. Egypt	18,100	17,700	18,600	18,700	18,700	2.6%
8. Turkey	17,100	17,300	18,100	17,500	17,750	2.5%
9. Iran	16,800	16,200	15,500	16,400	17,000	2.4%
10. Ukraine	12,300	11,600	14,950	11,800	11,500	1.6%
Others	185,502	185,072	205,680	190,636	205,514	29.1%
Total Demand	654,151	655,215	696,821	680,668	706,814	
Balance (Supply – Demand)	32,834	–2,800	347	–25,473	–1,436	

Source: USDA. World Wheat Production, Consumption and Stocks. As of September 2013.

TABLE 10.16 Global Top 10 Wheat Exporters and Importers

Wheat (thousand metric tons)

	Exports	July 2012	June 2013		Imports	July 2012	June 2013
1.	U.S.	27,695	*18.8%*	1.	Egypt	8,300	*5.6%*
2.	EU-27	22,200	*15.1%*	2.	Brazil	7,548	*5.1%*
3.	Australia	21,300	*14.5%*	3.	Indonesia	7,140	*4.9%*
4.	Canada	18,581	*12.6%*	4.	Japan	6,598	*4.5%*
5.	Russia	11,289	*7.7%*	5.	Algeria	6,273	*4.3%*
6.	India	8,619	*5.9%*	6.	Korea	5,439	*3.7%*
7.	Argentina	7,449	*5.1%*	7.	Iran	5,400	*3.7%*
8.	Ukraine	7,190	*4.9%*	8.	EU-27	5,300	*3.6%*
9.	Kazakhstan	7,000	*4.8%*	9.	Nigeria	4,150	*2.8%*
10.	Turkey	3,583	*2.4%*	10.	Iraq	3,960	*2.7%*
	Others	12,078	*8.2%*		Others	86,876	*59.1%*
		146,984				146,984	

Source: USDA. World Wheat, Flour and Products Trade. As of September 2013.

There are a few exchanges that trade wheat futures; however, the CBOT wheat futures contract is deliverable in soft red winter (nos. 1 and 2), hard red winter (nos. 1 and 2), dark northern spring wheat (nos. 1 and 2), and northern spring wheat (nos. 1 and 2), making it the most widely accepted futures contract. It also has the greatest majority of liquidity. One bushel of wheat is equivalent to 60 pounds of wheat. On the CBOT, W 1 <Comdty> is the first contract for wheat futures. They are quoted in cents (600 = $6.00) and the contract size is 5,000 bushels per contract. One contract in this example would have a notional of $30,000. The contract trades for delivery months March (H), May (K), July (N), September (U), and December (Z) on the CBOT.

Soybeans

The word "soy" originates from the Japanese word *shōyu*. The soybean, which is native to East Asia, is considered to be an oil seed and has many dietary uses. Soybeans have a lot of protein and not the same disadvantages of eating

FIGURE 10.32 Wheat Crop Calendar

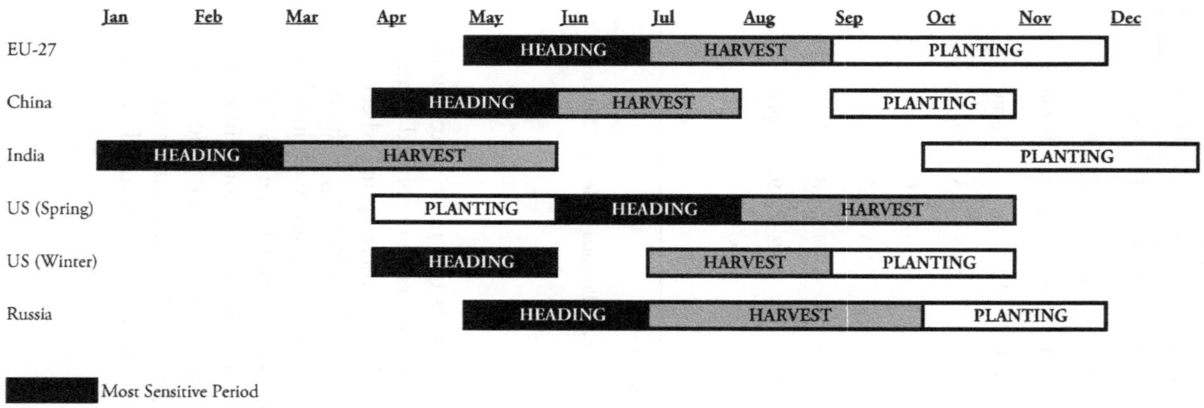

Most Sensitive Period

Source: Author's estimate.

250

FIGURE 10.33 Soybeans Front Contract Historical Price Chart

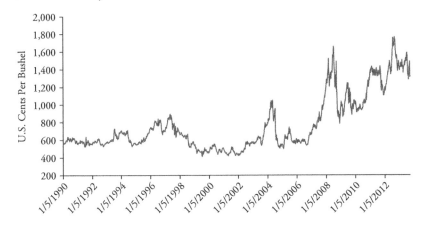

Source: Bloomberg.

meat (saturated fats and cardiovascular disease). Soybeans can be used in soybean meal, vegetable oil, soy milk, soy sauce, edamame, tofu, and industrial applications. Also, soybeans can be used as feedstock, which is a common practice in North and South America.

The United States is the largest producer by a small margin and the second largest exporter of soybeans in the world, at 31 percent and 37 percent, respectively (see Figure 10.33, Table 10.17, and Table 10.18). Production from Brazil and Argentina combined exceed that of the United States by a wide margin, which can be a little deceiving because weather patterns in South America are very critical. On aggregate, Brazil and Argentina neighbor each other and any adverse change in weather can affect the price and supply in both countries.

Soybeans typically take four to six months to mature after planting. In the United States, soybeans are planted in May or June and harvested in October or November. In Brazil, soybeans are planted in October, November, or December and harvested in March, April, or May. Soybeans are most vulnerable during the flowering stage (see Figure 10.34).

Today, more than 90 percent of all soybeans are genetically engineered (GE). The advantage of using GE soybeans is that it lowers the cost for growers because they do not need to use pesticides, and less pesticide means consumers are better off because the crop is healthier.

Soybeans trade most heavily on the CBOT in Chicago and the Dalian Exchange in China. On the CBOT, S 1 <Comdty> is the first contract

TABLE 10.17 Global Top 10 Soybean Producers and Consumers

Soybeans (thousand metric tons)	2009–2010	2010–2011	2011–2012	2012–2013	
Production					
1. United States	91,417	90,605	84,192	82,055	30.7%
2. Brazil	69,000	75,300	66,500	82,000	30.7%
3. Argentina	54,500	49,000	40,100	49,400	18.5%
4. China	14,980	15,100	14,480	12,800	4.8%
5. India	9,700	9,800	11,000	11,500	4.3%
6. Paraguay	6,462	7,128	4,043	9,367	3.5%
7. Canada	3,581	4,445	4,298	4,930	1.8%
Others	10,763	12,546	14,539	15,431	5.8%
Total Supply	**260,403**	**263,924**	**239,152**	**267,483**	
Consumption (Crush)					
1. China	48,830	55,000	60,970	64,650	28.3%
2. United States	47,673	44,851	46,348	45,994	20.1%
3. Brazil	33,700	36,330	38,083	34,840	15.2%
4. Argentina	34,127	37,614	35,886	33,350	14.6%
5. EU-27	12,595	12,355	12,245	12,470	5.5%
6. India	7,400	9,400	9,600	9,700	4.2%
7. Mexico	3,600	3,625	3,675	3,650	1.6%
8. Paraguay	1,558	1,570	950	3,000	1.3%
9. Russia	1,950	2,170	2,400	2,440	1.1%
10. Taiwan	2,010	2,060	2,020	2,040	0.9%
Others	15,673	16,285	15,651	16,425	7.2%
Total Demand	**209,116**	**221,260**	**227,828**	**228,559**	

Note: Most countries are on an October-September marketing year (MY). The United States, Mexico, and Thailand are on a September-August MY. Canada is on an August-July MY. Paraguay is on a March-February MY.
Source: USDA. Oilseeds: World Markets and Trade. As of September 2013.

TABLE 10.18 Global Top Soybean Exporters and Importers

Soybeans (000's metric tons) 2012–2013

	Exporters				Importers		
1.	Brazil	41,000	*41.9%*	1.	China	59,500	*62.7%*
2.	United States	35,788	*36.6%*	2.	EU-27	12,250	*12.9%*
3.	Argentina	6,425	*6.6%*	3.	Mexico	3,350	*3.5%*
4.	Paraguay	5,500	*5.6%*	4.	Japan	2,700	*2.8%*
5.	Canada	3,500	*3.6%*	5.	Taiwan	2,400	*2.5%*
6.	Others	5,530	*5.7%*	6.	Thailand	1,925	*2.0%*
				7.	Indonesia	1,920	*2.0%*
				8.	Egypt	1,650	*1.7%*
				9.	Vietnam	1,350	*1.4%*
				10.	Korea	1,150	*1.2%*
					Other	6,637	*7.0%*
	Total	97,743			**Total**	94,832	
	Balance (Supply – Demand)					2,911	

Source: USDA. Oilseeds: World Markets and Trade. As of September 2013.

for soybeans futures. They are quoted in cents (1,500 = $15.00) and the contract size is 5,000 bushels per contract. One contract in this example would have a notional of $75,000. The contract trades for delivery months January (F), March (H), May (K), July (N), August (Q), September (U), and November (X).

Cotton

The word cotton originates from the Arabic word *qutn* and was first cultivated by the Indus Valley civilization near modern-day Pakistan and India. It was also believed to be used in Mexico around the same period. Cotton is the most important textile fiber and has three classifications: character, grade,

FIGURE 10.34 Soybeans Crop Calendar

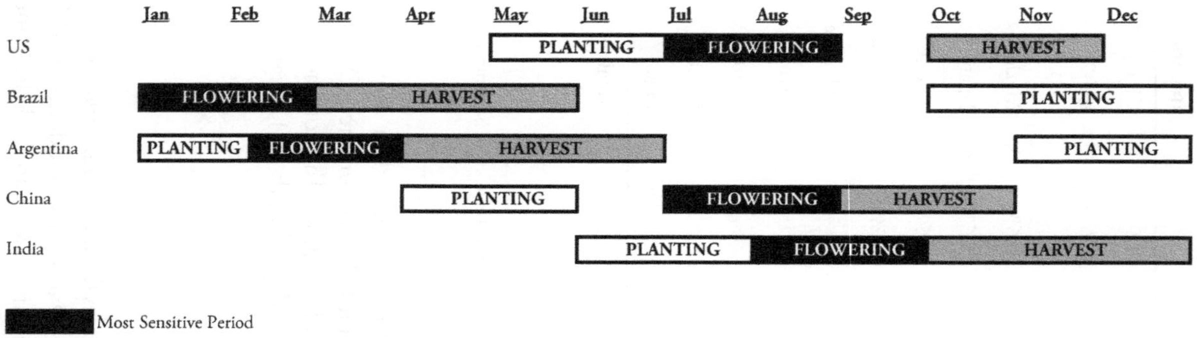

Sources: USDA, IBGE, and author estimates.

254

FIGURE 10.35 Cotton Front Contract Historical Price Chart

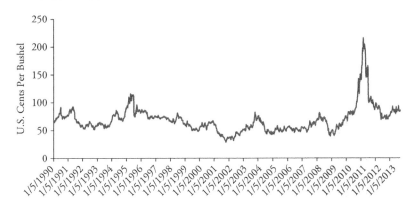

Source: Bloomberg.

and staple. Character is the strength of the fiber, grade is a measure of color and purity, and staple is the length of the fiber.

China, India, and the United States are the largest producers of cotton in the world, accounting for 65 percent of production in 2013 (see Table 10.17). China is the largest producer and consumer of cotton since they are the biggest player in the textile industry. The United States is the third-largest producer of cotton in the world (Table 10.19) and the largest exporter, accounting for almost 30 percent of global exports (Table 10.20). See Figure 10.35 for a historical price chart on cotton front contracts.

In the United States, cotton is typically planted from March to May and harvested in September to December. In China, cotton is planted in April and May to be harvested in September and October (see Figure 10.36). During the flowering stage (sometimes called the blooming stage), cotton is most vulnerable, though cotton is more drought-resistant relative to other crops.

Cotton trades most heavily on the Zhengzhou Commodity Exchange in China and the ICE. Cotton futures also trade in India and in Brazil (on the BM&F) but we will only cover the ICE contract. On the ICE, CT1 <Comdty> is the first contract for cotton futures and one bale of cotton is equivalent to 480 pounds of cotton. They are quoted in cents per pound and the contract size is 50,000 pounds per contract or roughly 104 bales of cotton. The contract settles with physical delivery with delivery points in Galveston, TX; Houston, TX; New Orleans, LA; Memphis, TN; and

TABLE 10.19 Global Top 10 Cotton Producers and Consumers

Cotton (000s 480-pound bales)

	August 2012–July 2013						
Production				**Consumption**			
1.	China	35,000	28.9%	1.	China	36,000	33.6%
2.	India	26,500	21.9%	2.	India	22,500	21.0%
3.	United States	17,315	14.3%	3.	Pakistan	11,000	10.3%
4.	Pakistan	9,300	7.7%	4.	Turkey	6,000	5.6%
5.	Brazil	5,800	4.8%	5.	Brazil	4,100	3.8%
6.	Australia	4,600	3.8%	6.	Bangladesh	3,600	3.4%
7.	Uzbekistan	4,500	3.7%	7.	U.S.	3,500	3.3%
				8.	Indonesia	2,550	2.4%
				9.	Vietnam	2,300	2.1%
				10.	Mexico	1,800	1.7%
	Other	18,020	14.9%		Other	13,923	13.0%
	TOTAL	121,035			**TOTAL**	107,273	
	Balance (Supply – Demand)					13,762	

Sources: National Cotton Council of America and USDA Foreign Agriculture Service.
As of September 2013.

Greenville/Spartanburg, SC. The contract trades for delivery months March (H), May (K), July (N), October (V), and December (Z).

Coffee

Coffee was named after the Ethiopian province of *Kaffa* where legend has it that an Ethiopian goat herder noticed his goats were more lively after consuming berries from a coffee tree. From 2000 years ago until the European exploration, coffee has consistently been a highly demanded commodity. There are two types of coffee that come from two different trees: arabica and robusta. Arabica makes up roughly 60 percent of global production and is a higher-grade coffee. It is more labor-intensive and is typically grown

TABLE 10.20   Global Top 10 Cotton Exporters and Importers

Cotton (000s 480-pound bales)

August 2012–July 2013						
Exporters				**Importers**		
1. United States	13,026	*27.9%*	*1*	China	20,327	*43.8%*
2. India	7,600	*16.3%*	*2*	Turkey	3,800	*8.2%*
3. Australia	6,179	*13.2%*	*3*	Bangladesh	3,600	*7.8%*
4. Brazil	4,307	*9.2%*	*4*	Indonesia	2,600	*5.6%*
5. Uzbekistan	3,200	*6.8%*	*5*	Vietnam	2,425	*5.2%*
6. Greece	1,200	*2.6%*	*6*	Pakistan	2,200	*4.7%*
7. Burkina	1,150	*2.5%*	*7*	Thailand	1,511	*3.3%*
8. Turkmenistan	1,075	*2.3%*	*8*	Korea	1,314	*2.8%*
9. Mali	875	*1.9%*	*9*	India	1,300	*2.8%*
10. Malaysia	725	*1.6%*	*10*	Mexico	950	*2.0%*
Other	7,406	*15.8%*		Other	6,401	*13.8%*
Total	**46,743**			**Total**	**46,428**	
Balance (Supply – Demand)					**315**	

Source: National Cotton Council of America and USDA Foreign Agriculture Service.
As of September 2013.

in higher altitudes. Most arabica coffee comes from Brazil, Colombia, and Central America. Robusta on the other hand has a stronger taste and more caffeine. It originates mostly from Africa and Asia and is grown in lower altitudes.

With the exception of Brazil, there is a large disparity of wealth between countries that import and export coffee (see Table 10.21). The income disparities are very large and this is unique to coffee as opposed to most other agricultural products. To combat this, and to protect the poor, Fair trade coffee has been established to ensure labor practices are more just. Additionally, the International Coffee Organization was established in 1963 in London to protect the interests of coffee exporters and consumers and to maintain

FIGURE 10.36 Cotton Crop Calendar

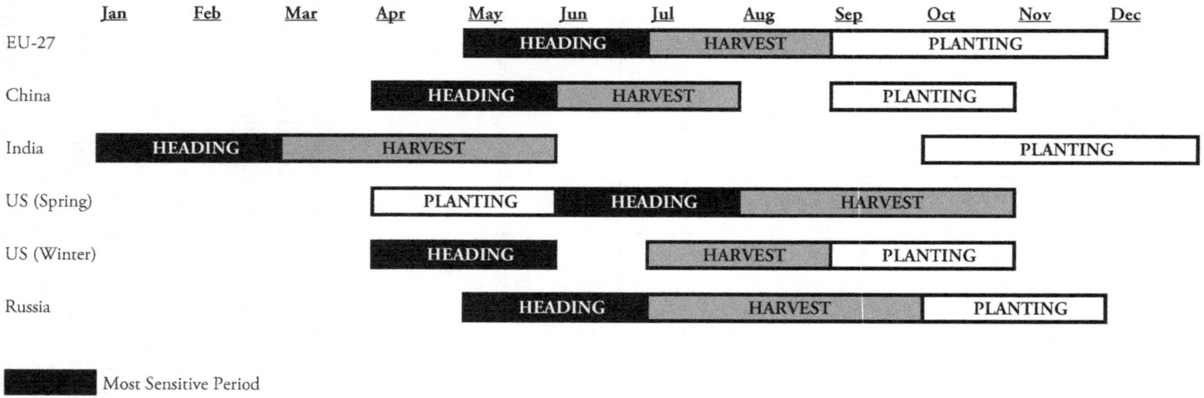

Source: Author estimates.

258

TABLE 10.21 Global Top 10 Coffee Producers and Consumers

Coffee (000 bags)	Primary Crop	Secondary Crop	2008–09	2009–10	2010–11	2011–12	June 2012–13	
Production								
1. Brazil	Apr/Mar	A	R	53,300	44,800	54,500	49,200	56,100	37.2%
2. Vietnam	Oct/Sep	R		16,980	18,500	19,415	26,000	24,950	16.6%
3. Indonesia	Apr/Mar	R	A	10,000	10,500	9,325	8,300	10,500	7.0%
4. Colombia	Oct/Sep	A		8,664	8,100	8,525	7,655	9,000	6.0%
5. Ethiopia	Oct/Sep	A		5,500	6,000	6,125	6,320	6,325	4.2%
6. India	Oct/Sep	R	A	4,375	4,825	5,035	5,230	5,250	3.5%
7. Honduras	Oct/Sep	A		3,225	3,550	3,975	5,600	4,600	3.1%
8. Mexico	Oct/Sep	A		4,550	4,150	4,000	4,300	4,300	2.9%
9. Peru	Apr/Mar	A		4,000	3,300	4,100	5,200	4,300	2.9%
10. Guatemala	Oct/Sep	A	R	3,980	4,010	3,960	4,410	4,210	2.8%
Others	–	–		21,665	20,756	21,487	21,583	21,176	14.1%
Total Supply				136,239	128,491	140,447	143,798	150,711	

(*Continued*)

259

TABLE 10.21 Continued

Coffee (000 bags)	Primary Crop	Secondary Crop	2008–09	2009–10	2010–11	2011–12	June 2012–13	
Consumption								
1. EU-27			39,575	49,505	41,730	45,730	44,250	31.4%
2. United States			22,650	22,060	22,888	23,405	22,798	16.2%
3. Brazil			18,030	18,760	19,420	20,025	20,615	14.7%
4. Japan			6,915	6,780	6,860	6,965	7,340	5.2%
5. Russia			3,190	3,805	4,190	3,700	4,350	3.1%
6. Canada			2,865	3,170	3,375	3,390	3,550	2.5%
7. Ethiopia			2,500	2,800	2,860	3,050	3,055	2.2%
Other			28,894	30,302	32,260	35,302	34,757	24.7%
Total Demand			124,619	137,182	133,583	141,567	140,715	
Balance (Supply – Demand)			11,620	–8,691	6,864	2,231	9,996	

Note: A = arabica and R = robusta. 1 bag = 60 kilograms
Source: USDA Table 3 Coffee Production and Table 4 Coffee Consumption and Coffee: World Markets and Trade.

TABLE 10.22 Global Top 10 Coffee Exporters and Importers

Coffee (000 bags)

	2012–2013						
	Exporters				Importers		
1.	Brazil	27,465	*27.1%*	1.	EU-27	45,000	*46.0%*
2.	Vietnam	23,200	*22.9%*	2.	United States	22,400	*22.9%*
3.	Colombia	7,700	*7.6%*	3.	Japan	7,000	*7.1%*
4.	Indonesia	6,900	*6.8%*	4.	Canada	2,400	*2.5%*
5.	Honduras	4,400	*4.3%*	5.	Algeria	2,300	*2.3%*
6.	Peru	4,100	*4.0%*	6.	Switzerland	2,275	*2.3%*
7.	Guatemala	3,800	*3.7%*	7.	Russia	2,000	*2.0%*
8.	India	3,750	*3.7%*	8.	Korea	1,650	*1.7%*
9.	Ethiopia	3,280	*3.2%*	9.	Malaysia	1,400	*1.4%*
10.	Uganda	3,200	*3.2%*	10.	Ecuador	1,350	*1.4%*
	Other	13,641	*13.4%*		Other	10,155	*10.4%*
	Total	101,436			Total	97,930	
	Balance (Supply – Demand)					3,506	

Note: A = arabica and R = robusta. 1 bag = 60 kilograms
Sources: USDA, ICE, International Coffee Organization, USDA Table 3 Coffee Production and Table 4 Coffee Consumption and Coffee: World Markets and Trade.

proper standards to protect poorer workers. It is also considered the most respected source for coffee data, alongside the USDA.

The United States and the European Union make up almost half of all demand for coffee, while Brazil, Vietnam, and Colombia make up almost 60 percent of the export market (see Table 10.22). Brazil and Colombia are the largest producers of arabica and more than 70 percent of Brazil's coffee is arabica. Vietnam also started growing significantly more amounts of coffee in the late 1990s, which caused the price to fall dramatically. It is now the second largest exporter. Coffee prices experience high volatility due to various factors. One of the biggest causes is weather. For instance, La Nina,

FIGURE 10.37   Coffee Front Contract Historical Price Chart

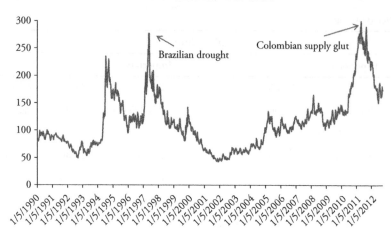

Source: Bloomberg.

cold weather in Brazil, or changes in weather conditions can adversely affect the price of coffee (see Figure 10.37).

During the blooming stage, water is critical for coffee, and often determines the forecasts for production. The harvest period is when coffee becomes available (see Figure 10.38).

Many coffee trees have a two-year planting cycle, meaning that one year the crop will have a strong yield and the second year will be a lighter crop. This causes a fluctuation in the supply of coffee (see Figure 10.39), though this fluctuation is forecasted and growers are trying to even the crop out. To complicate matters further, a coffee tree's life cycle is around 20 years, so growers are not quite certain how long the tree will be able to yield coffee. To combat this, growers are spreading high and low-yield crops more efficiently, but it will take several years for this to smooth out.

There are two types of coffees and several markets that trade coffee. The most liquid is traded on the ICE (KC), and is quoted in cents per pound of arabica. One contract is equivalent to 37,500 pounds. So if the price of arabica coffee is 150 ($1.50), then the notional is $56,250 ($1.5 × 37,500 lbs). Ironically enough, the industry standard is to measure coffee in bags of 60 kilograms, or roughly 132 pounds. Traders not only play the underlying commodity of coffee but they also play the spreads of the LIFFE Robusta contract (DFA Comdty CT), so the arabica/robusta spread and/or the spread of the BMF Arabica (AXA Comdty CT), which is a spread on arabica coffee.

FIGURE 10.38 Coffee Crop Calendar

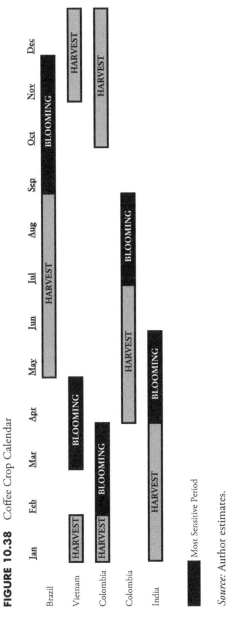

Source: Author estimates.

FIGURE 10.39   Coffee Crop: High- and Low-Yielding Years

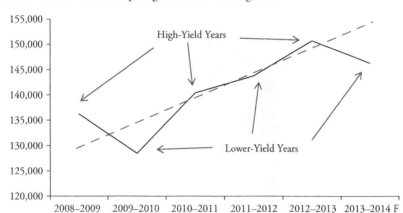

Source: USDA Coffee World Markets and Trade 2013.

Bloomberg Shortcuts

Oil Markets

> **OIL <Go>** Oil Markets Menu
> **CRUD <Go>** Crude Oil Price Monitors Menu
> **CRKS <Go>** Crack Spreads by Region
> **REFO <Go>** Refinery Outage Coverage
> **PVMO <Go>** OTC Broking of Swaps, Forwards, Crude Oil, and Refined Products
> **CLOP <Go>** Crude Oil Swaps Prices

Natural Gas Markets

> **NATG <Go>** Natural Gas Menu
> **NGAS <Go>** Natural Gas Fundamentals
> **ICE <Go>** Intercontinental Exchange Spot Indices
> **EGAS <Go>** Monitor European Natural Gas Prices
> **LNG <Go>** Liquefied Natural Gas Menu
> **BTU <Go>** Compare Global Thermal Values
> **BURN <Go>** Determine Natural Gas Demand

Metals Monitors

MINE <Go> Main Bloomberg Metals Menu
METL <Go> Metal Markets
MB <Go> Base Metals Pricing
MTL <Go> Gold, Silver, and Platinum Metals
CFVL <Go> Bloomberg Fair Values
LME <Go> London Metals Exchange
LMEI <Go> Display London Metal Exchange Warehouse Stocks Menu
USME <Go> USA Base Metal Spot Prices
CHIS <Go> China Metals Prices
RARE <Go> Steelhome Rare Earth Prices
COMX <Go> View Comex Metal Warehouse Inventories
MMST <Go> View Metals and Mining Statistics

Agriculture

CCAL <Go> Global Crop Calendar Analysis
GRCC <Go> U.S. Grain Cash and Carry Analysis
GRPM <Go> Gross Planting Margin Calculator
WETR <Go> Global Weather Platform
BWS <Go> Commodities Weather Forecasts
USDM <Go> U.S. Drought Monitor
YELD <Go> Crop Production Yield Estimates
AGSD <Go> Agriculture Supply and Demand Data
AGRI <Go> Calendar of Leading Agriculture Events
CRPM <Go> Agriculture Marketplace Trade Info
YTOP <Go> Top Agriculture News
BSHIP <Go> Shipping Markets Menu
WEAD <Go> Global Weather Data

Other

CTM <Go> Contract Table Menu
NRGF <Go> Access a Menu of Energy Futures Monitors
N <Go> Energy Industry Reports
SWPP <Go> Access a Menu of Swaps Markets Functions
CRCK <Go> Monitor Monthly Crack Spreads
CFTC <Go> Commitments of Traders Reports (COT)
NRGS <Go> Calculate Strip Prices

CRR <Go> Commodity Ranked Returns
CMBQ <Go> Commodity Composite Quote
CFVL <Go> Commodity Fair Value Curves
ENST <Go> Search International Energy Statistics
DOE <Go> U.S. DOE Statistics
APIS <Go> American Petroleum Institute Statistics
ECO10 <Go> Economic Releases for Energy/Commodities
ECO17 <Go> Metals Calendar and Release Data
OPEC <Go> OPEC Coverage Menu
CMDX <Go> Commodity Prices and Data by Country

Contract Analysis

CT <Go> Futures Spreads and Strategies
GP <Go> Price Graphs and Events
EXS <Go> Stock Futures Expiration Dates
COT <Go> CFTC and ICE COT Reports
CARC <Go> Regional Arbitrage and COC Analysis
CCRV <Go> Forward Curve Analysis
SEAG <Go> Seasonality and Spread Analysis
CTM <Go> Exchanges by Product and Region
SECF <Go> Security and Contract Search

Analytics

VCA <Go> Volatility and Correlation Analysis
UNTC <Go> Commodity Unit and Currency Converter
CCRV <Go> Analyze Futures and OTC Forward Curves
CMSP <Go> Create Crack, Spark, Crush, and Frac Spreads
WETR <Go> Global Weather Data Platform
CARC <Go> Commodity Arbitrage Calculator
BMAP <Go> Interactive Weather Platform
STRM <Go> Storm Impact Analysis

Comparative Return

CRR <Go> View Commodity Ranked Returns
CRB <Go> View CRB Commodity Movers
GSCC <Go> View Goldman Sachs Commodity Movers
DAIG <Go> View Dow Jones/AIG Commodity Movers

Summary

The goal of this chapter is to provide the reader with a broad introduction to commodities and the subcategories of energy, precious metals, industrial metals, and agriculture. Commodity prices, in their most basic form, are a function of supply and demand, so any change in either side of the equation can cause a change in price. By understanding the background of each type of commodity, as well as the supply and demand dynamics, a global macro trader has a better chance at success in trading this product group.

CHAPTER 11

The Role of Central Banks in Global Macro

A central bank is defined by the Federal Reserve Bank of Cleveland as:

> [T]he authority responsible for policies that affect a country's supply of money and credit. More specifically, a central bank uses its tools of monetary policy which include changing interest rates, open market operations, discount window lending, changes in reserve requirements—to affect short-term interest rates and the monetary base (currency held by the public plus bank reserves) and to achieve important policy goals.[1]

Central banks are referred to as both reserve bank and monetary authority, among other names.

This chapter outlines the key roles and activities of central banks, to help you better understand how they can signal traders and provide recent context to certain policies following the financial crisis.

Monetary Policy Goals

Modern-day monetary policy has several goals. The first and single-most important is price stability, also known as *inflation*. Most central banks release an inflation target and attempt to stay as close to that target or target range as possible. Another goal of a central bank like the U.S. Federal Reserve is

---

[1] Michael D. Bordo, "A Brief History of Central Banks," Federal Reserve Bank of Cleveland, December 1, 2007, www.clevelandfed.org/research/commentary/2007/12.cfm.

to keep unemployment levels low. Central banks want to ensure that business cycles run as smoothly as possible to maintain economic stability while achieving their inflation targets.

Following are the official statements from the major central banks.

U.S. Federal Reserve

The Board of Governors of the Federal Reserve System and the Federal Open Market Committee shall maintain long run growth of the monetary and credit aggregates commensurate with the economy's long run potential to increase production, so as to promote effectively the goals of maximum employment, stable prices, and moderate long-term interest rates.[2]

European Central Bank

The primary objective of the ECB's monetary policy is to maintain price stability. The ECB aims at inflation rates of below, but close to, 2 percent over the medium term.[3]

Bank of England

The Bank of England exists to ensure monetary stability and to contribute to financial stability. Monetary stability means stable prices and confidence in the currency. Stable prices are defined by the Government's inflation target. Financial stability entails detecting and reducing threats to the financial system as a whole.[4]

Swiss National Bank

The mandate is explained in detail in the National Bank Act (art. 5 para. 1 NBA), which requires the SNB to ensure price stability and, in so doing, to take due account of economic developments. The SNB is thus charged with resolving in the best general interests any conflicts arising between the objective of price stability and business cycle considerations, giving priority to price stability. The requirement to act in the interests of

---

[2] "Federal Reserve Act," Federal Reserve, updated May 23, 2013, www.federalreserve.gov/aboutthefed/section2a.htm.

[3] "Monetary Policy," European Central Bank, www.ecb.int/mopo/html/index.en.html.

[4] "Core Purposes," Bank of England, www.bankofengland.co.uk/about/Pages/corepurposes/default.aspx.

the country as a whole also means that the National Bank must gear its policy to the needs of the entire Swiss economy rather than the interests of individual regions or industries.[5]

Tools Used by Central Banks

Central banks use various different tools to monitor and maintain price stability. Additionally, they control the cost of marginal liquidity in a liquidity constrained system. This section covers a number of tools that central banks find useful.

Reserve Ratio

The reserve requirement, or reserve ratio, is the amount of reserves the central bank makes mandatory in customer deposits that each bank must hold as capital. The reserve ratio is very closely related to monetary policy, and at times, the two are even interchangeable. For example, raising the reserve requirement forces banks to keep more money aside rather than lending it out, which decreases the money supply. In the United States, the reserve ratio is 10 percent, while in China, the reserve requirement ratio is changed frequently as a monetary policy tool to control the money supply and, in turn, inflation. The term *money multiplier* is often used in economics to describe the relationship that the reserve ratio has on the money supply. It is often defined as 1/Reserve Ratio. The idea is that each dollar that is lent then gets spent somewhere else, and then spent again, keeping the cycle going. Base money enables banks to lend. With the United States reserve ratio of 10 percent, for each $1, the money multiplier is 10.

Interest Rate

Monetary policy is set by changing the overnight rate at which banks lend and borrow reserves to meet reserve requirements. Each country has its own respective rates that can be changed by the central bank. Central banks will increase the target rate in order to combat an overheating economy and inflationary regimes. Conversely, central banks lower interest rates in attempts to become more pro-growth and inflationary. Most of the time, changing the target rate is the single strongest action that a central bank can take.

---

[5] "Monetary Policy Strategy," Swiss National Bank, www.snb.ch/en/iabout/monpol/id/monpol_strat.

Open Market Operations

Open market operations are another policy tool central banks use to affect the money supply and, in turn, inflation. Open market operations refers to the process of buying or selling, usually government bonds in local currency. Buying domestic bonds increases bank reserves (see Figure 11.1), which then increases the bank's reserve account at the Fed. The bank can then lend the excess reserves. Selling bonds has the opposite effect and decreases the money supply since it reduces excess reserves.

Repurchase agreements, or "repos" for short, are similar to open market operations, but are shorter-term. Repos are agreements in which the bank agrees to repurchase securities purchased by the Fed within a specified amount of time. The Fed defines repos as follows:

> The Fed uses repurchase agreements, also called "RPs" or "repos" to make collateralized loans to primary dealers. In a reverse repo, or "RRP," the Fed borrows money from primary dealers. The typical term of these operations is overnight, but the Fed can conduct these operations with terms out to 65 business days. The Fed uses these two types of transactions to offset temporary swings in bank reserves; a repo temporarily adds reserve balances to the

FIGURE 11.1 Example of Balance Sheet Transactions between Bank and Fed

Original

Bank

Assets		Liabilities	
Securities	$1,000	X	

Fed Buying OMO

Bank

Assets		Liabilities	
Securities	$0	X	
Reserves	+$1,000		

Fed

Assets		Liabilities	
Securities	+$1,000	Reserves	+$1,000

[6]"Repurchase and Reverse Repurchase Transactions," Federal Reserve Bank of New York, August 2007, www.newyorkfed.org/aboutthefed/fedpoint/fed04.html.

banking system, while reverse repos temporarily drain balances from the system. Repos are the most common form of temporary open market operation.[6]

The discount window allows banks to borrow money directly from the central bank. When a bank cannot access capital in the money markets through unsecured borrowing, it borrows from the central banks at the discount rate. This usually has a negative stigma, but during the 2008 financial crisis, many banks jointly used the discount window for liquidity to ameliorate the stigma.

Currency Intervention

Currency intervention is also a policy tool used by many central banks. It entails a central bank buying or selling its own currency with the intent to affect the exchange rate. Currency intervention by central banks is a way to control inflation and demand for imports and exports, and establish exchange-rate stability. There are two methods through which a central bank can intervene in its currency: sterilized and unsterilized intervention. The Monetary Authority of Singapore, for example, uses currency intervention as its main monetary policy tool by maintaining a basket of currencies as reserves against the Singapore dollar.

Sterilized Intervention

Sterilized intervention involves the act of buying and selling a country's currency via foreign exchange reserves. If a country wanted to strengthen its currency, it would sell the foreign currencies it has on reserve and buy its own currency. Further, the central bank engages in open market operations to offset the change in the monetary base. For instance, if a country sold foreign currencies and bought its own currency by selling foreign currency reserves, its monetary base would increase and, to offset this increase, the central bank would need to sell securities in open market operations. The United Kingdom attempted this policy while it was in the exchange rate mechanism (ERM) and it caused the eventual collapse of the pound and exit from the ERM, which is covered in more detail later in this chapter. When a country wants to weaken its currency, it should take the reverse action, selling its own currency and accumulating other currencies.

Sterilized intervention is a methodology that China uses by setting its exchange rate and selling renminbi to buy dollars. The objective is to keep the currency artificially low in order to induce countries like the United States to continue to buy cheap Chinese goods. To offset the loss in the monetary base, the People's Bank of China (PBoC) issues liabilities and uses its reserve ratio to control the monetary base. When Chinese exporters get paid in dollars, they in turn exchange dollars for renminbi at a local bank. The local bank then deposits the dollars at the PBoC in exchange for renminbi. Once the local bank gets renminbi, it immediately causes the monetary base to increase. This is offset by the PBoC issuing an equivalent amount of T-Bills or other debt securities, which the local bank purchases, which results in no change in the monetary base. This policy has also been one of the biggest contributors to China's building of foreign reserves and holding of U.S. debt.

Unsterilized

Unsterilized intervention allows for changes in the monetary base. If the monetary base increases, then the supply of money increases, which in turn causes a decrease in short-term domestic interest rates and, ultimately, more inflation. The combination of lower interest rates and inflation would cause the value of the currency to eventually depreciate. This is a more passive approach to currency intervention. However, it is also a frequently used tool.

Taylor Rule

As a result of high unemployment and inflation in the 1970s, President Jimmy Carter signed into law the Full Employment and Balanced Growth Act, better known as the Humphrey-Hawkins Law. The objective of the law was to pursue, "maximum employment, production, and purchasing power." Additionally, the law sought to minimize inflation and reach for full employment. Upon the advent of this new law, using a new technique for central banking would prove useful for future decision making.

Stanford economist John Taylor proposed the Taylor Rule in 1992 as a tool for central banks to gauge appropriate monetary policy. The rule was designed to help banks like the Federal Reserve set short-term interest rates in the face of changing economic conditions in order to help work toward goals of both stabilizing the economy and eventual inflation. The Federal Reserve Bank of Kansas City defines the Taylor rule as follows:

> Specifically, the rule states that the "real" short-term interest rate (that is, the interest rate adjusted for inflation) should be determined according to three factors: (1) where actual inflation is relative to the targeted level that the Fed wishes to achieve, (2) how far economic activity is above or below its "full employment" level, and (3) what the level of the short-term interest rate is that would be consistent with full employment. The rule "recommends" a

relatively high interest rate (that is, a "tight" monetary policy) when inflation is above its target or when the economy is above its full employment level, and a relatively low interest rate ("easy" monetary policy) in the opposite situations. Sometimes these goals are in conflict: for example, inflation may be above its target when the economy is below full employment. In such situations, the rule provides guidance to policy makers on how to balance these competing considerations in setting an appropriate level for the interest rate.[7]

This could be summed up by the following formula:

Nominal Interest Rates = Inflation + Real Interest Rate + ½ (Actual Inflation − Inflation Target) + ½ (Logarithm of Output − Potential Output)

or

$$r = p + \left(\frac{1}{2y}\right) + \frac{1}{2} \times (p - 2) + 2$$

Forecasting the Taylor Rule can prove quite challenging. The idea is to estimate inflation with the market forecast of one-year CPI. Estimating the output can be done by looking at industrial production today and the last five years of change (growth) and then forecasting one year out against the expectations. In the United States, nominal rates can be compared again Fed fund futures.

The Impossible Trinity

The impossible trinity (see Figure 11.2) is derived from Nobel Prize–winning economist Robert Mundell's work. The impossible trinity is the concept that central banks have the constraints of only being able to have two of the following choices, but not all three.

Three Objectives/Choices

1. Fixed Exchange Rate
2. Free Capital Flows
3. Independent Monetary Policy

---

[7] Pier Francesco Asso, George A. Kahn, and Robert Leeson, "The Taylor Rule and the Transformation of Monetary Policy," The Federal Reserve Bank of Kansas City, December 2007. www.kc.frb.org/Publicat/RESWKPAP/PDF/RWP07-11.pdf.

FIGURE 11.2   Impossible Trinity

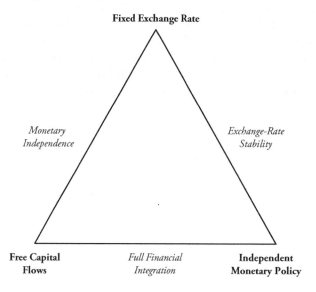

By selecting two of the three, a country, according to economist Jeffrey Frankel, who expanded on Mundell's work, finds itself in monetary independence, full financial integration, or exchange-rate stability.

Monetary Base

On the central bank's balance sheet, the sum of its monetary liabilities, currency in circulation, plus reserves is the monetary base, expressed as follows:

$$MB = C + R$$

The monetary base is also known as "high-powered money," which can only be controlled by the central banks via open market operations.

Money Supply

The money supply is defined as the amount of money available in a particular country at any specific point. Changes in the supply are used as one of the best predictors of change in GDP, growth, and inflation. The Quantity Theory of Money is a common equation used to show the effects of change in the money supply. It provides an explanation as to why both GDP and inflation change with money supply.

Where M = Money in circulation, V = Velocity of money, P = Average price, and Q = Quantity of goods and services sold

As the M × V increases, P × Q rises proportionally.

$$M \times V = P \times Q$$

By monitoring changes in the velocity of M1, M2, and M3 (defined in Table 11.1) one can get a sense of the money supply and better predict growth. The conundrum is that the higher the money supply, the higher the growth and inflation, and the lower the money supply the lower the growth and inflation. Historically, M2 tends to be a reliable predictor of nominal GDP growth with variable lags.

Reserves

The IMF defines reserve assets as external assets that are readily available to, and controlled by, monetary authorities for direct financing of payments imbalances, indirectly regulating the magnitude of such imbalances through intervention in exchange markets to affect the currency exchange rate, and/or

TABLE 11.1 Types of Money

M1	Currency (and traveler's checks)
	Demand deposits
	NOW and similar interest-earning checking accounts
M2	M1
	Savings deposits and money market deposit accounts
	Small time deposits*
	Retail money market mutual fund balances**
M3	M2
	Large time deposits
	Institutional money market mutual fund balances
	Repurchase agreements
	Eurodollars

*Time deposits in amounts of less than $100,000, excluding balances in IRA and Keogh accounts at depository institutions.
**Excludes balances held in IRA and Keogh accounts with money market mutual funds.
Source: Federal Reserve, www.federalreserve.gov/pf/pdf/pf_2.pdf.

for other purposes. The category of reserve assets is composed of monetary gold, SDRs, foreign exchange assets, and other claims. In 2012, the U.S. dollar accounted for 62 percent of total reserves.

An advantage of accumulating reserves is that it is a way for a country to acquire wealth. Additionally, large amounts of currency reserves allow a central bank to manipulate its currency via sterilized interventions, and to promote stability, as is the case with China. The largest disadvantage of holding large foreign reserves is that inflation erodes purchasing power. In effect, if a central bank were to just hold the reserves, they would be losing money every year. Since the U.S. dollar is the global reserve currency, it indirectly forces countries like China and Japan to buy U.S. Treasuries. Recently, depending on what part of the curve one is observing, yields on U.S. Treasuries are less than expected inflation, which means that the real yield is negative and holders of U.S. debt will see a reduction in purchasing power. It is also worthwhile to examine the cost of sterilization against the erosion of purchasing power to understand the real opportunity cost.

Asian countries by far have the biggest piece of the pie in reserves, accounting for greater than 50 percent of total reserves (see Figure 11.3). This has come under intense scrutiny, especially as it relates to U.S.-China relations, where China has almost 30 percent of global reserves alone. By fixing the Chinese renminbi, the Chinese make their goods artificially much cheaper than they would be under a free-floating currency regime. This in turn helps them build the largest reserves of any country by three times. One of the other interesting facts about Asian countries and reserves is that gold accounts for a small percentage of reserves relative to their Western counterparts.

FIGURE 11.3   2011 Top 10 Countries by Total Reserves ($ in billions)

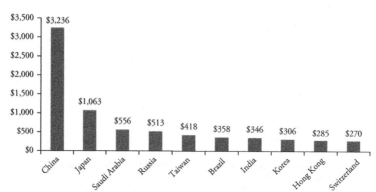

Sources: CIA Factbook, IMF, and Bloomberg.

Zero Lower Bound and the Liquidity Trap

The zero lower bound refers to the central bank rate that is at or near zero. Presently, the Fed, ECB, BOE, BOJ, and SNB are in or near this territory. Zero lower bound, or ZLB, typically implies low levels of growth and the danger of entering a liquidity trap. A liquidity trap is where a central bank infuses large amounts of excess reserves into the banking system and yet has no effect on institutions saving money as opposed to lending it out or investing it in securities. The reason a liquidity trap is so dangerous is that it typically implies a deflationary environment. Imagine a world where the view for economic growth is negative, such that no matter how much capital is invested, people do not want to invest and, because deflation is likely—even with 0 percent rates—earning nothing on money in a deflationary environment is still increasing purchasing power. The Fed is fully aware of this and is afraid of its implications. As a result, by performing quantitative easing (QE) and flattening the yield curve, the Fed indirectly aims to avoid a liquidity trap. Effectively, the Fed has conceded the fact that we are at ZLB, and if one is going to play it safe and hold cash, the Fed will incentivize people to invest by effectively inflating their money away, which is something many refer to as financial repression. If short-term real yields are negative, the Fed will do anything it can to avoid this in the United States and not allow the United States to fall into the same trap as Japan and experience years of deflation. Central banks no longer control the price of liquidity in a liquidity-constrained environment; rather excess liquidity is renumerated at a deposit rate at the respective central bank, creating an interest rate floor.

Quantitative Easing

Quantitative easing is a process by which central banks purchase financial assets, such as domestic government debt, and then create electronic reserves in order to increase the money supply. Quantitative easing works as an open market operation in that the central bank buys securities and holds them. QE has become common in the United States and United Kingdom since the financial crisis and it is used as a policy tool. If central bank rates are near the zero bound, they use it as a stimulant to the economy. The Fed first announced QE on November 25, 2008 (see Table 11.2), and the United Kingdom first announced QE on March 5, 2009 (see Table 11.3). One of the biggest criticisms of QE, which the Fed rejects, is that QE is debt monetization and money-printing. The Fed claims that electronic reserves

TABLE 11.2 Fed Quantitative Easing Program and Operation Twist

Date	Amount	Amount	Total
November 25, 2008	QE 1	$500 billion	$500 billion
March 18, 2009	QE 1 Expanded	$750 billion	$1.25 trillion
March 31, 2010	QE 1 Ends	—	$1.25 trillion
August 27, 2010	QE 2 Indication (Jackson Hole)	—	$1.25 trillion
November 3, 2010	QE 2	$600 billion	$1.85 trillion
June 30, 2011	QE 2 Ends	—	$1.85 trillion
September 21, 2011	Operation Twist 1	$400 billion	$1.85 trillion
June 30, 2012	Operation Twist 1 Ends	—	$1.85 trillion
June 20, 2012	Operation Twist 2	$267 billion	$1.85 trillion
December 31, 2012	Operation Twist 2 Ends	—	$1.85 trillion
September 13, 2012	QE 3	$40 billion MBS Monthly/$45 billion Treasuries Monthly	Open
December 12, 2013	QE 3	$45 billion Treasuries Monthly	Open

Source: Federal Reserve. As of September 2013.

TABLE 11.3 Bank of England Quantitative Easing Program

Date	Amount	Total
March 5, 2009	£75 billion	£75 billion
May 7, 2009	£50 billion	£125 billion
August 6, 2009	£50 billion	£175 billion
November 5, 2009	£25 billion	£200 billion
October 6, 2011	£75 billion	£275 billion
February 9, 2012	£50 billion	£325 billion
July 5, 2012	£50 billion	£375 billion

Source: Bank of England. As of September 2013.

do not qualify as money-printing. While this assertion is technically true because they are technically not printing money on a press, it does increase the money supply to new levels that are not physically backed by anything. In Ben Bernanke's paper, "Deflation: Making Sure It Does Not Happen Here," he analyzes how mistakes from the past have gotten Japan and other countries into a deflationary spiral. He effectively provides a roadmap of what he has done during the crisis, and he will always increase the supply at all costs to ensure inflation instead of deflation.

The original Operation Twist began in 1961 when the Fed sold shorter-term debt to purchase longer-term debt in order to flatten the yield curve. It is worth noting that this policy doesn't necessarily expand base money. Since then, the Fed has on two occasions announced that it would sell maturities of three years or less to purchase maturities of 6 to 30 years. The first Operation Twist was announced on September 21, 2011, and averaged $45 billion worth of securities per month. This extends the Fed's duration of its fixed income portfolio and flattens the yield curve. One could argue that this does not help the American people because when the yield curve is flattened it makes it harder for banks to make a profit and creates a need for a larger credit spread on longer-term loans.

The effectiveness of QE is diminishing. A recent study by the San Francisco Fed has demonstrated that in the time since QE1, both QE2 and Operation Twist (the Fed calls Operation Twist the maturity extension program, or MEP), each program has had consistently lowered effects (see Table 11.4). It's likely that two factors are contributing to this, the first being that the yield on 10-year Treasuries is substantially lower than in 2008,

TABLE 11.4 Effects of Past Large-Scale Asset Purchases on Interest Rates

	10-Year Treasury Yield	BBB Corp. Yield	30-Year MBS Yield
QE1	−1.00	−0.89	−0.93
QE2	−0.14	−0.13	−0.14
MEP	−0.08	−0.03	−0.25

Note: Cumulative change of key interest rates in percentage points over the announcement days of the three past Large Scale Asset Purchase (LSAP) programs.
QE1: 11/25/2008, 12/1/2008, 12/16/2008, 1/28/2009, 3/18/2009.
QE2: 8/10/2010, 9/21/2010, 11/3/2010.
MEP: 9/21/2011.
Source: Michael Bauer, "Fed Asset Buying and Private Borrowing Rates" (San Francisco Fed, May 21, 2012).

and the second being that the market is already pricing in QE and more Operation Twist programs. So, while the Fed does use this in its toolkit, the efficacy is significantly lower.

The statement the FOMC released on September 13, 2012, announcing QE3 was powerful on many fronts. While some may have expected U.S. government fixed income purchases in addition to the $40 billion per month in MBS purchases, the Fed communicated its intentions very clearly. It said that if the labor market did not improve substantially, it would "undertake additional asset purchases." It also mentioned that "a highly accommodative monetary policy will remain appropriate for a considerable time after the economic recovery strengthens." While many might criticize this move, the Fed is attempting to communicate its intentions to the market. If the economy improves, the Fed doesn't want people to believe the punch bowl will be taken away too early and cause a selloff that might bring us back to a difficult period. Additionally, rather than blatantly announce an open-ended QE, the FOMC signals that as the economy worsens, they will make additional asset purchases.

Interpreting Central Bank Communication

Statements

Following central bank statements is perhaps one of the most critical foundations one can have in global macro trading. Simply put, the statements are a foundation that one can use to understand the mindset of each central bank. It gives the global macro trader a perspective on how each central bank views its own economy, the global economy, and other factors that could affect monetary policy.

Since the United States is the most significant economy in the world, many people view Federal Reserve Bank statements as a key indicator. The Fed gives projections and insights as to what it believes is going on in the economy. As discussed above with hawkish and dovish policies, oftentimes the market perceives the Fed's statements to be loose policy or a tightening policy. In fact, you will see that oftentimes when the Federal Reserve Bank statement is released, markets typically move right after the release. This demonstrates the power of central bank statements. If a central bank changes its language on its expectation on inflation or potential rate paths (hikes or cuts), this can have a significant impact on the price of the local currency, fixed income, and equities.

Hawks and Doves

Central banks like the Federal Reserve Bank or the Bank of England have several central bankers who vote to affect policy. The central bankers each have their own particular methods that shape the way they view the world. For instance, the Bank of England has nine central bankers who determine the monetary policy rate for England. Each central banker has his or her own bias, which many people who follow global macro trading refer to as "hawkish" or "dovish." Hawks are typically viewed as being very wary of inflation and having concern for the currency's value. Conversely, dovish central bankers are viewed as those who tend to favor higher growth with looser policy and do not worry as much about inflation.

In addition to knowing which central bankers are hawkish or dovish, it is also useful to know that central bank statements tend to have a hawkish or dovish tone. The most challenging part in determining whether a particular view is hawkish or dovish is that there is no definite answer, and oftentimes people interpret these particular sets of views differently, so that one person could view the reserve Bank of Australia statement as hawkish and another could view it as dovish.

Even though the case is still open, it is important to be aware that this bias exists and that one should look for it in all central bank statements and policies. In addition to understanding hawks and doves in central bank statements, it is very useful to know whether the central bankers themselves are hawkish or dovish. When Adam Posen was a member of the Bank of England, he was extremely dovish, having made clear that he considered inflation protection to be a key goal. Because Posen was a dove, if he made dovish statements (such as advocating keeping central bank policy low for an extended period of time or saying that quantitative easing expansion is necessary), it would not be as significant as a hawk making the same kind of statements, which would catch the market completely by surprise. If a hawk made a statement that was viewed to be very dovish, it would likely have a very bearish impact on the pound sterling, while if Posen made the exact same statement, it would have little or no impact. It is always important to follow every central banker to know exactly what he or she is saying.

A great example in the United States is Federal Reserve Bank chairman Charles Evans from Chicago, who is seen as an ultra-dove. He has made many statements in favor of keeping the central bank policy rate at a very low rate for an extended period of time. Knowing this, if Evans made statements that were viewed to be dovish, this would come as no surprise. However, if Jeffrey Lacker, a hawk from the Richmond Fed, came out with the same dovish statements, it would be a big deal because Lacker typically defends the value of the currency.

Minutes

When a central bank has a meeting, the decision it releases is of the utmost importance. However, in situations when no decision is made, it would still be useful to know if the board members of a particular central bank were split or unanimously against it. The more insight one can gain on a central bank decision, the more clarity one has as to what potential actions might be taken in the future.

A great illustration is the Bank of England in the spring and summer of 2012. The United Kingdom had double dipped into recession and it was clear that more easing, likely in the form of QE, was on its way. The question wasn't if more QE would be done, but when it would be done. The Bank of England met on May 9 and 10, 2012, releasing their statement on Thursday, May 10. The statement read, "The Bank of England's Monetary Policy Committee today voted to maintain the official Bank Rate paid on commercial bank reserves at 0.5 percent. The Committee also voted to maintain the stock of asset purchases financed by the issuance of central bank reserves at £325 billion." It was impossible to know whether this was unanimous, or if there was dissent among members. The minutes for the May 9 and 10 meeting were released on May 23rd and read:

> The Governor invited the Committee to vote on the propositions that: Bank Rate should be maintained at 0.5%; The Bank of England should maintain the stock of asset purchases financed by the issuance of central bank reserves at £325 billion.[8]

Regarding bank rate, the committee voted unanimously in favor of the proposition.

> Regarding the stock of asset purchases, eight members of the Committee (the Governor, Charles Bean, Paul Tucker, Ben Broadbent, Spencer Dale, Paul Fisher, Adam Posen and Martin Weale) voted in favor of the proposition. One member of the Committee (David Miles) voted against, preferring to increase the size of the asset purchase programme by a further £25 billion to a total of £350 billion.[9]

---

[8] "Minutes of the Monetary Policy Committee Meeting 6 and 7 June 2012," Bank of England, www.bankofengland.co.uk/publications/minutes/Documents/mpc/pdf/2012/mpc1206.pdf.
[9] Ibid.

From the May minutes, one can gather that the bank rate will likely stay at 0.50 percent for quite some time, since the decision has been unanimous for quite some time (9-0). In regards to QE, which the BOE calls "asset purchases," the committee voted 8-1 to keep the program at a total of £325 billion, which means no additional QE.

Moving to the June 7, 2012, meeting, the Bank of England released the same headline as the May 10 release, "The Bank of England's Monetary Policy Committee today voted to maintain the official Bank Rate paid on commercial bank reserves at 0.5 percent. The Committee also voted to maintain the stock of asset purchases financed by the issuance of central bank reserves at £325 billion." Yet again, the same issue arose, where the breakdown of the committee's votes was unknown. It could be that the vote for additional QE remained at a total £325 billion, with an 8-1 vote, or it could be that others had changed their minds. The June minutes, which were released on June 20, 2012, were very telling.

The Governor invited the Committee to vote on the propositions that:[10]

- Bank Rate should be maintained at 0.5 percent.
- The Bank of England should maintain the stock of asset purchases financed by the issuance of central bank reserves at £325 billion.

Regarding bank rate, the committee voted unanimously in favor of the proposition.

> Regarding the stock of asset purchases, five members of the Committee (Charles Bean, Paul Tucker, Ben Broadbent, Spencer Dale, and Martin Weale) voted in favor of the proposition. Four members of the Committee voted against the proposition. The Governor, David Miles, and Adam Posen preferred to increase the size of the asset purchase programme by £50 billion to a total of £375 billion. Paul Fisher preferred to increase the size of the asset purchase programme by £25 billion to a total of £350 billion.[11]

Four members voted against the proposition of keeping the asset purchases at £325 billion, meaning that they support additional QE. The minutes from the June meeting clearly show a drastic shift in the committee, having a vote 5-4 against additional QE when just one month prior, they voted 8-1 against additional QE. The results of these minutes show that the

---

[10] "Minutes of the Monetary Policy Committee Meeting 6 and 7 June 2012," Bank of England.
[11] Ibid.

BOE is likely to do QE in the next meeting or two, and markets will react accordingly the instant these new minutes were released. Sure enough, at the July meeting, the committee voted 7-2 for more QE and increased the asset purchases by £50 billion for a total of £375 billion.

The Governor invited the Committee to vote on the propositions that:[12]

- Bank Rate should be maintained at 0.5 percent.
- The Bank of England should finance a further £50 billion of asset purchases by the issuance of central bank reserves, implying a total quantity of £375 billion of such purchases.
- Regarding Bank Rate, the Committee voted unanimously in favor of the proposition.
- Regarding the stock of asset purchases, seven members of the Committee (The Governor, Charles Bean, Paul Tucker, Paul Fisher, David Miles, Adam Posen and Martin Weale) voted in favor of the proposition. Spencer Dale and Ben Broadbent preferred to maintain the stock of asset purchases, financed by the issuance of central bank reserves, at £325 billion.

Another interesting point about minutes is that they reveal the hawkish and dovish tone of the central bankers. Notice how in the May minutes, David Miles was the only committee member to vote for additional QE; this information is very telling in that we can conclude he was in the Dovish camp. What is also telling is who voted against QE in the July minutes. Ben Broadbent was one of the newest members of the committee, and was one of two to vote against QE. This puts him in the hawkish camp and is very useful information because, given that Broadbent is relatively new, it wasn't clear which camp he was in. This vote reveals his tone towards hawkishness.

Central Banks

The objective of this section is to provide a brief history and background on the Fed, European Central Bank, Swiss National Bank, and Bank of England. Additionally, since the advent of the financial crisis, this section will detail many of the unprecedented measures taken by the Fed and ECB that can be used as a reference tool.

---

[12]"Minutes of the Monetary Policy Committee Meeting 4 and 5 July 2012," Bank of England, www.bankofengland.co.uk/publications/minutes/Documents/mpc/pdf/2012/ mpc1207.pdf.

The Federal Reserve

In the nineteenth century, the United States was reluctant to found a central bank in fear that states would lose sovereignty and the U.S. government would gain too much power. Since the United States gained independence in 1776, many citizens feared that centralization of any form could impede rights. The First Bank of the United States was founded in 1791 with a 20-year charter, which ran out in 1811. This was followed by the Second Bank of the United States, which closed in 1836 due to a veto for renewal by President Andrew Jackson.

The close of the Second Bank of the United States in 1836 left the United States vulnerable to bank runs and financial panics, since there was no lender of last resort. The Panic of 1907 occurred when the stock market fell precipitously, and there were major runs on banks, which burned depositors and led to the collapse of countless numbers of banks. It was agreed that having a central bank that could act as a lender of last resort was a necessity for stability and, as a result, the Federal Reserve Act of 1913, which replaced the National Bank Act of 1863 and 1864, created the Federal Reserve Bank, or the Fed, as we know it today. The Fed has a dual mandate, which is to have full employment and stable prices.

FOMC

When the Fed was created in 1913, one of the main goals was to limit its powers. This led to the creation of 12 district Federal Reserve banks. The Federal Open Market Committee (FOMC) was created to oversee the Fed's open market operations. The FOMC has seven governors and the president of the New York Fed. Of the remaining 11 presidents from the Federal Reserve Banks, four are on the FOMC on a rotating basis. The Board of Governors are appointed by the president and confirmed by the Senate for fourteen-year terms. The FOMC meets eight times a year to determine monetary policy on open market operations as well as the discount rate and reserve requirements. Four to five of the eight meetings are accompanied by Fed projections and a press conference with Ben Bernanke. The projections are a useful tool that macro traders can use to get a sense of what the Fed thinks GDP growth, inflation (core PCE), and unemployment will be. The projections also provide bands where the FOMC believe these outputs will be and offer a map of policy makers' projected rate moves. Following each FOMC meeting, the FOMC releases a statement on their summary view of the economy, which is released around 2:15 P.M. EST.

During the FOMC meeting, the beige, green, and blue books are distributed to the Board of Governors to help get a full handle on economic conditions. The beige book is a survey on financial conditions performed by the twelve FRBs in their respective districts to gauge the state of the economy. The beige book is the only one of the three books that is publicly released. The green book provides a forecast for the next three years, produced by each of the twelve Federal Reserve Banks. The blue book contains projections of the money supply. All of the books have a cover with the color of its name, so the green book for instance has a green cover, and this is where the nicknames originated from.

Federal Reserve Banks

The 12 Federal Reserve Banks oversee their respective regions (see Figure 11.4). The three largest FRB's are New York, San Francisco, and Richmond, which together account for almost three quarters of the total assets. The New York Fed is the largest, accounting for more than half of all assets, which is a by-product of the new asset purchase programs put in place after the financial crisis. FRBs are partially private and partially publicly owned; the government owns a part of each FRB and each bank in each district owns shares in the local FRB. Each district bank elects six directors and the Board of Governors appoints three; collectively, these nine directors appoint the president of their local FRB. The FRBs clear checks, issue currency, make loans to

FIGURE 11.4 The Twelve Federal Reserve Districts

Source: The Federal Reserve Board.

banks only through the discount window (unless you are in section 13(3)) in their district, and monitor local economic activity.[13]

The New York Fed

The New York Fed is a unique Federal Reserve Bank relative to the other 11 district banks. A number of factors make the New York Fed unique. First of all, the New York Fed is where all open market operations take place in the bond and foreign exchange market. Despite criticism of the Fed, the New York Fed publishes all of its operations, often ahead of time.

The second factor that makes the New York Fed unique is that it is the only Federal Reserve Bank with a permanent member of the FOMC and serves as the vice chairman of the committee. Thirdly, the New York Fed owns roughly half of all U.S. assets in the banking system and is the home to some of the largest banks in the United States.

Fourth, the president of the New York Fed, William Dudley, is automatically a member of the Bank for International Settlements (BIS) and has regular meetings with the BIS along with Ben Bernanke. Lastly, the New York Fed is the repository for large amounts of gold, holding even more than Fort Knox.

Fed Sources and Uses of Reserves

The Federal Reserve Sources and Uses of Reserves is released weekly in a form known as the H.4.1. In the H.4.1, as of November 1, 2007, before the financial crisis and the failure of Bear Stearns (on March 16, 2008 they signed a merger agreement with JP Morgan), the "Total Factors supplying reserve finds" were $921,341 (in millions). Now they total over $3,700,000 (in millions, as of September 26, 2013), which is a proxy for the Fed balance sheet and has quadrupled in size. To observe these effects and any additional add-ons to QE, it is very helpful to watch the change in U.S. Treasury securities. Over 95 percent of this change is a result of U.S. Treasury security and MBS purchases (Federal Agency and MBS were 0 precrisis).

European Central Bank

The Treaties of Rome led to the founding of the European Economic Community (EEC), which aimed to remove trade barriers, help integrate Europe and form a common market. The treaty was signed on March 25, 1957, by West Germany, France, the Netherlands, Italy, Belgium, and Luxembourg.

---

[13] Fed H-41.

While the Treaties of Rome did not establish the European Union as we know it today, it was the groundbreaking agreement that laid out the foundation.

After the United States left the gold standard following the Bretton Woods conference in August 1971, the European member states wanted a method to control currency fluctuations. In April 1972, the EEC created the "snake," which attempted to narrow the margins of fluctuations to ±2.25% between currencies, effectively creating a peg to one another.

In March 1979, the European Monetary System (EMS) was built on the concept of stable but adjustable exchange rates defined in relation to the newly created European Currency Unit (ECU)—a currency basket based on a weighted average of EMS currencies, which the "snake" did not have. The exchange rate mechanism (ERM) kept within ±2.25% band, with the exception of the Italian lira, the Spanish peseta, and the Portuguese escudo, which were allowed to fluctuate by ±6%.

Jacques Delors, then the president of the European Commission, recommended that the Economic and Monetary Union (EMU) be achieved in three "discrete but evolutionary steps," which were laid out in April 1989 in the Delors Report. The Delors Report led the European Commission to agree that the EMU should be achieved in three steps, or pillars (see Figure 11.5).

EU or Maastricht Treaty

The EU Treaty, which is commonly known as the Maastricht Treaty, established the European Union upon its signing on February 7, 1992. It laid out the foundations of the EMU and set out a method and timetable for the implementation and realization of the euro single currency (see Table 11.5). The Maastricht Treaty also established the European Central Bank (ECB), and specified that the ECB has the exclusive right to authorize the issue of euro banknotes. The European Union totals 27 countries, even ones that do not use the euro, like the United Kingdom, Sweden, and Denmark. Presently there are 17 countries in the euro area and on the euro: Germany, France, Italy, Spain, the Netherlands, Belgium, Finland, Ireland, Slovakia, Slovenia, Austria, Portugal, Greece, Luxembourg, Cyprus, Estonia, and Malta. The Eurosystem is composed of the ECB and the national central banks (NCBs) of the 10 countries not on the euro.

The ECB

The ECB was established in June 1998, taking over its predecessor, the European Monetary Institute (EMI). It is headquartered in Frankfurt,

FIGURE 11.5 EMU: Three Steps

Maastricht Treaty Signed in February 1992

- Established the European Union
- Led to the creation of a single European currency, the euro
- Implemented the 3-stage process for EMU to be achieved
  - Often referred to as "Pillar structure"

EMU Stage 1   July 1, 1990 –December 31, 1993

- Member states established the free movement of capital between their respective territories with closer coordination of economic policies and cooperation of their central banks

ECB June 1, 1998

- ECB (European Central Bank), replaces the EMI

EMU Stage 2   January 1, 1994 –December 31, 1998

- Created the EMI (European Monetary Institute)
  - Technical preparations for the creation of a single currency, the avoidance of excessive deficits, and enhanced convergence of the economic and monetary policies of the member states

EMU Stage 3   January 1, 1999 –Present

- The irrevocable fixing of exchange rates, the transfer of monetary policy to the ECB and the introduction of the euro as a single currency

Euro January 2002

- Euro banknotes and coins introduced

Source: European Central Bank and author.

TABLE 11.5 The Maastricht Convergence Criteria

What Is Measured	How It Is Measured	Convergence Criteria
Price stability	Harmonized consumer price inflation rate	Not more than 1.5 percentage points above the rate of the three best-performing member states
Sound public finances	Government deficit as % of GDP	Reference value: not more than 3%
Sustainable public finances	Government debt as % of GDP	Reference value: Not more than 60%
Durability of convergence	Long-term interest rate	Not more than 2 percentage points above the rate of the three best-performing member states in terms of price stability
Exchange rate stability	Deviation from a central rate	Participation in ERM for two years without severe tensions

Source: The Road to the Euro. European Commission, 2014.

Germany. The ECB typically announces its policy on the first Thursday of each month and the Governing Council usually meets twice a month to discuss. The ECB's Governing Council decides on monetary policy and the Executive Board implements policy. The ECB meets to develop one forecast, which is then presented to the Governing Council, unlike the Fed where each of the twelve FRBs have different forecasts, which are then presented to the FOMC. Price stability is defined by the ECB as a year-on-year increase in the Harmonized Index of Consumer Prices (HICP) for the euro area to be at or lower than 2 percent over the medium term.

The Governing Council of the ECB is the decision-making body and the determinant of monetary policy. It consists of two groups, the Executive Board and the NCBs of the 17 euro area countries. The Executive Board is composed of six people, including the president of the ECB, Mario Draghi, Vice President Vítor Constâncio, and four other rotating members. The Governing Council has a total of 23 members. The main refinancing operations (MRO) is the interest rate on marginal lending facility and the deposit rate is the interest rate on the deposit facility at the ECB. The MRO is a weekly OMO conducted by the Eurosystem. Effectively, it is the equivalent to the Fed funds rate and what the ECB targets, however the Fed performs overnight operations. The MRO and deposit rate create a corridor; pre-crisis the MRO was the main rate, while post-crisis the deposit rate is the main rate.

Capital Keys

The capital of the ECB comes from the national central banks (NCBs) of all EU Member States. It amounts to €10,760,652,402.58 (as of December 29, 2010). The NCBs' shares in this capital are calculated using a key, which reflects the respective country's share in the total population and gross domestic product of the EU. These two determinants have equal weighting. The ECB adjusts the shares every five years, and also whenever a new country joins the EU. The adjustment is made on the basis of data provided by the European Commission (see Table 11.6).

Longer-Term Refinancing Operations (LTROs)

Longer-term refinancing operations (LTROs) were initially set up by the ECB to "give a good opportunity for smaller banks which have limited or

TABLE 11.6 Euro Area NCBs' Contribution to the ECB's Capital

NCB	Capital Key %	Paid-Up Capital (€)
Nationale Bank van België/Banque Nationale de Belgique	2.4256	220,583,718.02
Deutsche Bundesbank	18.9373	1,722,155,360.77
Eesti Pank	0.1790	16,278,234.47
Central Bank of Ireland	1.1107	101,006,899.58
Bank of Greece	1.9649	178,687,725.72
Banco de España	8.3040	755,164,575.51
Banque de France	14.2212	1,293,273,899.48
Banca d'Italia	12.4966	1,136,439,021.48
Central Bank of Cyprus	0.1369	12,449,666.48
Banque centrale du Luxembourg	0.1747	15,887,193.09
Central Bank of Malta	0.0632	5,747,398.98
De Nederlandsche Bank	3.9882	362,686,339.12
Oesterreichische Nationalbank	1.9417	176,577,921.04
Banco de Portugal	1.7504	159,181,126.31
Banka Slovenije	0.3288	29,901,025.10
Národná banka Slovenska	0.6934	63,057,697.10
Suomen Pankki – Finlands Bank	1.2539	114,029,487.14
Total*	69.9705	6,363,107,289.36

*Due to rounding, the total may not correspond to the sum of all figures shown.
Source: European Central Bank.

no access to the interbank market to receive liquidity for a longer period." They had a three-month maturity, unlike the biweekly maturities of MROs. LTROs have changed drastically since then, becoming a policy tool that the ECB uses to combat the financial crisis and economic uncertainty in Europe. When European banks were under severe stress due to the worries in Portugal, Ireland, Italy, Greece, and Spain, the ECB announced on December 8, 2011, LTRO 1 and 2, which allowed European banks to post securities for three years with the ECB, providing liquidity to the European banking system.

LTRO 1 resulted in €529.5 billion and LTRO 2 was performed on February 29, 2012, totaling €489.2 billion. Many people perceive this as the European recipe for QE since it adds over €1 trillion into the banking system. However, the ECB dismisses this notion, since even though it is unlikely, the banks have the ability to get out of the three-year LTRO after one year. Internally at the ECB, they refer to these new LTROs as VL-LTRO (very long LTRO). This data can be retrieved on an ongoing basis on the ECB website under "History of all ECB open market operations." The LTRO was successful in that prior to the announcement and after LTRO I and II, the ECB managed to lower yields significantly in Italy and Spain and steepen the yield curve (see Figure 11.6).

European Debt Problem

While it is true that the 2008 financial crisis that originated in the United States significantly hurt Europe, the fact remains that Europe was on an unsustainable path, considering that several countries in Europe had debt/GDP exceeding 100 percent with a negative budget deficit and cur-rent account in violation of the Maastricht Treaty—even Germany (see Table 11.7). This coupled with the fact that many countries in Europe are still in recession means that they cannot outgrow their debt. If the growth in

FIGURE 11.6   Chart of Italian Sovereign Curve before LTRO Announcement after LTRO I and II

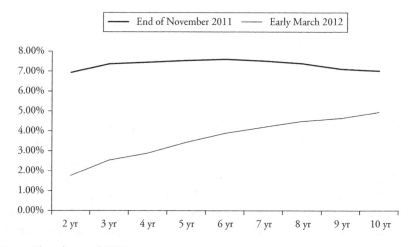

Source: Bloomberg and ECB.

TABLE 11.7 European Debt/GDP

	Gov't Debt ($ in Billions)			GDP			2012 Est Budget Surplus/Deficit	2012 Est Current Account	Gov't Debt/GDP %		
	2010	2011	2012	2010	2011	2012	% GDP	% GDP	2010	2011	2012
Euro Area*	$10,310	$11,428	$11,053	$12,073	$13,090	$12,200	-3.7%	1.4%	85%	87%	91%
Austria	$272	$302	$293	$377	$418	$400	-2.5%	1.6%	72%	72%	73%
Belgium	$472	$504	$482	$469	$514	$484	-4.0%	-2.0%	101%	98%	100%
Cyprus	$14	$18	$19	$23	$25	$23	-4.6%	-6.5%	61%	72%	84%
Estonia	$1	$1	$1	$19	$22	$22	-0.3%	-1.8%	7%	6%	6%
Finland	$114	$129	$133	$235	$263	$250	-1.8%	-1.8%	48%	49%	53%
France	$2,100	$2,393	$2,357	$2,548	$2,780	$2,613	-4.8%	-2.2%	82%	86%	90%
Germany	$2,739	$2,902	$2,784	$3,284	$3,601	$3,400	0.1%	7.0%	83%	81%	82%
Greece	$417	$479	$391	$292	$290	$249	-9.0%	-2.4%	143%	165%	157%
Ireland	$195	$239	$249	$206	$221	$210	-8.2%	4.4%	95%	108%	118%
Italy	$2,432	$2,633	$2,557	$2,042	$2,192	$2,013	-3.0%	-0.5%	119%	120%	127%

(Continued)

TABLE 11.7 *Continued*

	Gov't Debt ($ in Billions)			GDP			2012 Est Budget Surplus/ Deficit % GDP	2012 Est Current Account % GDP	Gov't Debt/GDP %		
	2010	2011	2012	2010	2011	2012			2010	2011	2012
Luxembourg	$10	$10	$11	$53	$59	$57	-1.1%	5.7%	20%	17%	19%
Malta	$6	$7	$6	$8	$9	$9	-3.3%	1.1%	69%	72%	72%
Netherlands	$486	$544	$549	$775	$836	$772	-4.1%	9.4%	63%	65%	71%
Portugal	$213	$256	$263	$227	$238	$212	-6.4%	-1.6%	94%	108%	124%
Slovakia	$36	$42	$48	$87	$96	$92	-4.5%	1.4%	41%	43%	52%
Slovenia	$18	$21	$24	$47	$50	$45	-3.8%	3.3%	39%	42%	53%
Spain	$829	$1,012	$1,135	$1,380	$1,477	$1,349	-10.6%	-1.1%	60%	69%	84%

*Includes 17 countries listed and may be subject to rounding error.
Sources: Bloomberg, Eurostat, CIA Factbook, OECD, IMF, and World Bank.

296

debt and interest expense is higher than the rate of growth, then over time, this presents a huge concern. Financial markets and banks simply stopped trusting the creditworthiness of many European sovereigns, which is also true of the CDS markets. This has led to capital flowing out of Europe and a decline in the euro. Additionally, there has been selling of periphery debt in exchange for buying bonds and German debt. The German two-year went negative in yield at one point, which means that people effectively stopped trusting their banks but felt that if the euro collapsed, Germany would back up their money, and if they didn't receive euros, they would get deutschemarks.

European Financial Stability Facility (EFSF)

The European Financial Stability Facility (EFSF) was created by the euro area member states on May 9, 2010, within the framework of the Ecofin Council. The EFSF's mandate is to safeguard financial stability in Europe by providing financial assistance to euro area member states.

EFSF is authorized to use the following instruments linked to appropriate conditionality:

- Provide loans to countries in financial difficulties.
- Intervene in the debt in primary and secondary markets. Intervention in the secondary market will be only on the basis of an ECB analysis recognizing the existence of exceptional financial market circumstances and risks to financial stability.
- Act on the basis of a precautionary program.
- Finance recapitalizations of financial institutions through loans to governments.

The EFSF issues bonds and has done so in bailouts for Ireland, Portugal, and Greece. Of the €85 billion that went to Ireland, €35 billion went to the banking sector. EFSF is backed by guarantee commitments from the euro area member states for a total of €780 billion, and has a lending capacity of €440 billion, which came from an amendment on June 24, 2011. The EFSF is based in Luxembourg and is presided over by Klaus Regling.

In addition to the EFSF, the European Financial Stabilization Mechanism (EFSM) was created on May 10, 2010, with a total of €60 billion and was used in the Ireland, Portugal, and Greece bailouts.

European Stability Mechanism (ESM)

The European Stability Mechanism (ESM) had €500 billion in capital and was originally intended to start July 1, 2013, but this date was amended by the European Council for immediate use on June 24, 2011. The biggest difference between the ESM and EFSF is that the ESM has paid in capital, meaning that member states will put €80 billion in total with five tranches of €16 billion euros to back the €700 billion of subscribed capital (see Figure 11.7). The first two tranches will be paid in the second half of 2012, the third and fourth tranches will be paid in 2013, and the fifth, final tranche will be paid in the first half of 2014. The ESM, like the EFSF, is only available to the euro area and requires an 85 percent majority to pass, unlike the EFSF, which must be unanimous.

Securities Market Program (SMP)

The Securities Market Program (SMP) started on May 10, 2010. The SMP is probably the closest program to QE, though size is not nearly as large. The SMP was very controversial within the ECB and led to the resignation of Juergen Stark of Germany. Stark was on the governing council and was also the chief economist and, though he said he left for "personal reasons," it was widely known that he refused to see the ECB monetize debt on his watch. The SMP program totaled €208.8 billion and performed weekly purchases (or at times none at all), which were released on the ECB website.

FIGURE 11.7   Lending Capacity of EFSF/ESM and Timetable

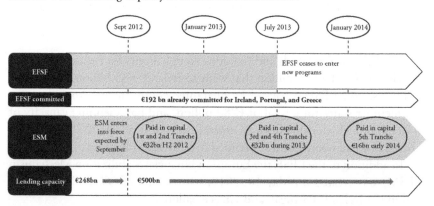

Source: European Financial Stability Facility (EFSF).

FIGURE 11.8 SMP Total Weekly Purchases

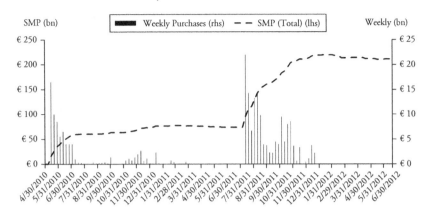

Source: Bloomberg and ECB.

On September 6, 2012, upon the announcement of the Outright Monetary Transactions (OMT) program, the ECB announced that the SMP would be terminated (see Figure 11.8).

Outright Monetary Transactions (OMT)

On September 6, 2012, while simultaneously closing the SMP, the ECB announced the Outright Monetary Transactions (OMT). The OMT was viewed as a significant announcement due to its open-ended nature. This was viewed as a necessary step for the ECB, though it remains to be seen what will happen with longer-duration assets and how the ECB will punish those who do not comply (or if they will actually punish countries). The ECB outlined several conditions for the OMT:

- Participating country must be in the EFSF/ESM.
- ECB will continue OMT in participating countries as long as conditionality is fully respected.
- The ECB will target one- to three-year maturities.
- There are no limits to size of OMT.
- The OMT will be "fully" sterilized.
- The ECB will maintain transparency and publish holdings and values on a weekly basis. Country holdings and duration breakdown by country will be done on a monthly basis.

- Transactions receive pari passu treatment as private or other creditors with respect to bonds issued by euro area countries and purchased by the eurosystem through OMT.

Covered Bond Purchase Program

The ECB's definition of a covered bond is as follows: dual-recourse bonds, with a claim on both the issuer and a cover pool of high-quality collateral (which the issuer is required to maintain), issued under specific covered bond legislation (or contracts, which emulate this). The recourse to the issuer and consequent lack of credit risk transfer distinguishes covered bonds from asset-backed securities, with significant implications for issuers and investors.

In order to further ease credit markets in the eurozone, the ECB announced on May 7, 2009, the start of the Covered Bond Purchase Program 1 (CBPP1), which would start July 6, 2009. The CBPP1 was for €60 billion and as of June 30, 2010, had an average duration of 4.12. Four hundred twenty-two bonds were purchased, 27 percent on the primary market and 73 percent on the secondary market. CBPP1 saw its conclusion in June 2010. The ECB estimates that covered bond yields fell 12 bps as a result of the CBPP1.

On October 6, 2011, at the ECB meeting, the ECB decided to create CBPP2, which would start in November 2011 and end in October 2012 in the amount of €40 billion to serve the same purpose as CBPP1. CBPP2 required that the bonds purchased were at least BBB-rated.

Emergency Liquidity Assistance (ELA)

The emergency liquidity assistance (ELA) was initially designed to provide liquidity to banks that were in stress and could not access capital. As defined by the ECB, "the (ELA) protects individual credit institutions with adequate collateral. Generally, this tool consists of providing liquidity support in exceptional circumstances to a temporarily illiquid credit institution which cannot obtain liquidity through either the market or participation in monetary policy operations." This policy was created before the financial crisis and is controversial because no one foresaw the problem that ensued. The ELA was used in the Irish bailout to capitalize Ireland's banks, and by summer 2012, as estimated, €200 billion had been given out. There are moral hazards because the ELA doesn't require the banks asking their NCBs to be held to the same ECB borrowing standards, which has led to an increase in borrowing of the ELA.

TARGET2

TARGET2 (Trans-European Automated Real-Time Gross Settlement Express Transfer System) was created as a single IT platform for settling almost all heavily traded securities in Europe, eliminating any differences between the settlement of domestic and cross-border transactions. The objective is to reduce transaction costs and centralize all transactions to integrate the euro area. The Bundesbank estimates that an average of 350,000 payments with a value of just under €2.5 trillion are processed using TARGET2 each working day. TARGET2 has grown into a gauge for tension in the euro area since recently significant credits and debits have emerged.[14]

At inception, TARGET2 was a well-intentioned working mechanism. To demonstrate the way TARGET2 works, let's say, for example, a Spanish company purchases certain machinery from Germany. The Spanish company would get a debit from a local Spanish bank, which then gets a debit from the Bank of Spain (NCB). After that, the Bank of Spain receives a TARGET2 debit for the purchase from the ECB and then a credit is established to the Bundesbank. The Bundesbank then credits the German company for the purchase. So the Bundesbank has a credit with the ECB and the Bank of Spain has a debit. To finance the transaction made by the Spanish bank, it may issue debt and sell it to a German bank. In this transaction, the Spanish Bank gets a credit and the German bank gets a debit netting out the initial loan made to the company.

The problem in this instance is that when the Spanish bank tries to make the offsetting transaction of selling debt to get a credit, the German bank doesn't want to buy it. Effectively, Germany is financing Spain's trade deficit and is taking on large credit risk to the periphery. As Figure 11.9 shows, the periphery countries rely on external financing. The problem is that if one of these countries defaults or leaves the euro, Germany could potentially be on the hook for hundreds of billions of euros, meaning that over the crisis, Germany's credit risk to countries like Spain has risen to around €700 billion. Many people closely monitor TARGET2's, as they are one of the best gauges of the financing needs of member states.

The Bundesbank

Given the size of the German economy in the eurozone, the Bundesbank is the most important NCB in Europe, similar to the New York Fed in the United States. It was founded on July 26, 1957, and independent of instructions

---

[14] Bundesbank.

FIGURE 11.9   European TARGET2 by Country

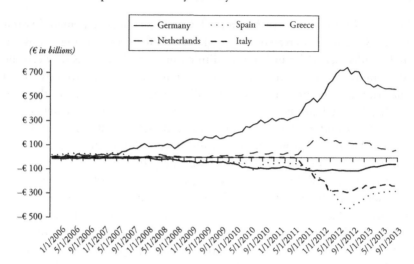

Sources: Bundesbank, Nederlandsche Bank, Bank of Spain, Banca D'Italia, Bank of Greece, and Bloomberg.

from the German federal government, and had the objective of safeguarding the currency. Being separate from the government was important to provide integrity to monetary policy of the Bundesbank. Upon the integration of the euro as its currency, the Bundesbank gave away its power to control monetary policy to the ECB.

In addition to being the largest and most important NCB, the Bundesbank is in Frankfurt, as is the ECB. The Bundesbank has unique duties to the euro area that include issuing bank notes (though other NCBs do also), managing currency reserves, and acting as a clearinghouse and bank supervisor. Though not directly through the Bundesbank, the German Debt Management Office provides front, bank office, cash management, and risk management for EFSF bonds. Even though the Bundesbank is separate from the government, it is clearly more intertwined with the ECB than any other NCB.[15]

Greece

Greece is at the epicenter of the European economic crisis and is responsible for much of the uncertainty. Greece suffers from negative GDP growth, which

---

[15] Bundesbank.

FIGURE 11.10   Greece Debt/GDP and Real GDP Growth

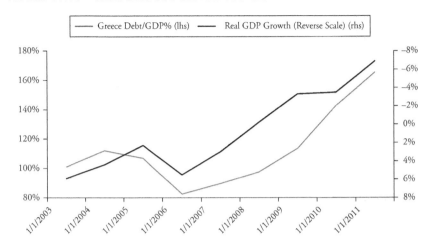

Sources: Bank of Greece, World Bank, CIA, Eurostat, and Bloomberg.

means that even if their debt is constant, their debt-to-GDP ratio continues to rise, as do government deficits, resulting in an unsustainable amount of debt (see Figure 11.10).

For years before the financial crisis, Greece spent money on credit, and their borrowing far outpaced their growth in income, leading to a severe current account deficit. Labor productivity in Greece fell drastically as the expense of Greek workers, relative to other workers in Europe, grew.

Fears in Greece led to selling of Greek bonds and yields rose, which resulted in more expensive issuance of debt. Five-year CDS went from 345 bps in the beginning of April 2010, to 890 bps in a month, along with credit downgrades that only exacerbated the deterioration. On May 2, 2010, Greece agreed to its first bailout from the IMF, European Commission, and ECB, for a total amount of €110 billion, with €30 billion coming from the IMF in exchange for austerity.

Even with the bailout package, Greece's yields continued to rise and the curve remained inverted, which typically implies a high probability of default. Though Greece had a received a bailout, its high yields meant that it was borrowing additions at unsustainable rates. This was coupled with the political difficulty of implementing austerity measures. Additionally, Greece had certain debt repayments due and the market questioned its ability to pay these obligations back. This all led to a second bailout of Greece for €109 billion on July 21, 2011, with the aid of the IMF, and an intention to use

15- to 30-year EFSF bonds. It was also in this bailout that the IMF proposed a private sector haircut Greek debt. While the bailouts of Greece were a short-term solution, it would be impossible for Greece to pay all of its debt of in its current situation. Later, on February 21, 2012, the ECB, EU via the EFSF, and IMF agreed to increase the amount to €130 billion which came with a private sector haircut of 53.5 percent.

The world is well aware of the issues that Greece faces now. There have been constant headline risks, from Moody's downgrading Greek banks in September 2011, to Prime Minister Georgios Papandreou resigning in November 2011, and all of this has certainly tired many market participants.

Ireland

On November 28, 2010, the European Commission and the ECB provided loans to Ireland for €85 billion. €35 billion was for the banking sector and €50 billion was for the government. The IMF agreed to match 50 percent of the entire bailout, which was financed by €22.5 from the EFSM, €22.5 from the EFSF €22.5 from the IMF and €17.5 billion coming from Ireland (the Treasury and Pension Reserve).

The problems in Ireland originated from a housing property bubble. After the financial crisis, property prices crashed and banks were left with huge loses. By 2010, Ireland ran a budget deficit greater than 20 percent and unemployment skyrocketed. Ireland's biggest competitive advantage in the euro area is their unusually low corporate tax rate. Even though Ireland needed a bailout, they agreed to fiscal cuts but refused to raise their corporate taxes in fear that businesses would leave.

Portugal and Spain

On April 7, 2011, Portugal was provided with €78 billion in assistance, having €26 billion shared equally from the EFSM, EFSF, and the IMF. In exchange for the bailout, the Portuguese government agreed to cut its budget deficit from 9 percent to 3 percent by 2013.

Spain has a low debt-to-GDP standing at roughly 60 percent, which is much lower than most of its fellow euro area countries. However, Spain had arguably the biggest housing bubble in Europe and public and bank debt is significantly higher, amounting to 355 percent in 2010 (this includes government, corporate, and household) (see Table 11.8). The precipitate fall in housing prices caused Spanish banks to be incredibly weak. While some have passed European bank stress-tests, it is clear that these tests were not stringent

TABLE 11.8   OECD Household, Corporate, and Government Debt as a Percentage of Nominal GDP

	Levels				Changes[2]		
	1980	1990	2000	2010[1]	1980–90	1990–2000	2000–10
United States	151	200	198	268	49	−2	70
Japan	290	364	410	456	75	46	46
Germany	136	137	226	241	1	89	15
United Kingdom	160	203	223	322	43	20	99
France	160	198	243	321	37	45	78
Italy	109	180	252	310	71	72	58
Canada	236	278	293	313	42	15	20
Australia	128	174	185	235	46	11	49
Austria	162	178	205	238	16	27	32
Belgium	170	264	298	356	94	34	58
Denmark			259	336			77
Finland	146	173	222	270	26	49	48
Greece	92	139	195	262	47	55	67
Netherlands	205	265	294	327	60	29	33
Norway			256	334			78
Portugal	144	141	251	366	−2	110	115
Spain	172	187	258	355	15	70	97
Sweden	219	289	320	340	70	31	21
Total of above							
Median	160	192	251	322	45	40	58
Weighted average[3]	172	218	246	306	47	28	61
Simple average	168	211	255	314	43	44	59
G7	177	223	264	303	45	41	55
Other advanced	160	201	249	321	41	46	61
Memo: Std deviation	*50*	*64*	*54*	*43*			

[1] Some figures refer to 2009.
[2] In percentage points of GDP.
[3] Based on 2005 GDP and PPP exchange rate.
Sources: OECD; national data, authors' estimates.

enough. Given that most Spanish banks did not take proper write-downs, they were severely undercapitalized and not equipped for the write-downs. This, coupled with large budget deficits, over 10 percent, eventually led to Spanish 10-year yields rising to 7 percent, which is not sustainable. Bankia, one of Spain's largest financial institutions, received a €19 billion bailout in May 2012. Global markets continued to have stress and the Bankia bailout led to suspicion that other Spanish banks were undercapitalized. On June 25, 2012, it was decided that Spanish banks would receive a loan of €100 billion with an average maturity of 12.5 years.

The Swiss National Bank

The Swiss National Bank, or SNB, sets the target range for three-month Swiss franc LIBOR and has an inflation target of less than 2.0 percent. It meets four times a year, typically in March, June, September, and December. Recently, the SNB has received big attention for setting a minimum exchange rate for the euro against the Swiss franc of 1.20 CHF per euro, which was announced on September 6, 2011.

Since the beginning of the financial crisis in 2008, the Swiss franc saw massive currency appreciation as a flight to quality, which caused the Swiss franc to appreciate significantly against the euro. Combined with currency strength, Switzerland has experienced deflation, which the SNB also feared could affect exports. To fight the strong appreciation in the Swiss franc and deflation in the country, the SNB lowered three-month Swiss franc LIBOR to a 0.00 to 0.25 percent target range and devalued its currency. To protect the ceiling and strengthening in the Swiss franc, the SNB has electronically created Swiss francs, sold them on the open market to weaken its currency, and then bought euros and other currencies (see Figure 11.11).

Ultimately, the creation of Swiss francs to maintain the 1.20 ceiling against the euro will have inflationary repercussions, but since CPI remains negative, policy makers are presently more focused on creating some inflation. The goal is to deter capital inflows as a haven, since there are fears that the euro may devalue or dissolve. Many lessons in Switzerland can be taken from the late 1970s, when the SNB was in a similar predicament. A strong appreciation in the Swiss franc caused low inflation along with fear that Swiss exports would decline. Initially, the SNB made interest rates negative and created capital controls, which failed to weaken the Swiss franc. In October 1978, inflation reached 0.40 percent and the SNB announced a ceiling on the Swiss franc against the deutschmark of 0.80 Swiss francs per deutschmark

FIGURE 11.11   SNB Reserves

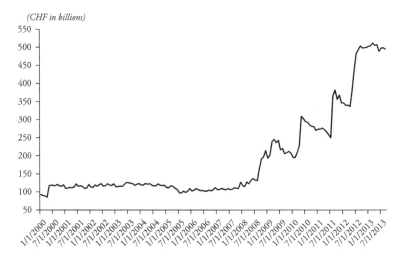

Sources: Bloomberg and SNB.

FIGURE 11.12   Swiss CPI 1978 to 1983

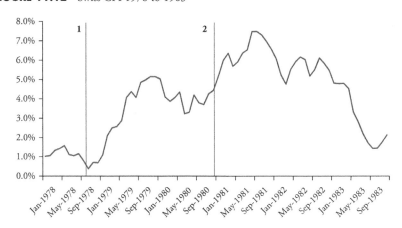

Sources: FRED Data, St. Louis Fed, and the Swiss National Bank.

(Figure 11.12, Point 1). The policy was successful, initially seeing both an increase in inflation and GDP growth. However, as a result of the SNB's policy, inflation moved from under 1.0 percent to 5.0 percent (Figure 11.12, Point 2) in a little over than a year, which led to the SNB removing the ceiling on the Swiss franc. After removing the ceiling on the Swiss franc, Switzerland went into recession in 1982.

The Bank of England (BOE)

The Bank of England, or BOE, was founded in 1694 to act as the government's banker and debt manager. Since then, its role has evolved to monitoring inflation and providing financial stability to the United Kingdom. The BOE was on the gold standard until 1931. In October 1990, the British pound joined the exchange rate mechanism (ERM) and since leaving the ERM has maintained its independence by not joining the euro. Before 1997, the chancellor of the exchequer determined interest rate policy, but now the Bank of England is independent. Mervyn King has been the governor of the BOE since June 2003. The BOE targets inflation of 2 percent and, most recently has had inflation well above its target, which the BOE attributes to high energy prices and VAT hikes, though inflation has moderated. The BOE currently has nine committee members, all of whom vote on a majority for monetary policy, meeting typically on the first Thursday of each month. On March 5, 2009, the BOE announced it was conducting its first round £75 billion of quantitative easing for £75 billion.[16]

Black Wednesday

Through the 1970s and 1980s, the United Kingdom experienced periods of high inflation, multiple recessions, and extreme currency moves. The aftereffect of the 1973 oil crisis left the United Kingdom in periods of double-digit inflation, even years after the crisis. The United Kingdom turned down the opportunity to join the European exchange rate mechanism (ERM) during its formation in March 1979, and in May 1979, the conservative leader, Margaret Thatcher, became Great Britain's prime minister. Upon entering office, Thatcher wasted little time in making austerity cuts, which led to a recession in 1981. The GBP/USD exchange rate went as high as 2.45 in 1980, only to depreciate 57 percent to GBP/USD 1.05 in February 1985 and then rally 82 percent to GBP/USD 1.91 in April 1988. Many countries in Europe joined the ERM and, combined with extreme currency fluctuations, this led the United Kingdom to reconsider its original plan of staying out of the ERM. The economic picture for the United Kingdom consisted of low growth and low inflation, which in turn was conducive to a lower interest policy. However, since the pound was targeted against the deutschmark, central bank policies and economic conditions in Germany were also vitally important.

---

[16] Bank of England.

West Germany had a long history of low inflation, which was attributed to their strong, stable currency. The deutschmark was becoming increasingly attractive for the United Kingdom to target their currency against. The United Kingdom gradually considered joining the ERM in 1987–1988, when West Germany and East Germany were separate countries, with separate currencies. Ultimately, on October 8, 1990, the United Kingdom decided to fix their exchange rate against the German deutschmark (DEM) at a rate of £1/2.95 DEM with a lower band of 2.778 DEM to the pound, meaning that the United Kingdom would not allow their currency to weaken beyond their band.

With the fall of the Berlin Wall in November 1989, and unification of West and East Germany in early 1990, some issues began to arise in Germany. Since East Germany was under communism, its workers were not as productive and initially West Germany significantly outperformed in GDP growth as compared to East Germany. It simultaneously ran large government deficits to finance infrastructure and development in East Germany. This large disparity led to inflation higher than 6 percent in early 1992. As a result, on July 16, 1992, the Bundesbank (the German central bank) decided to raise its discount rate 75 bps from 8.00 percent to 8.75 percent to combat inflation.

Starting October 8, 1990, the Bank of England started lowering rates from a high of 14.875 percent, the same date the United Kingdom entered the ERM to target £1/2.95 DM. Because the United Kingdom had declining inflation and needed to stimulate growth, it made sense for them to cut rates. At the same time, it is worth keeping in mind that in June 1991, Germany's inflation was at 3.7 percent while the United Kingdom's was more than double at 8.4 percent. It wasn't until April 1992 that Germany had a higher inflation rate. The United Kingdom was in a continual rate-cutting cycle and the last cut they made before Black Wednesday was on May 5, 1992, when they cut the official bank rate 50 bps to 9.875 percent.

When the Bundesbank raised rates in July 1992, it put immense pressure on the Bank of England to prefer (sterilized) interventions to defend their currency. Due to interest rate differentials, the currency with higher rates tends to appreciate against the currency with lower rates. Because the United Kingdom had little to no GDP growth, it was not in a strong position to raise rates and was forced to intervene in the currency market to defend the lower band of £1/2.778 DEM.

George Soros successfully predicted that the Bank of England had only limited reserves and ultimately would not be able to support the lower band via sterilized intervention, which would cause an inevitable devaluation.

He had been building a short pound position with Stanley Druckenmiller, who worked with Soros at the time, and they also observed that, in a last-minute desperation, the Bank of England borrowed billions via a credit line to sell DEM in order to attempt to strengthen the £/DEM exchange rate. On September 16, 1992, the Bank of England raised interest rates to 15 percent, and later decided on the same day that it would no longer remain in the ERM, since all their efforts were prohibitive to maintaining the lower band. That same evening, the rate hike to 15 percent in an attempt to defend the currency was canceled and the British pound was no longer in the ERM. In less than a week, the British pound lost 10 percent of its value against the deutschemark.

The underlying core issue with the ERM was that, while having stable inflation is the main objective, it failed to realize that not all countries are in sync at all times. Some countries have high inflation and need tightening, while other countries might be in lower inflation regimes or need to stimulate their economy by lowering rates. Black Wednesday exemplifies this core issue at heart; George Soros's trade is likely the single greatest trade in history.

Similar to the British pound devaluation and ERM exit, the Italian lira suffered the same fate. The lira joined the ERM when it was formed in 1979 at an exchange rate of 457 lira per 1 DM and later had many of the same mirror-image problems as the United Kingdom. Italy had a higher infla-tion rate and it is estimated that by 1987 the purchasing power of the lira against the deutschmark had fallen by 50 percent on a trade-weight basis. On September 13, 1992, Italy devalued its currency by 7 percent and left the ERM on September 17, 1992.[17]

Bloomberg Shortcuts

CENB <GO>	Central Bank Menu
FED <GO>	Federal Reserve Bank
ECB <GO>	European Central Bank
BOE <GO>	Bank of England
BOJ <GO>	Bank of Japan
BOC <GO>	Bank of Canada
SNB <GO>	Swiss National Bank
RBA <GO>	Reserve Bank of Australia
RBNZ <GO>	Reserve Bank of New Zealand

---

[17] Federal Reserve Bank of Kansas City.

PBOC <GO>	People's Bank of China
BCB <GO>	Central Bank of Brazil
BDEM <GO>	Central Bank of Mexico
BDRC <GO>	Central Bank of Colombia
BOI <GO>	Central Bank of Israel
BCCE <GO>	Banco Central de Chile

Summary

The goal of this chapter is to provide a basic understanding of central banks and the role they play in global macro trading. Having a comprehension of the world's main central banks, their history, and how they interact with one another is crucial to becoming a successful trader. Central banks provide signals and give context to certain policies, and being aware of both bank statements and the tendencies of individual central bankers will give a trader essential advantages in global macro.

Appendix: Fed Programs during the Financial Crisis

Ben Bernanke has been a student of the Great Depression and has vowed that the Fed will never make the mistakes of the past. At the onslaught of the 2008 financial crisis, beginning with the Bear Stearns and the Lehman Brothers bankruptcy, the confidence among lenders began to dissipate and liquidity was drained from the system. To combat any further catastrophes, the Fed implemented several programs with the intent to increase liquidity into the system.

- **Central Bank Liquidity Swap Lines:** The first announcement came on December 12, 2007, with several other announcements. The dollar LIBOR market for funding is critical for unsecured bank borrowing. During periods of crisis, LIBOR can move drastically higher because the loans are unsecured. To avoid having LIBOR spike, the Fed provided liquidity for the ECB, SNB, and later other central banks. As a result, the cost of LIBOR priced of dollar funding in the interbank market fell drastically, as did the LIBOR (90-day)/Overnight Index Swap (OIS) Spread (see Figure 11.13), which can be a proxy for credit risk.[18]

---

[18] "Central Bank Liquidity Swap Lines," Federal Reserve, updated August 2, 2013, www.federalreserve.gov/newsevents/reform_swaplines.htm.

FIGURE 11.13 Dollar Liquidity Swaps, More Than 30 Days

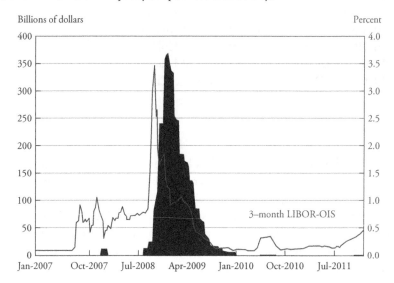

Billions of dollars   Percent

3–month LIBOR-OIS

Sources: Federal Reserve Board; Bloomberg. www.clevelandfed.org/research/
trends/2012/0112/01monpol.cfm.

- **TAF (Term Auction Facility):** TAF was first announced on December 12, 2007, prior to the financial crisis. When banks need liquidity and unsecured funding, going to the discount window had stigma. TAF was intended to provide banks with unsecured borrowing for 28 days, and this was later expanded to 84-day loans. In order to fund banks, TAF held three auctions in 2010. January 11, 2010, TAF offered up to $75 billion in credit, having $38.5 billion submitted, February 8, 2010, offered up to $50 billion in credit, having $15.4 billion submitted, March 8, 2010, offered up to $25 billion in credit, with $3.4 billion submitted for a total of $57.3 billion.[19]
- **TSLF (Term Securities Lending Facility):** TSLF was announced on March 11, 2008. Under the TSLF, the Fed loaned up to $200 billion of Treasury securities to primary dealers secured for a term of 28 days (rather than overnight, as in the existing program) by a pledge of other securities, including federal agency debt, federal agency residential-mortgage-backed securities (MBS), and nonagency AAA/Aaa-rated private-label residential MBS.[20]

---

[19] "Term Auction Facility (TAF)," Federal Reserve, updated August 2, 2013, www.federalreserve.gov/newsevents/reform_taf.htm
[20] "Term Securities Lending Facility (TSLF) and TSLF Options Program (TOP)," Federal Reserve, updated August 2, 2013, www.federalreserve.gov/newsevents/reform_tslf.htm.

- **PDCF (Primary Dealer Credit Facility):** The PDCF began March 17, 2008, and was closed on February 1, 2010. After the collapse of Bear Stearns, the Fed wanted to ensure that the repo market functioned properly and that banks could post collateral as they normally did in the course of business.[21]
- **AMLF (Asset-Backed Commercial Paper Money Market Mutual Fund Liquidity Facility):** The AMLF began operations on September 22, 2008, and was closed on February 1, 2010. During the crisis, the money markets were starting to show signs of weakness and significant withdrawals. The AMLF intended to finance purchases of commercial paper from money market mutual funds in order to protect everyday investors who were exposed.[22]
- **MMIFF (Money Market Investor Funding Facility):** The MMIFF was created on October 21, 2008, and was closed on October 30, 2009. It was introduced to complement AMLF in providing liquidity to money market mutual funds. This facility was created under the Federal Reserve Act, which permitted the Fed to take this type of bold step under unusual circumstances.[23]
- **CPFF (Commercial Paper Funding Facility):** The commercial paper market is over $1 trillion dollars and is one of the most important funding mechanisms in the global financial system because it allows companies to meet their short-term obligations—it acts as the lifeblood for all international trade and transactions among companies by allowing companies to fund themselves. Commercial paper is an unsecured loan for 1 to 365 days. When Lehman Brothers went bankrupt, the commercial paper market was not functioning properly and there were worries of financing through this normally liquid market, which could have caused the entire global financial system to collapse had something not been done.[24]

  CPFF began operating October 27, 2008, and was closed on February 1, 2010. Under the CPFF, the Federal Reserve Bank of New York financed the purchase of highly rated unsecured and asset-backed commercial paper from eligible issuers via eligible primary dealers.

---

[21] "Primary Dealer Credit Facility (PDCF)," Federal Reserve. updated August 2, 2013, www.federalreserve.gov/newsevents/reform_pdcf.htm.

[22] "Asset-Backed Commercial Paper Money Market Mutual Fund Liquidity Facility (AMLF)," Federal Reserve, updated August 2, 2013, www.federalreserve.gov/newsevents/reform_amlf.htm.

[23] "Money Market Investor Funding Facility (MMIFF)," Federal Reserve, updated August 2, 2013, www.federalreserve.gov/newsevents/reform_mmiff.htm.

[24] "Commercial Paper Funding Facility (CPFF)," Federal Reserve. www.federalreserve.gov/newsevents/reform_cpff.htm.

- **TALF (Term Asset-Backed Securities Loan Facility):** Announced November 25, 2008, TALF was intended to provide up to $200 billion on a nonrecourse basis to holders of AAA-rated asset-backed securities (ABS), which included student loans, credit cards, auto loans, and loans guaranteed by the Small Business Association (SBA). Later, on March 19, 2009, the Fed announced that TALF would be expanded.[25]
- **Agency Mortgage-Backed Securities (MBS) Purchase Program:** The Fed announced on November 25, 2008, that it would purchase MBS backed by Fannie Mae, Freddie Mac, and Ginnie Mae in order to support the mortgage and housing markets. Originally, the Fed intended to purchase $100 billion in GSE direct obligations and up to $500 billion in MBS; however, with the expansion of QE, it ended up purchasing a total of $1.25 trillion in agency MBS between January 2009 and March 2010.[26]

---

[25] "Term Asset-Backed Securities Loan Facility (TALF)," Federal Reserve, updated August 2, 2013, www.federalreserve.gov/newsevents/reform_talf.htm.

[26] "Agency Mortgage-Backed Securities (MBS) Purchase Program," Federal Reserve, updated August 2, 2013, www.federalreserve.gov/newsevents/reform_mbs.htm.

CHAPTER 12

Economic Data Releases and Demographics

This chapter begins with an overview of economic indicators and demographics to illuminate the dynamic factors that drive different countries. It will also address important data releases that give both lagging and leading economic information; these can be used for detailed economic research and analysis or short-term trades. The chapter will also address the topic of demographics as they relate to global macro. Demographics are one of the best predictors of success of any country in the long run and one of the least studied fields in global macro. For very long-term trades, understanding the basics of demographics is critical.

Measuring Growth

GDP

A country's GDP growth is likely the single most important statistic of economic data. Most other important economic data points are either a part of GDP or give insight to the likelihood of GDP growth. GDP is measured in two ways: nominal and real.

Nominal GDP is a measure of total economic activity in current prices. This is what most central banks target when they measure growth. Nominal GDP is an accurate measure of total production in current prices, which is why it includes inflation. The data is released for quarterly and annual figures of ranging frequency, depending on the country.

$$GDP = \text{Consumption} + \text{Investment} + \text{Government Spending}$$
$$+ \text{Net Exports (Exports} - \text{Imports)}$$

Real GDP is a measure of total economic activity in constant prices (see Figure 12.1). Because it is measured in constant prices, it must be adjusted for inflation. Long periods of data can be more useful in analyzing real GDP growth as opposed to nominal growth. Like nominal GDP, real GDP data is released for quarterly and annual figures of ranging frequency, depending on the country.

Inflation

Inflation and growth are the two most important factors to an economy (see Figure 12.2). Inflation is defined as the general change in the price level. Most economies have inflation, as opposed to deflation, which is a decrease in the price level. Most central banks have an explicit inflation target and most of them cite maintaining stable prices as their primary objective. Central banks typically use consumer price index (CPI) to measure inflation. CPI refers to the prices paid by consumers for a representative basket of goods and services, according to the Bureau of Labor Statistics. Supply shock and demand pull are the causes of inflation. In supply shock, prices are higher, because input costs, such as raw materials or wages, increase, which in turn increases the

FIGURE 12.1   Real GDP Growth: Average Annual Percent Change 2003–2012

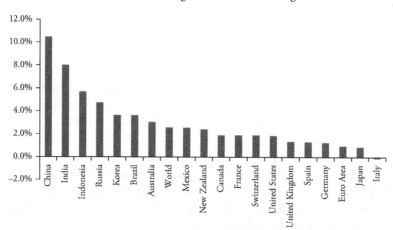

Sources: IMF, World Bank, OECD, and Bloomberg.

FIGURE 12.2   CPI Year-over-Year: Average Annual Percentage Change, 2003–2012

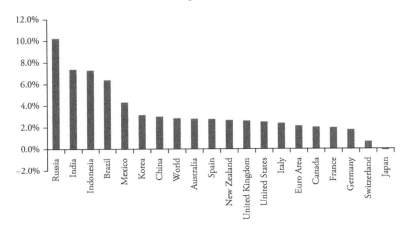

Sources: IMF, World Bank, OECD, and Bloomberg.

price of goods. Demand pull is increased because people continue to spend more than is available (i.e., scarcity) and prices move higher. This can result from tax cuts, an overheating economy or an increase in the money supply. Many emerging markets experience demand pull because growth and wealth increases so rapidly that citizens demand more and more goods and services.

Knowing which CPI each central bank follows is of the utmost importance. For example, the Fed targets core PCE (personal consumption expenditures) index, which excludes food and energy and targets urban consumers. That is significant in this case, because food and energy tend to be more volatile in the short term and the Fed is trying to avoid medium-term decisions based on price changes in oil. The ECB targets Harmonized Index of Consumer Prices (HICP), which targets rural consumers. The Producer Price Index (PPI), according to the BLS program, measures the average change over time in the selling prices received by domestic producers for their output, whereby the price includes the first commercial transaction for many products and some services. The PPI is useful from the supply side; however, CPI is a more of a real-time statistic, while PPI can take longer to affect inflation.

Employment and Population

The unemployment number is defined as the number of people who are unemployed divided by the labor force. This figure is calculated by the Bureau of Labor Statistics in the United States. There are several global variations in accounting for the labor force—some countries count total population instead of those of working age. The overall unemployment rate is one of the most important data points we have in the United States, and in general. The U.S. nonfarm payroll number is released on the first Friday of the month and is another incredibly important piece of data, showing how many jobs were added or lost on a seasonally adjusted basis. Since consumption accounts for a majority of the U.S. economy, if unemployment is high, consumption could fall over time, hurting GDP. The employment picture also gives insight into whether businesses are hiring or not, which in itself is an indication of where the economy is headed (see Figure 12.3).

When looking at the nonfarm payroll number (see Figure 12.4) there are several numbers to which one should pay attention. First is the overall unemployment number. Next is the labor force, since it provides you with a general sense of workers' feelings toward the economy by giving you a proxy for the denominator in the unemployment rate. Disgruntled workers, or workers who stop looking for jobs, are not included in the labor force. If the economy is bad and people exit the work force, then the labor force drops, which makes the unemployment rate lower. The participation rate attempts to find a relative measure by taking the labor force as a percentage of the civilian

FIGURE 12.3   Global Unemployment Rates: Annual Average, 2003–2012

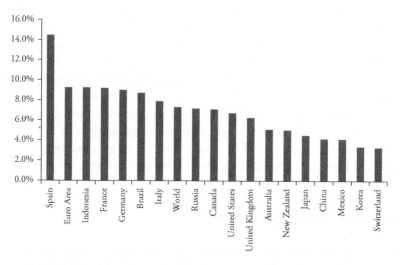

Sources: IMF, World Bank, OECD, and Bloomberg.

FIGURE 12.4 U.S. Payrolls and U.S. Real GDP Change

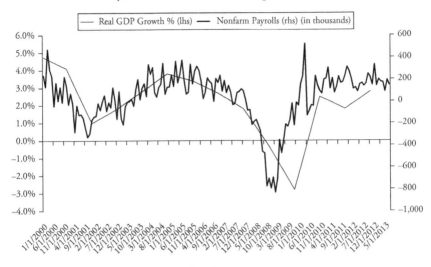

Sources: Bureau of Labor Statistics and Bloomberg.

noninstitutional population.[1] This way one can see in percentage terms if people are entering or leaving the workforce. However, if the economy was doing well, many of these disgruntled workers likely would reenter the workforce, so one would need to examine other factors in addition to the unemployment rate. According to the Bureau of Labor Statistics, the U6 is the total number of unemployed plus all people working part-time for economic reasons, as a percentage of the labor force. The U6 is also an important number in the nonfarm payroll data release, because many people who cannot find work opt to work part-time to make at least some income. This can give a proxy to unemployment because it measures the number of unemployed and those who likely want more work but cannot get it. Another number to monitor on the nonfarm payroll release is the average hourly earned. This provides a good sense of whether workers are making more or less money per hour over the course of time.

There are several types of unemployment:

- **Structural unemployment** arises when workers' skills are obsolete or no longer needed. In the auto sector, machines are now performing the jobs that used to require human workers. Sadly, with structural unemployment, many

---

[1] Bureau of Labor Statistics.

workers get displaced because their skills do not fit what other industries need. This has been a big problem in the United States after the latest recession.

- **Frictional unemployment** arises when people change jobs within industries. If someone leaves a job and then enters a new position, they are still included in the unemployment rate.
- **Seasonal unemployment** arises due to the time of year. For example, many retailers hire temporary workers during Christmas season and then have to end their employment come January or February. Industries like tourism, construction, and agriculture are also subject to seasonal unemployment.

Population is also critical in many factors. If real GDP does not rise as quickly as population growth, then living standards fall. Not only does the size of the population matter, the age demographics are also a large determinant of a country's success or ultimate decline. This is so critical because while people in a country are young, they work and contribute to society by paying taxes. In a sense, when we retire we become a burden on society because we no longer work but are still supported by the government. This is certainly fair because citizens work their whole lives in order to obtain these benefits, but a problem arises when there are more retirees than young people. The tax revenues of that government drop significantly while the amount of expenses and commitments increase. The fact that governments have been completely irresponsible by spending and spending and racking up large debts only exacerbates this problem, so the piggy bank, so to speak, is not only empty, but also has loans against future income.

Balance of Payments

Balance of payments are financial transactions a nation incurs over the course of a year. Financial inflows include foreign capital investment and foreign payments for exports. Financial outflows include paying for imports and having capital leave to invest in other countries. Balance of payments follow accounting principles, maintaining debits and credits on all transactions (double entry system). These debits and credits are composed of current account, trade balance, exports, and imports (net exports).

Current Account

The current account is equal to the change in net foreign assets, which is composed of net exports (exports – imports), net foreign investment (foreign income – foreign payments), and transfer payments. Current account data is released monthly for most countries and a positive current account means that a country is gaining foreign assets. When a country is running a large current account deficit, it is likely the cause of negative net exports. The concern is that if that pattern persists over time, a country must finance these transactions and deplete reserves (which is another way of saying it loses its relative wealth). See Figure 12.5 for a comparison of current account surplus and deficits by country.

Exports and Imports

It is useful to observe exports and imports separately prior to looking at net exports. For example, if a country's exports are rising, it's likely that GDP is growing, which causes imports to increase. Exports are also important to monitor for commodity-exporting countries because they are vulnerable to changes in commodity prices and demand. For example, the Netherlands and Belgium are heavily dependent on exports as a percentage of GDP, accounting for 70 to 90 percent of GDP. Their largest trading partners are in the European Union, so weakness in the EU will likely result in a challenging export environment for the Netherlands and Belgium. Imports as a percent of GDP can provide a gauge of a country's dependence on imports. If imports

FIGURE 12.5   Current Account as a Percent of GDP: Annual Average Change, 2003–2012

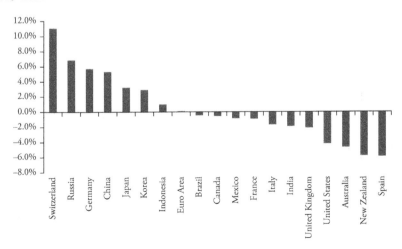

Sources: IMF, World Bank, OECD, and Bloomberg.

are a high percentage of GDP, then a country is also more vulnerable to rises in import prices (like commodities). Imports also have a strong link to exports; as exports rise, countries import more goods as GDP rises.

Trade Balance

Trade balance is the difference between exports and imports (net exports). Small incremental changes in exports or imports, relative to one another, can have a big impact on the trade balance (as a percentage of GDP). If the trade balance goes into deficit, it usually implies that domestic production is not significant enough to meet a country's domestic demand or could also imply a loss of competitiveness in the global economy. One way a country can deal with a trade balance deficit is by weakening its currency, making its exports more attractive and imports less attractive. It is useful to compare the trade balance and current account of a country side by side.

Terms of Trade (ToT)

Terms of trade (ToT) indicates a country's exports by the amount of imports it can purchase. It is calculated by taking the price of exportable goods divided by price of imported goods in an index of goods. Terms of trade improves as export prices rise relative to import prices, and it acts as a measure of purchasing power. Terms of trade is an important measure to monitor in foreign exchange. Typically, when a country's currency weakens, its terms of trade worsen, since it takes more of its currency to buy imports and its exports are cheaper globally. Conversely, a stronger currency would improve terms of trade.

Reserves

Countries hold reserves that can be used for various economic goals. Foreign central banks with large reserves can intervene in the foreign exchange market to weaken or strengthen their currency based on their desire to affect trade and other factors. Reserves also allow one to see which countries are accumulating wealth as a result of trade. Asian counties have large reserves as a percent of GDP, and countries such as China use their reserves to weaken their currency as a policy tool, making their exports attractive in the global trading environment. Observing changes in foreign reserves can provide an indication of what a country is doing in the foreign exchange market and in local investment.

Government Indicators

Fiscal indicators revolve around revenue and expenditures. Much like a company has revenues and expenses, every country does as well. Tax revenues qualify as revenues; government spending is an expense. The difference between revenues and expenditures yields a budget balance, which can be in surplus or deficit. To help facilitate a budget deficit, countries need to borrow. Debt-to-GDP is a ratio that aims at making debt a more relative measure on a country-by-country comparison. The following are useful tools in watching for fiscal indicators.

Government Expenditures and Revenues

Government expenditures provide a proxy for how much the government spends while government revenue gives an indication of how much a government takes in, the bulk of which is taxes. The two combined give us the budget balance, which can be in surplus or deficit. In most countries, both data points are released monthly.

Budget Balance

A government's budget is a calculation of the amount it spends minus the amount it receives in revenues (see Figure 12.6). The budget can either be in surplus or in deficit. Running a budget deficit is in many ways like a government using a credit card. The government can use the additional borrowed capital to stimulate demand, build infrastructure, support defense, and pay for government entitlement programs. There is nothing wrong with running a budget deficit unless it becomes habitual, similar to a consumer continuously spending money he or she doesn't have on a credit card. The United States has consistently had a budget deficit and has not been in surplus since the Clinton administration. If a government wants to save for future outlays, such as pensions, it makes sense to run a budget surplus to ensure that there will enough saved for citizens when they need these types of benefits. In most countries, the budget deficit is typically released every month.

Government Debt and Debt-to-GDP

Government debt is a measurement of how much a government borrows. However, the measure of borrowing is relative to the size of a country's

FIGURE 12.6 Budget Surplus/Deficit as a Percent of GDP: Annual Average Percent, 2003 to 2012

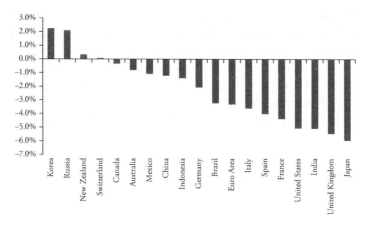

Sources: IMF, World Bank, OECD, and Bloomberg.

FIGURE 12.7 2012 Country's Debt-to-GDP

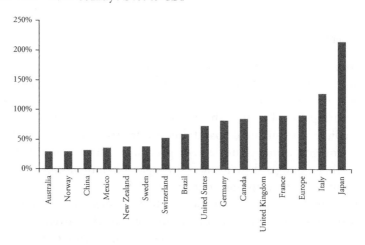

Sources: IMF, World Bank, OECD, and Bloomberg.

economy (see Figure 12.7). Debt-to-GDP is one relative measure that aims to measure a country's health. The higher the debt-to-GDP ratio, the more it signifies an unhealthy economy. Reinhart and Rogoff (2010) argue that once a country's debt-to-GDP ratio exceeds 90 percent, it becomes more difficult to grow. An argument many economists use is that debt is fine as long as a country can outgrow its own debt. One flaw in this argument is that debt has interest payments that must be met. As the great Albert Einstein said, "compound interest is the most powerful force in the universe." As time and debt progress, the interest payments become increasingly more difficult to pay, typically enticing governments to borrow more until their debt becomes insurmountable. Additionally, as debt payments increase, the government typically has to cut into federal programs since they can no longer afford them.

Consumption Indicators

Consumption refers to how much consumers are spending on goods and services. Because consumption is part of the GDP calculation, it is a critical indicator. In the United States, for instance, consumption accounted for more than 70 percent of GDP in 2011. The United States accounted for approximately 20 percent of global GDP, so by these figures the U.S. consumer accounts for a little more than 15 percent of global GDP alone. Gauging this number can help predict the path of GDP as well as the GDP of a country's import and trading partners.

As a result, observing overall consumption is the starting point for observing consumer spending. As consumers get higher wages and save more, they in turn tend to spend more, so monitoring savings rates over time can provide insight to future spending. Lastly, consumer sentiment is a great leading indicator. If consumer confidence is murky regarding the economy, then consumers are more likely to spend less in the short run. Monitoring consumer confidence is a very powerful tool to try to capture patterns in consumption and general GDP growth. The following are useful tools in monitoring consumption.

Savings Rate

When workers earn personal income they have the choice to spend it (consumption) or to save it (savings rate). Consumption boosts the economy. However, if a country does not save, then it will make future expenditures more difficult. Conversely, if households save, they build wealth over time but short-term consumption suffers. The savings rate is equal to disposable income minus consumption, but consumers have the luxury to borrow as well. Countries that have households that save are better off over the long run. The United States has had a continual decline in its savings rate, which

FIGURE 12.8   Country's 2012 Gross Domestic Savings as a Percentage of GDP

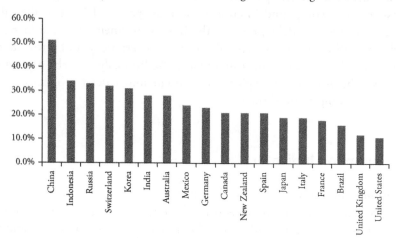

Note: Gross domestic savings are calculated as GDP less final consumption expenditures (total consumption).
Sources: IMF, World Bank, OECD, and Bloomberg.

means that citizens have less savings and wealth. Figure 12.8 shows gross domestic savings as a percentage of GDP.

Consumer Confidence

Consumer confidence is a survey that attempts to give an overall indication of how consumers feel about the economy. If consumers are worried about the economy, they are likely to spend less in the short run in order to save for a rainy day, whereas if they are confident about economic prospects, they will be more likely to spend. There are several companies that perform consumer confidence surveys. Citigroup has a good global standard for measuring individual consumer confidence; in the United States, the Conference Board runs surveys as well.

Industry and Services Indicators

Though there are a great number of industry and services indicators, this book outlines the more powerful ones available. PMIs, such as the ISM in the United States, are great predictors for an economy and are one of the most watched data releases. Other useful indicators are industrial production (which is a good leading indicator and is more sensitive to economic cycles), building permits, and capacity utilization.

Business Conditions

Purchasing managers' indices (PMIs) are one of the best indicators that we have for projecting future economic conditions. The PMIs survey business managers on employment, new orders, inventories, production, supplier deliveries, customer inventories, prices, backlog of orders, imports, and exports. Managers are surveyed on all these economic activities by responding better, same, or worse than a month ago to each. Most PMIs range from 0 to 100, but some are −50 to 50. On a 0-to-100 scale, 0 is worse than a month prior, 50 is the same, and 100 is better. If PMIs are above 50, that typically indicates expanding output, while below 50 indicates contracting output.

For the United States, the Institute for Supply Management (ISM) conducts the survey (see Table 12.1). Most other countries' PMIs are surveyed by Markit. Canada's survey is conducted by the Richard Ivey School of Business and the Purchasing Managers Association of Canada, also called the Ivey PMI, or Ivey for short. The PMI is viewed as a leading indicator for growth.

Industrial Production

Industrial production measures growth in the manufacturing sector, utility companies, and the mining industry. Some countries include other factors like construction, while others do not. While the services side of the economy is greater than the manufacturing side for many economies, Industrial production is more sensitive to economic cycles than services, so it is broadly viewed as a leading indicator for GDP forecasting. Another great method of using industrial production in one's forecast is to use analysts' forecasts. If analysts forecast industrial production higher, then GDP growth is likely to be higher than expected.

Building Permits

Housing starts are counted when construction begins. They can act as a gauge for housing demand and also lead construction increases. In many ways, building permits lead housing starts. Before a house is built, one must acquire a permit. This is why building permits are good indicators of housing starts;

TABLE 12.1   ISM Manufacturing at a Glance, September 2013

Index	Series Index Sep.	Series Index Aug.	Percentage Point Change	Direction	Rate of Change	Trend* (Months)
PMI	56.2	55.7	+0.5	Growing	Faster	4
New Orders	60.5	63.2	−2.7	Growing	Slower	4
Production	62.6	62.4	+0.2	Growing	Faster	4
Employment	55.4	53.3	+2.1	Growing	Faster	3
Supplier Deliveries	52.6	52.3	+0.3	Slowing	Faster	3
Inventories	50.0	47.5	+2.5	Unchanged	From Contracting	1
Customers' Inventories	43.0	42.5	+0.5	Too Low	Slower	22
Prices	56.5	54.0	+2.5	Increasing	Faster	2
Backlog of Orders	49.5	46.5	+3.0	Contracting	Slower	5
Exports	52.0	55.5	−3.5	Growing	Slower	10
Imports	55.0	58.0	−3.0	Growing	Slower	8
Overall Economy				Growing	Faster	52
Manufacturing Sector				Growing	Faster	4

*Number of months moving in current direction.
Source: Institute for Supply Management.

monitoring the number of permits is a more aggressive way to observe the level of housing in the United States.

While housing starts are also an important data point, being able to gauge future housing demand is more useful in economic forecasts. For longer-term trends, household formations are a very important data point. Since the recent economic downturn, household formations have slightly declined, which means that over time fewer families will demand homes. Many are hoping that this is a temporary effect; however, in Europe many children live with their parents into adulthood, which decreases household formations. This data point is released monthly in the United States.

Capacity Utilization

Total capacity is the maximum output an economy can produce at any given point. Capacity utilization aims to measure how far away the current economy is from total capacity. If the capacity utilization is lower than 100 percent, that means the economy is growing at below trend growth. Capacity utilization over 100 percent indicates that an economy may be overheating. This data point is released monthly in many countries.

Demographics

Demographics is one of the least studied fields in investing and one of the most important factors in long-term investing. Middle-aged workers are likely to be net savers, who are willing to take more risks than retirees. Hence, all else being equal, a larger proportion of middle-aged workers are more bullish on equities. Conversely, workers who are near or approaching retirement are far more risk-averse and less likely to hold equities. One method of measuring the amount of people in the workforce in relative terms is the dependency ratio. The dependency ratio is a portion of the population that is not in the labor force. The higher the number of dependents, especially those 65 and older, the more vulnerable an economy is. The dependency ratio and labor productivity are negatively correlated with equity returns over time.

$$\text{Dependency Ratio} = \left(\frac{\text{Ages 0 to 14} + \text{Ages 65 and Older}}{\text{Ages 15 to 64}} \right) \times 100\%$$

While the dependency ratio is a useful relative measure across countries, it also helps to look at a country's retirement ages to help assess when the aging population will begin to collect pension and retirement money. Retirement ages for many countries have not changed, but life expectancy continues to increase, which also increases expense for governments. It is also worth noting that in some countries women have different retirement ages than men (see Figure 12.9).

Demographics affect government fiscal positions over time. As a population ages and the dependency ratio increases, the pressure on fiscal spending increases drastically. The European Union has age demographics that work against it. As time progresses, there will be more and more people retiring and

FIGURE 12.9 Effective Retirement Age for Men, 2002–2007

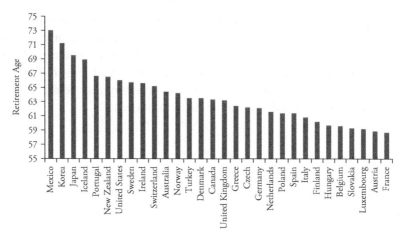

Source: OECD.

FIGURE 12.10 Social Benefit by Function as a Percentage of GDP, EU-27

	2010			
	Pensions	Health Care	Long-Term Care	Total
EU-27	10.2%	6.8%	1.3%	18.3%
	2035			
	Pensions	Health Care	Long-Term Care	Total
EU-27	11.8%	7.7%	1.8%	21.3%

Sources: ECP, Eurostat, ECB, and Hagist and Kotlikoff "Who's Going Broke" (working paper, National Bureau of Economic Research, 2005).

fewer middle-aged workers to support them. Figure 12.10 aims to show that, by current projections, the European Union will have to pay a higher percentage of GDP to retirees. The additional problem is that not only do expenses increase, but revenues will likely fall, since the amount of people working will decrease, unless their labor productivity increases by the same amount, which is highly unlikely if not impossible.

Global population has soared to parabolic growth proportions that civilizations have never seen before. Aside from overcoming starvation, which is a monumental task on its own, the developed world is going to have to face the fact that global demographics will affect their economies in a negative way. Since 1970, global population has grown by 90 percent, almost doubling (see Figure 12.11). And to make matters more difficult, the disproportionate amount of growth has come from an aging population. Since 1970, the number of people 65 and older grew by 180 percent, while the number of people aged 0 to 14 grew by only 33 percent. While the number of people aged 15 to 64 has also grown, it is difficult to see how developed economies will be able to sustain their current paths as the younger population approaches retirement over the coming decades. While looking at the wide range of 15 to 64 is useful, it also helps to look at a country's median age to get a better sense of the distribution. The median age for many European countries is in the 40s and, by comparison, emerging markets are in the 20s and 30s.

As an economy has more workers and a lower dependency ratio, economies tend to save more, which causes their current account to increase (see Figure 12.12). Because many developing countries are past their peak age of savings, over the next decade or two, they will see a continual decline in their current accounts, while emerging markets will see a continual increase. Japan, for instance, currently runs a current account surplus and most analyst forecasts will run current account deficits in 2025. Jean-Claude Trichet, the former ECB president, said that "Current account balance is an important summary indicator that signals losses of competitiveness and emerging imbalances."[2]

FIGURE 12.11   Age Demography Change from 1970 to 2012

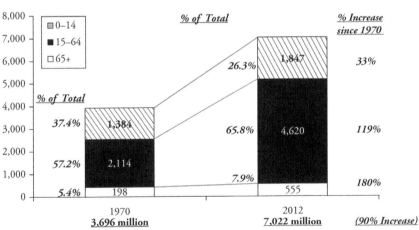

Sources: OECD, *CIA World Factbook*, World Bank, and the UN.

---

[2] Speech by Jean-Claude Trichet, February 23, 2011. Liège, Belgium. Available at www.bis.org/review/r110224b.pdf.

Because 15 to 64 is a broad age range, it's good to monitor peaks in a tighter window. Observing 35 to 69 years of age, and the year in which those peak ages are higher, can help one understand a country's place in the cycle shown in Figure 12.12. Understanding the peak ages can help one forecast years ahead for a country's current accounts. Table 12.2 shows the peak in prime age for saving, which helps forecast fiscal expenses that might build in the developing markets and the length of periods that emerging markets will have a current account surplus.

FIGURE 12.12 Demographic Implications on Savings and Current Account

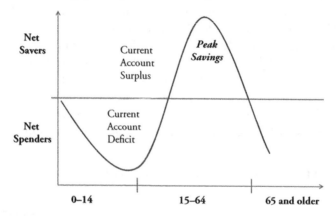

Source: Author's estimates.

TABLE 12.2 Age Demography by Country

Country	Year of Peak in Prime Age (35–69)	Year of Peak in Working Age (15–64)	Country	Year of Peak in Prime Age (35–69)	Year of Peak in Working Age (15–64)
Argentina	2045	2032	Mexico	2041	2021
Australia	2014	2009	Netherlands	2012	1989
Austria	2009	2004	New Zealand	2037	2011
Bangladesh	2050	2033	Nigeria	2050	2050
Belgium	2015	1987	Norway	2012	2009
Brazil	2037	2018	Oman	2050	2050

TABLE 12.2 *Continued*

Country	Year of Peak in Prime Age (35–69)	Year of Peak in Working Age (15–64)	Country	Year of Peak in Prime Age (35–69)	Year of Peak in Working Age (15–64)
Canada	2015	2008	Pakistan	2050	2041
China	2032	2011	Philippines	2050	2037
Denmark	2011	1992	Portugal	2024	2000
Egypt	2050	2030	Qatar	2020	2004
France	2016	1987	Russia	2025	2011
Germany	2006	1986	Saudi Arabia	2050	2043
Greece	2022	1998	South Africa	2050	2044
Hong Kong	2019	2011	Spain	2022	2004
India	2050	2027	Sweden	2010	2007
Indonesia	2050	2023	Switzerland	2013	1989
Iran	2032	2011	Thailand	2031	2013
Italy	2016	1991	Turkey	2035	2018
Japan	2016	1992	UAE	2050	2010
Korea	2023	2015	United Kingdom	2012	2009
Kuwait	2004	2004	United States	2016	2007
Malaysia	2050	2018	Vietnam	2032	2020

Source: U.S. Census Bureau.

Bloomberg Shortcuts

Economic Data

ECST <GO>	World Economic Statistics
ECOW <GO>	Key Indicators Snapshot
ECMX <GO>	World Economic Matrix
ECOF <GO>	Economic Data Finder
GEW <GO>	Global Economy Watch
STAT <GO>	Global Statistic Watch

Calendars

ECO <GO>	Economic Releases/Events
WECO <GO>	Calendar Country Browser
ECOS <GO>	Release Estimates/Rankings
ECOC <GO>	Economic Releases Schedule

Economic News/Commentary

N ECO <GO>	Top Economic News
NI ECO <GO>	Economic News
BRIEF <GO>	Economic Newsletter
BBSE <GO>	World Economic News

Summary

The aim of this chapter is to provide an introduction to economic data releases and demographics. Knowing which data releases are relevant to specific countries and trades is of the utmost importance in global macro trading. Data releases move markets for short-term traders and for people who are in particular positions. In the medium to long run, data releases are critical because they provide key insights as to how a particular economy is performing. Though not a short-term indicator, they are very useful for longer-term trading trends and for understanding which nations will fare better in decades to come.

References

The Federal Reserve Bank of Richmond. "Instruments of the Money Market."

Abner, D. 2010. *The ETF Handbook*. Hoboken: John Wiley and Sons.

Aronson, D. 2007. *Evidence-Based Technical Analysis*. Hoboken: John Wiley and Sons.

Asness, C., A. Frazzini, and L. Pedersen. 2012. "Leverage Aversion and Risk Parity." *Financial Analysts Journal* 68 (1): 47–59.

Asness, C., T. Moskowitz, and L. Pedersen. 2013. "Value and Momentum Everywhere." *Journal of Finance* 68 (3): 929–985.

Asness, C., A. Frazzini, and L. Pederson. *Leverage Aversion and Risk Parity*. CFA Institute. 2013.

Bain, C. *Guide to Commodities: Producers, Players and Prices; Markets, Consumers and Trends*. Profile Books. 2013.

Barsky, R. and L. Summers, "Gibson's Paradox and the Gold Standard." *Journal of Political Economy* 96 (3): 528–550.

Beirne, J., L. Dalitz, J. Ejsing, M. Grothe, S. Manganelli, F. Monar, B. Sahel, M. Susec, J. Tapking, and T. Vong. 2011. "The Impact of the Eurosystem's Covered Bond Purchase Programme on the Primary and Secondary Market." ECB Occasional Paper No. 122.

Bender, J., R. Briand, F. Nielsen, and D. Stefek. 2010. "Portfolio of Risk Premia: A New Approach to Diversification." *Journal of Portfolio Management* 36 (2): 17–25.

Bernanke, B., V. Reinhart, and B. Sack. 2004. "Monetary Policy Alternatives to the Zero Bound: An Empirical Assessment." Finance and Economics Discussion Series No. 2004-08. Washington, DC: Federal Reserve Board, Divisions of Research and Statistics and Monetary Affairs.

Black, F. and R. Litterman. 1992. "Global Portfolio Optimization." *Financial Analysts Journal* (September/October): 28–43.

Bollinger, J. 2001. *Bollinger on Bollinger Bands*. New York: McGraw Hill.

Brown, C. 2008. *Fibonacci Analysis*. Bloomberg Financial.

Buffett, W. and M. Olson. 2013. *Berkshire Hathaway Letters to Shareholders*. Max Olson Publishing.

Burghardt, G. 2003. *The EuroDollar Futures and Options Handbook*. New York: McGraw-Hill.

Chernow, R. 2010. *The House of Morgan: An American Banking Dynasty and the Rise of Modern Finance*. Grove Press.

Colvin, G. 2010. *Talent is Overrated: What Really Separates World-Class Performers from Everybody Else*. Portfolio Trade.

Corb, H. 2012. *Interest Rate Swaps and Other Derivatives*. New York: Columbia Business School Publishing.

Cornish, S. 2010. *The Evolution of Central Banking in Australia*. Reserve Bank of Australia.

Covel, M. 2009. *The Complete Turtle Trader: How 23 Novice Investors Became Overnight Millionaires*. Harper Business.

Davis, N. 2000. *Being Right or Making Money*. Ned David Research Inc.

Du Plessis, J. 2012. *The Definitive Guide to Point and Figure: A Comprehensive Guide to the Theory and Practical Use of the Point and Figure Charting Method*. Harriman House. 2012.

Edwards, R. and J. Magee. 2007. *Technical Analysis of Stock Trends*. AMACOM. 2007.

Fabozzi, Frank and Mann, Steven. *The Handbook of Fixed Income Securities, Eighth Edition*. New York: McGraw Hill. 2011.

Faith, Curtis. *Way of the Turtle: The Secret Methods that Turned Ordinary People into Legendary Traders*. New York: McGraw Hill. 2007.

Fama, E., and K. French. 1993. "Common Risk Factors in the Returns on Stocks and Bonds." *Journal of Financial Economics* 33 (1): 3–56.

Folkerts-Landau, D. 2011. *A User Guide to Commodities*. Deutsche Bank.

Frazzini, A., D. Kabiller, and L. Pederson. 2013. *Buffett's Alpha*. New York University (NYU); Copenhagen Business School; AQR Capital Management, LLC; Centre for Economic Policy Research (CEPR); National Bureau of Economic Research (NBER).

Frazzini, A. and L. Pedersen. *Betting Against Beta*. Working paper. AQR Capital.

Friedman, M. 2002. *Capitalism and Freedom*. Chicago: The University of Chicago Press.

Galen, B. 2003. The EuroDollar Futures and Options Handbook. New York: McGraw-Hill.

Greenblatt, J. 1999. *You Can Be a Stock Market Genius: Uncover the Secret Hiding Places of Stock Market Profits*. Touchstone.

Greider, W. 1989. *Secrets of the Temple: How the Federal Reserve Runs the Country*. Simon and Schuster.

Ilmanen, A. 2011. *Expected Returns: An Investor's Guide to Harvesting Market Rewards.* Hoboken, NJ: John Wiley and Sons.

Ilmanen, A., and J. Kizer. 2012. "The Death of Diversification Has Been Greatly Exaggerated." *Journal of Portfolio Management* 38 (3): 15–27.

Jaeger, L. 2008. Alternative Beta Strategies and Hedge Fund Replication. Hoboken, NJ: John Wiley and Sons.

Jorion, P. 1986. "Bayes-Stein Estimation of Portfolio Analysis." *Journal of Financial and Quantitative Analysis,* 21, 279–292.

Judd, J. P., and B. Trehan. 1995. "Has the Fed Gotten Tougher on Inflation?" *FRBSF Weekly* Letter, Number 95-13, (March 31).

Kamich, B. 2009. *Chart Patterns.* Bloomberg Financial.

Kan, R., and G. Zhou. 2007. "Optimal Portfolio Choice with Parameter Uncertainty." *Journal of Financial and Quantitative Analysis* 42 (3): 621–656.

Kaufman, P. J. 2005. *New Trading Systems and Methods, Fifth Edition.* Hoboken, NJ: John Wiley and Sons.

Kindleberger, C. 2011. *Manias, Panics and Crashes: A History of Financial Crises, Sixth Edition.* Palgrave Macmillan.

Kirkpatrick, C. D. and J. R. Dahlquist. 2011. *Technical Analysis: The Complete Resource for Financial Market Technicians Second Edition.* Upper Saddle River, NJ. Pearson Education.

Klein, R. W., and V. S. Bawa. 1976. "The Effect of Estimation Risk on Optimal Portfolio Choice." *Journal of Financial Economics* 3: 215–231.

Kleinman, G. 2013. *Trading Commodities and Financial Futures: A Step-by-Step Guide to Mastering the Markets Fourth Edition.* FT Press.

Krugman, P., and R. Wells. 2009. *Macroeconomics.* 2nd ed. New York: Worth Publishers.

Kydland, F. E., and E. C. Prescott. 1990. "Business Cycles: Real Facts and a Monetary Myth." *Federal Reserve Bank of Minneapolis Quarterly Review* 14 (2): 3–18.

Lipscomb, L. 2005. "An Overview of Non-Deliverable Foreign Exchange Forward Markets." Federal Reserve Bank of New York.

Lee, W. 2011. "Risk-Based Asset Allocation: A New Answer to an Old Question?" *Journal of Portfolio Management* (Summer): 11–28.

Lefervre, E. *Reminiscences of a Stock Operator.* 2006. Hoboken, NJ: John Wiley and Sons.

Levinson, M. 2009. *Guide to Financial Markets.* New York: Bloomberg Press.

Lindsay, R. R., and B. Schachter, eds. 2007. *How I Became a Quant: Insights from 25 of Wall Street's Elite.* Hoboken, NJ: John Wiley and Sons.

Luca, C. 2007. *Trading in the Global Currency Markets, Third Edition*. New York: Prentice Hall.

Lynch, P. 1994. *Beating the Street*. New York: Simon and Schuster.

Mackay, C. 1980. *Extraordinary Popular Delusions and the Madness of Crowds*. Harmony Books.

Mankiw, N. G. 2008. *Principles of Macroeconomics*. 5th ed. Mason, OH: South-Western Cengage Learning.

Markowitz, H. 1952. "Portfolio Selection." *Journal of Finance* 7 (1): 77–91.

Michaud, R.O. 1989. "The Markovitz Optimization Enigma: Is Optimized Optimal?" *Financial Analysts Journal* (January/February) 31–42.

Murphy, J. 1999. *Technical Analysis of the Financial Markets: A Comprehensive Guide to Trading Methods and Applications*. New York Institute of Finance.

Neely, G. and E. Hall. 1990. *Mastering Elliott Wave: Presenting the Neely Method: The First Scientific, Objective Approach to Market Forecasting with the Elliott Wave Theory*. Windsor Books.

Niederhoffer, V. 1997. *The Education of a Speculator*. Hoboken: John Wiley and Sons.

Nison, S. 2001. *Japanese Candlestick Charting Techniques, Second Edition*. New York: Prentice Hall.

Poundstone, W. 2006. *Fortune's Formula: The Untold Story of the Scientific Betting System That Beat the Casinos and Wall Street*. Hill and Wang.

Prechter, R. and A.J. Frost. 2005. *Elliott Wave Principle*. New Classics Library.

Pring, M. 1993. *Investment Psychology Explained*. Hoboken, NJ: John Wiley and Sons.

Pring, M. 2002. *Technical Analysis Explained: The Successful Investor's Guide to Spotting Investment Trends and Turning Points*. New York: McGraw Hill.

Qian, E. 2009. "Risk Parity™ : The Original." Boston: PanAgora Asset Management (June).

Rappoport, P., and N. Nottebohm. 2012. "Improving on Risk Parity." New York: J.P. Morgan Asset Management.

Reinhart, C. M. and K. S. Rogoff. 2010. "Growth in a Time of Debt." *American Economic Review* 100 (2): 573–578.

Meese, R. and K. Rogoff 1983. "Empirical Exchange Rate Model of the Seventies: Do They Fit Out of Sample?" *Journal of International Economics* 14: 3–24.

Romahi, Y. and K. Santiago. 2012. "Diversification—Still the Only Free Lunch?" New York: J.P. Morgan Asset Management.

Sadr, A. 2009. *Interest Rate Swaps and Their Derivatives: A Practitioner's Guide*. Hoboken, NJ: John Wiley and Sons.

Scheller, H. K. 2006. *The European Central Bank. History, Role and Functions.* 2nd ed. Frankfurt: European Central Bank.

Schwager, J. 2003. *Stock Market Wizards: Interviews with America's Top Stock Traders.* Harper Business.

Schwager, J. 2006. *Market Wizards. Interviews with Top Traders.* Marketplace Books.

Sharpe, W. F. 1964. "Capital asset prices: A theory of market equilibrium under conditions of risk." *Journal of Finance,* 19 (3): 425-442.

Soros, G. 2003. *The Alchemy of Finance.* Hoboken, NJ: John Wiley and Sons.

Stigum, M. 1989. *The Money Market: Third Edition.* New York: McGraw Hill.

Taylor, J. B. 1993. "Discretion Versus Policy Rules in Practice," Carnegie-Rochester Conference Series on Public Policy, 39: 195-214.

Tetlock, P. 2005. *Expert Political Judgment.* Princeton University Press.

Thorp, E. 1966. *Beat the Dealer: A Winning Strategy for the Game of Twenty-One.* New York: Vintage Publishing.

Tuckman, B. 2011. *Fixed Income Securities: Tools for Today's Markets.* Hoboken, NJ: John Wiley and Sons.

Tversky, A. and D. Kahneman. 1974. "Judgment under Uncertainty: Heuristics and Biases." *Science* 185 (4157): 1124-1131.

Wigmore, B. 1985. *The Crash and its Aftermath.* Westport, CT: Greenwood Press.

Yamarone, R. 2010. *The Trader's Guide to Key Economic Indicators: With New Chapters on Commodities and Fixed-Income Indicators.* New York: Bloomberg Financial.

About the Author

Greg Gliner most recently worked at AQR Capital Management on the Global Asset Allocation team and as an analyst at Tudor Investment Corporation, a global macro hedge fund, focusing on discretionary macro in equities, commodities, foreign exchange, and fixed income. Prior to this, he was with Thracian Capital (a hedge fund seeded by Man Group PLC/GLG), where he was a portfolio manager. Gliner also worked at BNP Paribas in their equity derivatives business and was also with Citigroup's Financial Institution Group in investment banking where he was involved in various M&A, equity, and debt transactions. He holds MBAs from Columbia Business School and London Business, and has a BS and BA from Miami University (OH) in finance and history. Gliner pledges all personal profits from the sale of this book to charity.

Index

343

Printed and bound by CPI Group (UK) Ltd, Croydon, CR0 4YY

16/04/2025